KRUGER NATI

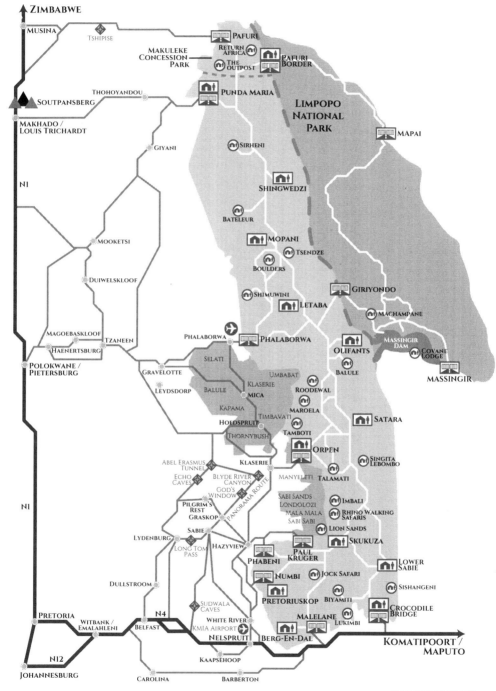

Other Books by David Fleminger

Back Roads of the Cape

Swaziland Travel Guide

Lesotho Travel Guide

Southbound Pocket Guides to the
World Heritage Sites of South Africa:
The Cradle of Humankind
Robben Island
Mapungubwe Cultural Landscape
The Vredefort Dome
The Richtersveld Cultural and Botanical Landscape

Fair Game –

a hidden history of the Kruger National Park

By

David Fleminger

dogdog
Publishing

First Edition, 2017

ISBN 978-0-620-64626-0

DogDog Publishing
P.O. Box 1816
Highlands North
Johannesburg, South Africa, 2037
www.dogdogpublishing.com

www.davidfleminger.com
davidfleminger@gmail.com

Cover Design and Maps by Ilan Mizrachi
Cover Photographs by David Fleminger

TABLE OF CONTENTS

Part One: Making Kruger

Part One:

Making Kruger

Introduction

Clocking in at nearly 2 million hectares (or 20 000 square kilometres), the Kruger National Park is an internationally renowned wildlife sanctuary and one of South Africa's top tourist attractions. And it's not hard to see why. This vast reserve is the size of a small country, providing an aegis for the flora and fauna of the southern African Lowveld region. In other words, it is one of the regrettably few game reserves on the planet where large herds of wild animals can still be viewed in a more-or-less natural state. As such, the Kruger Park is a globally important environmental asset and a priceless heirloom for future generations.

For South Africans, however, the Kruger Park is more than that. It's an evocative symbol of national pride and an integral part of our cultural identity. This is where we go to commune with nature; a place where the spirit of the wild reigns supreme. Indeed, over the last 75 years, conservation has become a way of life in South Africa and an appreciation of game is a central tenet of our culture (although, paradoxically, so is an appreciation of hunting and biltong). Nevertheless, at the heart of this love of nature lies the Kruger Park.

But this was not always the case. For most of our time on the planet, we humans had a pretty low opinion of wildlife. When we weren't running away from them in fear, we were hunting them down. And not just as food. In the last few hundred years especially, our strange species also started hunting animals for sport. For trophies. For fun?

Accordingly, hunters gleefully shot out the game for meat, hides, and/or entertainment. Livestock farmers reviled wild animals as either reservoirs for disease, or dangerous predators. And just about everyone tended to view game as a communal natural resource that was there to be exploited, and not always in a sustainable manner. In short, back then, the idea of preserving nature just so you could look at it was considered ridiculous.

Truth be told, nature conservation had a rocky start in South Africa and even the celebrated Kruger Park has been dogged with controversy throughout its 100-year history. Things were particularly bad during the first 30 years of the park's existence, when various parties made strenuous efforts to have the reserve deproclaimed, diluted or abandoned altogether. After all, land is a political issue and South Africa has always been a country overflowing with politics.

In fact, we are very lucky indeed that we have any game reserves in Southern Africa at all, let alone the mighty Kruger Park. So, let's take a trip back into the benighted past and track the spoor of the reserve to see how it all came about.

Kruger and the South African Identity

The Kruger National Park (KNP, or simply 'Kruger', for short) is the premier game reserve in South Africa. Even though the subcontinent is blessed with hundreds of beautiful and biologically diverse conservation areas, you still find that many people have a peculiar connection to Kruger as the greatest of them all.

The primacy of the KNP in our national consciousness is so strong that it even manifests itself in the subliminal vernacular of the local tourist. Thus, when a South African says that they are going to a game reserve for a holiday, they could be referring to any one of our fine national, provincial or private game parks. However, if they say that they are going to THE Game Reserve, odds are they are referring to Kruger.

But the international treasure that is the KNP had very humble beginnings. Its birth was exceedingly difficult and its origins were fraught with conflict. Most modern visitors simply aren't aware that the Kruger was ever anything but the popular and much-loved national treasure it is today. Nevertheless, in the first few decades of the park's existence, it came perilously close to being destroyed – several times.

Today's KNP is a very different proposition. It boasts rest camps of every description, picnic spots, game drives, walking trails, an extensive public road network, a staff of thousands and over 1.5 million visitors annually. It is a vital economic driver in the region and a keystone of South Africa's tourism industry.

So, why has all that past unpleasantness been written out of the history books? Perhaps it no longer fits in with the current narrative – or the previous one, for that matter. Perhaps we don't want to be reminded of our blinkered foolishness from 100 years ago. Or maybe it's just too obscure. Who wants to dwell on arcane eco-history when the KNP has grown in size and stature to become one of South Africa's 'Big 5' tourist attractions (along with Table Mountain, Robben Island, the Garden Route and cheap cosmetic surgery).

Perhaps some things are destined to remain much loved but little understood. Or maybe, it's time to finally pull back the covers and reveal the hidden history of the Kruger National Park.

The Lowveld

Literally meaning 'low-lying grasslands', the Lowveld is situated in the north-eastern part of South Africa, extending into Mozambique in the east, Zimbabwe in the north and Swaziland in the south. It is a region characterised by scrubby bush, comprised of smallish trees (such as the thorny acacia and leafy mopane families), shrubs and numerous grass species. Also called the 'Bushveld', this humid region is cut-off from the cooler, high-altitude grasslands of the interior (the Highveld) by a line of mountains that runs north to south in a great escarpment.

A sharp spine of rocks thus separates the high plateau in the west from the Lowveld and its adjoining coastal plains in the east. This 'Eastern Escarpment' is an extension of the famous Drakensberg mountain range in KwaZulu-Natal and, rather usefully, acts as a barrier for the malaria-carrying *Anopheles* mosquito. So, as a rule of thumb, if you descend from the mountains into the Lowveld, you are in a malaria area.

But avoiding malaria is only one reason to spend some time on top of the mountains. The sheer face of the Eastern Escarpment is spectacular and there are several viewpoints (such as the well-known God's Window) perched along the very lip of the range. Standing here on the edge of the Berg, in clear weather, you can look out over the trees and bushes of the sprawling Lowveld plains, nearly 1000 metres below. The famous Panorama Route from White River to the Blyde River Canyon takes in God's Window and a dozen similarly scenic delights, and can be easily incorporated into your KNP itinerary.

From the foot of this so-called 'Golden Escarpment', the flat plains of the Lowveld spool out to the East for about 100km, until they meet the Lubombo mountains. This rugged and remote range runs in a remarkably straight line from north to south, roughly parallel to the Drakensberg escarpment. The Lowveld of the KNP is thus cradled between these two mighty massifs.

Numerous rivers and streams run across the Lowveld. Most emanate in the Drakensberg and flow in an easterly direction through the Kruger Park. The major rivers, moving from south to north, are the Crocodile River, the Sabie River, the Olifants River, the Letaba River, the Shingwedzi, the Luvuvhu (or Pafuri) River and the Limpopo, which marks the border between South Africa, Zimbabwe and Mozambique. Where these rivers meet the Lubombo Mountains, they carve a passage or 'poort' through the rocks and continue flowing through Mozambique to end their journey in the Indian Ocean.

Geology

The bedrock of the KNP is granite. This layer of igneous rock was formed around 3.5 billion years ago and is one of the oldest rock layers found anywhere on Earth. The tough, weather-resistant granite has now eroded into the koppies and rolling hills that characterise the southern part of the park, notably around the Pretoriuskop area.

On top of the granite, a series of shale and sandstone layers were deposited. These contain animal and plant fossils along with deposits of coal; indications that the land was once wet, swampy and teeming with prehistoric wildlife. The soft shales have now eroded away to form the flat, grassy plains that run along the eastern side of the KNP.

After the sedimentary shales were deposited, there was a massive outpouring of volcanic matter that flooded the Lowveld. This flow of molten basalt was released when the super-continent of Gondwanaland split apart to form the southern land masses that we know today. The igneous layer of 'flood basalt' has now formed into flat plains, pockmarked with water holes.

Later, the land split again as the large island of Madagascar started moving away from the African mainland. This caused the land adjacent to the coast to tilt up, creating (amongst other things) the Lubombo mountain range that runs along the eastern boundary of the KNP.

In the north of the park, around the Punda Maria rest camp, the geology is characterised by sandy soils which have formed into beautiful sandstone mountains. This area is classed as Sandveld and chemical analysis has shown that the soil is similar to that found in the Kalahari. It has been proposed that an era of severe sandstorms transported this sand halfway across the country, from the Kalahari to the KNP, about 100 million years ago.

As each of these rock layers weather and crumble into small particles, they form soils with different chemical compositions. These soils, in turn, each support a distinct ecosystem with its own characteristic assortment of plants, trees and fauna. The eco-zones of the KNP therefore correspond with the underlying geology of each region.

In the Beginning

Since time immemorial, wild animals have flourished in the Lowveld. The warm temperatures and regular rainfall nurtured a remarkable bio-diversity, and the region supported thousands of plant and animal species. Back then, when the natural order was intact, the herds of game would drift with the seasons. Winters were spent grazing in the well-watered foothills of the escarpment. In summer, they migrated eastwards into the dense bush of the plains.

Weak and puny humans, however, have always had one big problem with the region: disease. The *Anopheles* mosquito, some of which carry the malaria pathogen, is endemic to the area. Other deadly diseases are (or were) also common in the Lowveld, including *nagana* (sleeping sickness, transmitted by the hated Tsetse fly), anthrax, foot and mouth, *dikkop,* black water fever and several other tropical maladies.

So, it took a very hardy type of hominin to settle among these pestilential plains. But that is not to say that the Lowveld was uninhabited.

The earliest evidence of human habitation indicates that *Homo erectus,* one of our evolutionary predecessors, walked the Lowveld plains around 500 000 years ago. Early modern humans (*Homo sapiens)* also lived in the Lowveld, and Kruger archaeologists have identified over 300 sites containing stone tools dating from the Later Stone Age, between 100 000 to 30 000 years ago.

As was the case throughout southern Africa, the first identifiable human civilisation to live in the KNP was the Bushmen (or San), who emerged as a distinct culture around 20 000 years ago. The size of this nomadic community of hunter-gatherers and the length of time they spent within the boundaries of the present day national park are hard to determine, but their unmistakable paintings and rock art have been found at over 130 sites throughout the KNP. There are also a couple of potential Khoikhoi rock art sites in the north of the park (the Khoikhoi, also derisively known as Hottentots, were relatives of the Bushmen who had adopted pastoralism from the Bantu tribes migrating southwards down the continent – see 'The Iron Age').

Surveys of these rock art sites are on-going and, in the future, several sites may be developed for tourism. At the moment, the best way to see the Bushman heritage of the KNP is through the guided Bushman Walking Trail near Berg-en-Dal camp (it is unclear whether the rock art site near the Hippo Pools at Crocodile Bridge is still accessible).

The Iron Age

From about 4000 years ago, a new kind of African began to move down the continent in a mass migration that came to be known as the Bantu Diaspora. These 'Bantu' tribes originated in western Africa, around modern-day Cameroon and the Niger Delta, and they spoke a root language called 'Ntu' – hence *Ba-Ntu* translates as 'the people of Ntu'. But what really made them stand out were the new technologies they had adopted from travellers plying the trans-Sahara trade route that linked west Africa with the Middle East. These new-fangled ideas included such innovations as metal work (iron smelting and casting), agriculture (sowing and reaping crops) and the keeping of domesticated animals (including cattle, goats and, later, sheep).

The initial Bantu migration was probably triggered because of population pressure and climate change in their home region but, whatever caused the initial wanderlust, the diaspora soon gathered its own momentum. Thus, armed with the Iron Age and pastoralism, the Bantu began to move slowly south; travelling in several distinct streams along the east and west coasts of Africa – slowly supplanting the Stone Age Bushman cultures they encountered *en route*.

As the Bantu journeyed, groups split away from the main body and established settlements which would, in time, develop their own distinct languages, cultures and identities. Eventually, the Bantu colonised the entire continent and most modern languages currently spoken in sub-Saharan Africa have their distant roots in the Ntu tongue.

The Bantu arrived in southern Africa between 2000 and 1500 years ago in the form of several early iron-age cultures that found a convenient home along the banks of the Limpopo River (such as the flourishing Mapungubwe civilisation, described in the next chapter). Subsequently, additional Bantu tribes arrived and moved south over the Limpopo and into what would become the country of South Africa.

Broadly speaking, one stream of these southern migrants – the Nguni – settled along the eastern coast of South Africa and eventually became the Swazi, Zulu and Xhosa nations. A short time later, another stream came through and settled across the high plateau of the interior. They would become the Sotho, Tswana and Pedi people.

Mapungubwe and Sofala

By the end of the first millennium of the Common Era, the east coast of Africa was bustling. Arab and Asian seafarers had discovered the seasonal trade winds, which enabled them to sail up and down the African shore where they snapped up animal skins, gold and ivory from the locals. Several trading stations were subsequently established at places such as Zanzibar, Mogadishu, Madagascar and Kilwa, creating a marine trade network that predated the European voyages of discovery by over 500 years.

The most southerly trading station was Sofala, located near the modern-day city of Beira, in Mozambique. As such, teams of African porters from the interior would carry their trade goods to the coast, where it was exchanged for glass beads, cowrie shells and the occasional piece of porcelain from the Far East.

Since the Limpopo region contained healthy supplies of wild elephants for ivory as well as nuggets of alluvial gold in the rivers, several tribes in the region became very prosperous. Gradually, these early entrepreneurs began to develop a sophisticated civilisation based on personal wealth and status. Fortunately, at the time, the climate was in a benevolent phase and the developing kingdoms were bolstered by fertile lands and bountiful herds.

A prominent centre of this mercantile Iron Age culture was located several hundred kilometres to the north-west of the KNP, near the junction of the Limpopo and Shashe rivers. By 1200, this society had developed into a considerable empire, exerting an influence over several hundred square kilometres in what is now the cross-border region between Botswana, Zimbabwe and South Africa.

Known today as the Mapungubwe civilisation, the capital city was built around a distinctive flat-topped hill on the southern side of the Limpopo River. On the summit of the hill lived the king and a small entourage. At the foot of the hill lived several thousand citizens, who literally looked up at their king as a sacred being. Clearly, the idea of politics as an Ivory Tower is nothing new...

Consequently, the king was not allowed to mix with the common folk and access to the royal personage was strictly controlled. Stone walls were also erected on top of the hill to further enhance the king's isolation. These were built using a distinctive dry walling technique, whereby stones are cut and stacked on top of each other without any kind of mortar. This dry-stone walling became a hallmark of the culture.

The people of Mapungubwe were also skilled craftsmen who fashioned beautiful objects and delicate beads from gold and ivory. The most famous of these artefacts include a miniature gold rhino, a gold bowl and a gold mace or sceptre. Meticulously created by hammering thin gold foil around a wooden base, these treasures are often called 'South Africa's Crown Jewels' and are held by the Mapungubwe Museum at the University of Pretoria.

For 100 years, the people living around Mapungubwe Hill flourished. Then, quite suddenly, the civilisation collapsed. It does not appear as if the hill was invaded by an external force, but climate change and drought may have forced the people to move on. Whatever the case, circa 1290, Mapungubwe was abruptly abandoned.

African tribes who subsequently lived in the area considered the hill to be taboo. It was said to be the home of ancestors and cursed would be the man who attempted to climb the hill. Mapungubwe was therefore shunned and the story of its people remained shrouded in mystery for 700 years.

It was only in the 1930s that white farmers in the area heard of the forbidden hill and, unconcerned with native superstition, climbed up its steep flanks. Their re-discovery of several royal graves on the hilltop, complete with golden grave goods, sparked off a 70-year excavation that is still on-going.

Today, Mapungubwe is safely located in the beautiful Mapungubwe National Park, about 100km to the west of Musina. Guided tours up Mapungubwe Hill are a fascinating excursion, the accommodation is lovely, the interpretation centre has won international awards for its unique design, and a visit to the region is highly recommended. More information can be found at the SA National Parks website.

Great Zimbabwe

After the collapse of Mapungubwe, many of its people moved north and east, where they joined another iron-age settlement that came to be known as Great Zimbabwe. Assimilation proved to be fruitful and the locals quickly embraced the culture, technology, spiritual beliefs and trading connections of the new arrivals.

Over the next 200 years, the power of Great Zimbabwe grew and an impressive capital city was constructed using those distinctive dry-stone walling techniques. Like Mapungubwe, the royal entourage lived on top of a large hill, with the common population living below, but the scale of Great Zimbabwe was immense. The settlement covered several square kilometres and boasted towering stone walls, monuments and large public enclosures. Many of these colossal structures still stand, near the modern city of Masvingo, and Great Zimbabwe is truly one of the wonders of the ancient world.

Then, around 1450, Great Zimbabwe also collapsed – probably because of poor climatic conditions and over-population. The inhabitants abandoned their great city and scattered. Several new stone cities were founded in modern-day Zimbabwe and Botswana, such as Khami and Dhlodhlo.

One section of this population also moved south of the Limpopo once again and established a number of stone citadels in South Africa. One of these,

Thulamela, is located in the north of the Kruger Park and it is an amazing place to visit. The associated Dzata ruins (home of the legendary 'Sleeping Drum' made of human skin) can also found to the west of the KNP, close to the Venda capital of Thohoyandou.

The displaced people of Great Zimbabwe would later mix with other tribes and ultimately became the Shona and Venda nations, among others. The Sotho-Tswana tribes also subsequently adopted the practise of building dry-stone walls and constructed many sprawling settlements, such as Kaditshwene near Zeerust (which lasted into the 1800s and contained up to 18 000 inhabitants).

Thulamela

In 1983, a KNP ranger named Philip Nel was doing a foot patrol in the far north-west region of the park, between the Limpopo and Luvuvhu rivers. This part of the KNP is wild and mountainous and, on top of one of these rocky outcrops, Nel stumbled upon thousands of evenly shaped stones, scattered in roughly linear heaps. It was clear he had found the remains of a stone wall that had once been part of a large fortification.

Nel reported his find, but it was only in 1991 that the first proper archaeological survey was conducted. The importance of the site was soon confirmed and a full excavation and reconstruction project began in 1993. Operating under the auspices of Sydney Miller, the project ran for four years.

First, Miller and his crew carefully cleared away the grass and bushes around the various enclosures. They then set about the painstaking task of rebuilding the stone walls, using only stones found on the site. No mortar or cement was used, as the original walls were dry-stacked.

Piece by piece, the stone citadel was resurrected. All in all, 350 metres of walling were reconstructed, consisting of about 2000 metric tonnes of rock. The restored complex was opened to the public in 1996.

Life at Thulamela

Modern tribes living in the area knew little about the hill, but they did call it by a rather singular name – Thulamela. According to David, my site guide, 'Thula' means to rise above and 'Mela' means to germinate, to give birth, or to grow. A more direct translation is 'place of giving birth'.

Although historical details are still sketchy, it is now accepted that Thulamela hill was originally inhabited around 800 years ago by an early tribe of uncertain provenance. After the fall of Great Zimbabwe, around 1450AD, some of the refugees from that city moved south and settled at Thulamela, either absorbing or transplanting the original inhabitants. According to some oral histories, these new arrivals were the Nyai division of the Shona-speaking Lembethu.

Between 1450 and 1550, Thulamela became a wealthy trading centre and, as was the case at Mapungubwe and Great Zimbabwe, the citizens built an impressive series of enclosures, surrounded by high dry-stone walls. The layout of the site also suggests that the king was considered sacred and was isolated from the population.

Additionally, there is evidence that the Thulamela-ites smelted gold and metal, and were skilled craftsmen. They were also astute businessmen with links to the Muslim traders at Sofala as well as indigenous settlements in southern and central Africa. This is evidenced by the gold artefacts and glass beads found in the graves, along with further evidence of trade that was uncovered from the settlement's ancient midden (a communal rubbish dump that was a common feature of many iron-age villages).

At its height, Thulamela was home to about 2000 people. The king and his entourage lived on top of the hill, of course, while the commoners probably lived close to their fields around the foot of the hill. The fertile soil was thus used to grow a variety of crops including sorghum, millet and cotton, which was spun on clay spindles and woven on 'low flat looms fixed to the ground'. Despite its wealth and size, however, the settlement appears to have been abandoned between 1650 and 1700.

After the fall of Thulamela, several smaller stone-walled settlements were built in the vicinity. The remains of some of these sites have now been identified by researchers, and there is a possibility that they will be excavated and rehabilitated in the future. Although none of these more recent 'towns' reached the size and power of Thulamela, local history does record the names of a couple of the kings who lived in the area – most notably the cruel and lazy Makahane who terrorised the people from atop his small stone palace.

Today, Thulamela is generally acknowledged as a Venda heritage site, but some Tsonga-Shangaan historians also lay claim to the citadel. They could well both be correct. The heritage of Thulamela is expansive, forming an essential but neglected part of our modern understanding of African history.

The reason for this lacuna is that, until recently, colonial and apartheid narratives portrayed Africa's pre-European past as savage and featureless. Accordingly, for previous generations of school kids, the history of southern Africa only began when Bartolomeu Dias sailed around the Cape in 1488 and kicked off in earnest with good old Jan Van Riebeeck landing at the Cape in 1652. But the discoveries from sophisticated iron-age communities such as Mapungubwe, Great Zimbabwe and Thulamela have shown that this was not the case. There is a rich African history that extends back several centuries before the Europeans pulled themselves out of the Dark Ages.

As Pallo Jordan, then minister of Environmental Affairs, said in his speech at the opening of Thulamela, "On the foundations of this African civilisation, we will build a better future for all South Africans. Our true origins have been captured by Thulamela and not by colonialism, which was just a passing phase in our history."

Queen Losha and King Ingwe

During the course of Thulamela's excavation, two significant skeletons were found. The first was discovered in the centre of the King's Hut – a small circular enclosure with a wonderful view out over the valley. It was named King Ingwe (leopard), because a leopard was seen prowling around the archaeologists' vehicles during the exhumation.

Upon closer inspection, the king's bones had been carefully arranged in their grave; the spinal column on one side, the ribs next to the spine and the skull next to the ribs. The spinal column had been snapped, suggesting that the king may have been stabbed. Another possibility is that the skeleton was exhumed from another grave and reburied at Thulamela.

In the Venda tradition, when one king dies the successor moves into the same hut, so it is possible that there are more skeletons buried underneath King Ingwe. But nothing has come to light so far.

The second important skeleton was a woman, found buried under the fireplace in a hut on the opposite side of Thulamela. Measuring around 5 feet 7 inches tall, this comparatively robust female had strong bones, which suggests that she led a very active lifestyle. Considering her physical condition and the prestigious location of her grave, she is thought to have been the first wife of a king.

The reasoning for this assumption is as follows: traditionally, the king can only trust his first wife and it would have been her job to prepare the food, make the beer and fetch water from the river at the foot of the hill. This would have made her a very fit wife (literally). It is also telling that the Queen's hut is overlooked by the hut of the King's mother, who would have wanted to keep a beady eye on her daughter-in-law. Some things never change...

The female skeleton was named Queen Losha, as she was buried on her side, with her hands tucked under her cheek – similar to the position you sometimes take when you are going to sleep. This is a traditional Venda posture, called 'Losha', and it indicates respect. There is a possibility that the Queen's Hut also contains the skeletons of other queens, but none have been found thus far.

Both the king and queen were buried with impressive funerary goods. These included hundreds of tiny gold beads, delicate ornaments made from ostrich eggs and glittering gold bracelets that were wound around the queen's arms.

Always on the lookout for a good story, the media usually presents King Ingwe and Queen Losha as a cosy iron-age couple who ruled over Thulamela together. Unfortunately, this romance is unlikely. Dating of the king's bones has shown that he died some time before Queen Losha.

It is gratifying to note that the excavation of Thulamela was conducted with the participation and support of the local communities. Every effort was made to respect the cultural significance of the site and the tribal authorities were consulted whenever possible. This approach stands in contrast to the excavators of old, who used to run roughshod over the sensibilities of the local people.

At the request of the local tribes, the skeletons of King Ingwe and Queen Losha were ceremonially re-interred at Thulamela after the laboratory studies had been completed. Some artefacts and implements from Thulamela are on display at the National Cultural History Museum (formerly the Transvaal Museum) in Pretoria.

Visiting Thulamela

The reconstructed Thulamela is a wonder to behold and a must-see if you are ever up in the north of Kruger. It is only accessible as part of a guided tour that leaves daily from Punda Maria rest camp. This restriction is necessary because Thulamela is a fragile archaeological site located in a wilderness area, and you really need an informed guide (armed with a rifle) to make the evocative location come alive.

The journey from Punda Maria to Thulamela takes about 90 minutes. The bush is thick in this part of the KNP, dominated by forests of Mopani trees. Nyala antelope are commonly seen grazing among the appropriately named Nyalaberry trees, and our guide also spotted Crested Guineafowl in the dense woods.

After about an hour, we left the main tar road and headed west into the mountains on an unmarked gravel track. The narrow path now twists through the tall trees, crossing several small streams as we ventured further into the deepening valleys. After several kilometres, the vehicle stopped in a small clearing at the foot of Thulamela Hill and we all clambered out. A bush toilet has been erected nearby, in case of emergencies.

The walk up the hill is short but quite steep. It's very manageable, however. The path is well maintained and there's no rush as you stroll beneath the awesome bulk of ancient baobabs that grow inexorably out of the hillside.

Once you gain the summit, the views are wonderful. Lush valleys cut through the sandstone hills, the sun plays on the red-rocked ridges and the golden stone walls of Thulamela run along the crest of the hill. It is a visually thrilling and emotionally resonant sight.

Before you enter the actual enclosures of Thulamela, however, you'll probably take a seat on the bulging roots of a particularly huge baobab to hear the story of Thulamela from your guide. Under the towering canopy, you'll be told about the history of the site and the lifestyle of Thulamela's inhabitants. The guide may also describe the lengthy and intricate site rehabilitation process, if you are interested. Then it's time to enter the portals of the citadel...

As you approach, it becomes clear that the walls are much higher than they look, reaching heights of more than 2 metres. They are made of light-yellow stones, each one carefully cut and placed together like an elaborate jigsaw puzzle made of masonry.

The tour wends its way through the various living enclosures, each with its own function and status. Appropriately enough, the King's hut is strategically located at the summit of the settlement, and it has beautiful views. A large circular courtyard stands a short distance away, which was probably used for public gatherings and as a stock pen.

All in all, Thulamela is a remarkable construction that bears testament to its builders, both in its original form and in its reconstructed state. Even though it's far off the usual tourist path, the tour of the hill is highly recommended.

Bookings for the Thulamela tour must be made at Punda Maria rest camp. Tours usually leave at 07:00 in the morning and the round trip takes about 5 hours. Basic refreshments may be served as part of the tour but you should bring along your own drinks and snacks to supplement the rations. Please note, for the sake of your own safety and the preservation of the site, you are only allowed to visit Thulamela as part of the guided tour. It is advisable to arrange your booking a week in advance to make sure there is availability.

Masorini Archaeological Site

Along with Thulamela, Masorini is the other major iron-age archaeological site in the KNP. It is located on the H-9 tar road, 12km from Phalaborwa Gate and 39km from Letaba Rest Camp, at the foot of a prominent hill.

Named after a former chief, Masorini is a later Iron Age settlement that was inhabited by the Sotho speaking BaPhalaborwa people during the 1700s and 1800s. Like the earlier people of Thulamela, the BaPhalaborwa had a sophisticated understanding of iron smelting technology and were able to skilfully mine and process various metals. Spearheads, arrowheads and agricultural implements were among the items they manufactured.

The Phalaborwa region is fantastically rich in copper and other metal ores, and local tribes have been mining these valuable minerals for at least 1000 years. Since copper was once a popular form of currency (carried about in the shape of a copper rod, or *Lerale)*, the Phalaborwa region used to enjoy some degree of wealth and fame.

Accordingly, during the time of the BaPhalaborwa, Masorini was part of an extensive trade network that included dealings with the Venda to the north and the Portuguese on the East Coast. Copper was thus exchanged for exotic glass beads, ivory and other trade goods, and the settlement of Masorini grew to be quite prosperous.

Today, the town of Phalaborwa is a significant mining centre and boasts one of the world's largest open-cast copper mines. First 'discovered' by a South African geologist named Hans Merensky in 1938, this colossal mineral deposit was based around a hill named Loolekop (situated about 20km to the west of Masorini). Subsequent investigations of Loolekop revealed that a number of shafts had been dug into the hillside by local tribes many hundreds of years previously.

These ancient, horizontal shafts (or adits) were generally around 20 metres deep and about 1 metre in circumference. There were no supports and it must have been a dark, dusty and dangerous job to scrape out the ore. Loolekop was clearly a very active iron-age mining site, but it was all blasted away in the name of progress when the modern copper mine was established. Much valuable archaeological evidence about the early African miners was thus destroyed.

The preservation of Masorini, within the confines of the KNP, is therefore of considerable importance. When the settlement was first identified, there were only a few scattered artefacts and ruins to be seen. Now, it has been reconstructed into an impressive open-air museum that attempts to re-create an authentic iron-age settlement.

The museum is attractively laid out along the slopes of the hill, and there is a full complement of huts to admire and explore. Agricultural implements are displayed and the distinctive dome-shaped furnaces, used to smelt iron, have been restored.

Masorini is open to visitors throughout the day and guided tours are available. It's a fascinating stop and an excellent way to get to grips with the society and technology of a typical iron-age village. It is also a convenient picnic spot and gas braais can be hired.

The Myth of the Golden City

Soon after the Europeans landed on the shores of southern Africa from the 1500s onwards, stories began to be told about a fabulous city of gold, located somewhere deep in the wild African interior. The myth varied with the telling. Some legends mentioned a great stone city of immeasurable wealth, ruled over by the fearsome Emperor Monomotapa. Others spoke of a white Christian king, Prester John, who ruled over the savage Africans and kept the whole enterprise organised in a suitably European fashion. In all cases, the story of a 'golden city' was told to explain the steady supply of gold nuggets that inexplicably dripped out of the dark continent.

With such a rich story to tempt them, the Europeans made several attempts to find this African El Dorado. In the wake of Vasco da Gama's exploratory voyage of 1492, the Portuguese had a head start on this quest as they quickly usurped older Arabic trading posts along the Mozambique coast or established their own, such the fort of Lourenço Marques (now Maputo) on Delagoa Bay.

As such, in 1512, they sent out an exploratory mission into the interior, led by a former convict named Antonio Fernandez who reported finding a 'fortress which he now makes of dry stone'. Several other expeditions were sent out between 1532 and 1575, and the Portuguese eventually established a relationship with 'Mwena Mutapa' – a Kalanga kingdom in the north.

When the Dutch arrived at the Cape in 1652, they too heard stories of the mythical golden city. Over the years, various expeditions were sent out from the Cape into Namaqualand and the interior, but all were unsuccessful and several met with outright disaster.

Then, in 1719, the Dutch established Fort Lydsaamheid on the shores of Delagoa Bay (Bay of the Lagoon). From this fresh vantage point, they decided to try and find the elusive city of gold once more. And so, in 1723, the authorities duly appointed Jan Stefler to set out on an expedition into the wild hinterland. This adventure ended badly for Stefler, who was killed in an altercation with native villagers near Komatipoort.

Two years later, in 1725, another attempt was made, under the leadership of Frans de Kuiper. De Kuiper left Delagoa Bay with several dozen well-armed men and journeyed across the coastal plains towards the Lubombo mountains. After crossing the mountains through a poort carved out by the Komati River, de Kuiper and his crew crossed the Crocodile River and entered what is now the KNP. Their destination was the famous 'iron mountain' at Ciremandelle (Phalaborwa) where they hoped to find out more about the locals' productive copper mine.

Unfortunately, a short distance to the north of the modern-day Crocodile Bridge, close to the banks of the Sabie River, the party was attacked by the warriors of Chief Dawano. The expedition suffered heavy losses and was forced to retreat across the Lubombo. Disheartened, De Kuiper returned to Delagoa Bay, where he died 2 years later of malaria. The Dutch would eventually abandon Fort Lydsaamheid in 1730.

The Sotho, the Zulu, the Swazi and the Tsonga-Shangaan

As we've mentioned, endemic malaria prevented the Lowveld from supporting a large, permanent human population. The cyclical waves of tsetse fly infestation also made the area hazardous for domestic animal stocks. Nevertheless, the history of the area's indigenous people is intriguing and vivid.

By the turn of the nineteenth century, the Lowveld was inhabited by several different tribal groups. In the north, the shifting populations of Mapungubwe, Great Zimbabwe and Thulamela had evolved into the Venda and Shona nations, including the Pafuri tribe. In the south-east, around the foothills of the Drakensberg, lived Sotho-speaking tribes that had spilled over from the interior, such as the Lobedu, Podile and Maake. In the south, Swazi people controlled most of the land between the Crocodile and Pongola rivers. The central Lowveld was also inhabited by several loosely affiliated clans who shared a common culture and language.

According to James Stevenson-Hamilton, this latter group included the Nondwane, Nkuna, Nwalungu, Hlangane, Hlabi, Hlengwe and Loyi. Later, the Zulus would collectively and contemptuously name these tribes 'BaThonga' (the slaves – now transliterated to Tsonga). Although they were not a prosperous people, these original Lowvelders often acted as go-betweens, facilitating trade between the coast and the wealthy tribes in the interior.

But this usually peaceful arrangement of tribal authorities was rudely shattered in the early 1800s by the exploits of the incorrigible Shaka Zulu. Born around 1785, Shaka was the illegitimate son of Senzangakhona, the chief of the small Zulu tribe that lived in the Stanger/KwaDukuza area (about 70km north of Durban in KwaZulu-Natal).

At that time, the humble Zulu polity operated under the auspices of King Dingiswayo of the Mthethwa nation. Despite (or perhaps because of) his ignoble birth, Shaka was determined to become a success and worked his way up the Mthethwa military hierarchy with ruthless efficiency. Soon, he was leading the Mthethwa army and, when Dingiswayo was killed in a battle with his arch-rivals, the Ndwandwe, Shaka took over as leader of the Mthethwa nation and renamed them as the Zulu – the people of heaven.

Next, Shaka built up the Zulu army into a fearsome fighting force; militarising social structures and developing new and brutal methods of warfare. After finally defeating the Ndwandwe, he embarked on an ambitious and often violent expansion policy in which he approached neighbouring tribes with what has been described as an 'open-door' policy. Basically, this consisted of an unpleasant choice between either joining the emergent Zulu nation or being conquered by force.

Many chiefs bowed to Shaka's will, took on the Zulu name and paid their new king many heads of cattle as a tribute. Others vowed to fight, and a series of bloody confrontations broke out across the region. Those that didn't want to fight had little choice but to flee, often displacing other tribes in the process. The result was an era of war, migration and instability that affected the entire southern African region. Shaka was later titled 'the Black Napoleon' by European historians.

This controversial period of history is known in isiZulu as the *Mfecane* - the crushing (in Sesotho, it's called the *Difaqane* - the scattering). Although traditionally the *Mfecane* was blamed mainly on Shaka and his imperialist impulses, the reality is that there were many causes with roots dating back decades before Shaka's rise. Population pressure, tribal aggression, drought, labour raiding by slave traders from Mozambique, and other socio-economic factors all contributed. In any event, the *Mfecane* soon enveloped the once placid Lowveld and several decades of chaos would ensue.

For the purposes of our story, however, things now get a little bit complicated. You see, the study of South Africa's indigenous history was often neglected or adulterated during the Apartheid era. Furthermore, much of the information we have about this pre-literate era has been handed down in the form of oral histories.

But the integrity of these oral histories was weakened by the cultural ravages of the twentieth century. Even in the best of times, verbal record keeping has a reach of only a couple of hundred years before things get hazy, and certain tales may become unreliable through the partisan attitudes of the teller (the latter being a pitfall that often affects written history as well). As a result, there are often conflicting reports about events during this time and such is the case with what happened next.

Best I can make out, the basics are as follows: After years of bitter conflict, Shaka finally defeated Zwide - chief of the Ndwandwe - around 1820, at the Battle of Mhlatuze River. In the aftermath, one of Zwide's generals named Soshangane (also known as Manukosi) fled the region and headed north where he met another former Ndwandwe chief named Zwangendaba. At first, the two men formed an alliance, but they soon quarrelled and Zwangendaba decided to push further north (into modern day Zambia, Malawi and Tanzania) where his people would become known as the Angoni (or baNgoni).

Soshangane, meanwhile, went forth with his army into the Lowveld. They raised hell as they marched, terrorising the local tribes, until they finally halted on the banks of the Limpopo river. Thus encamped, Soshangane took a look around and liked what he saw. This would make a good place for an empire of his own, he thought, especially since the resident Thonga tribes were too disorganised to mount a united defence.

In short order, Soshangane conquered and united the disparate Thonga tribes under a new name - the Shangaan. He then embarked on a military campaign that extended his power base over the area between the Zambezi River and Delagoa Bay (what is now southern Mozambique along with parts of Zimbabwe, Mpumalanga and Limpopo). He called his new state the Gaza (or Gasa) Empire, which he named after either his grandfather or the Nguni word for 'blood'.

Shaka Zulu, however, didn't take kindly to the upstart kingdom to his north and sent a regiment (an *impi)* to unseat Soshangane. Unfortunately, the warriors got lost in the thick bush and began to run out of food. Malaria also took its toll and when the *impi* reached the broad Olifants River, they decided to return home and risk Shaka's wrath. Luckily for them, once they limped back into Shaka's capital, they found that Shaka had been assassinated by his half-brothers Dingane and Mlangana. Such is the price of power.

Once he was firmly installed, Soshangane's people began to assimilate with the Thonga people; mixing their own Nguni heritage with the local customs. There was the occasional upset, admittedly, and Soshangane had a tendency to run amok every few years to subdue his enemies. These ructions caused several Thonga tribes to move to the west, through the KNP, where they sought protection from Sotho or Venda tribes. These refugees included the Boloyi, Maluleke, Tshauke and Sono. By the 1850s, some Thonga travellers had settled as far west as the Soutpansberg, where they were recruited by the influential trader, Joao Albasini, for his network of porters.

By this time, Soshangane's Gaza Empire was firmly established - his army even raided the settlements at Delagoa Bay and Inhambane once or twice, forcing the Portuguese to pay tribute for a time. Around 1856, however, Soshangane died and two of his sons, Muzila and Mawewe, got locked into a battle for succession. One was the favoured son, nominated by Soshangane to take over the throne. The other was first born son of the head wife, a traditional heir. Each son had their own supporters, and the two factions battled for several years. Succession battles of this type are a familiar part of many tribal histories (including the fractious European kings).

At first, Muzila held the upper hand as he was supported by Joao Albasini, the Boers and the traders at Lourenço Marques (Maputo), who gave him access to guns on the understanding that he would keep open the trade route between the Soutpansberg and Delagoa Bay. Mawewe fled into Swaziland and appealed to the King, Mswati, for assistance. Mswati (who was married to Mawewe's sister) obliged and sent three divisions through the Lowveld to roust Muzila. This military force, keening for action, devastated everything in their path. Muzila, however, withdrew to the north and the wide barrier of the Olifants River turned back the Swazi army.

Thereafter, there was a long series of destructive Swazi raids that devastated the Lowveld. Most of the human inhabitants fled, and those that chose to remain lived in fear for their lives. The constant war parties also took a heavy toll on the herds of wild animals, which were consumed by the ravenous troops.

Then, towards the end of 1861, Muzila concluded a treaty with the Portuguese in which he acknowledged their sovereignty over the southern part of his realm and became, in effect, a Portuguese subject. In exchange, an armed entourage of Portuguese settlers helped Muzila finally defeat Mawewe at a definitive battle on the Nkomati River.

Muzila continued to rule over the remainder of the Gaza Empire until his death in 1884, after which he was succeeded by his son, Ngungunyane. Keen to restore his waning influence in the face of European expansion across the sub-continent, Ngungunyane rebelled in a campaign that created new waves of disruption and migration, and brought Ngungunyane (now called the Lion of Gaza) into the Portuguese's black books.

Finally, in 1895, the Portuguese sent a force from Lisbon to defeat Ngungunyane. This was efficiently done and Ngungunyane was exiled first to Lisbon and then to the Azores. The next in line to the throne was a young boy with a redoubtable name, Thulilamahanxi. He and his regent (Mpisane) fled over the Lubombo mountains into the KNP and settled in the foothills of the Drakensberg, near the present-day district of Mhala.

In short order, the Gaza Empire had been broken. Some of the remaining citizens headed west to join their juvenile chief in the Lowveld, others spread out into Swaziland, Mozambique, Malawi, Zambia and Zimbabwe. Today, the polity is known by a number of different names but in South Africa, they are generally called the Tsonga-Shangaan (or Vatsonga) and people who speak Xitsonga (pronounced Shi-Tsonga) as a first language make up about 4.5% of the South African population.

Interestingly, most of the Tsonga clans currently living in South Africa do not recognise the lineage of the Gaza kings as part of their heritage as they claim their ancestors fled west of the Limpopo when Soshangane first moved in. Told you it was confusing.

The Voortrekkers

In the 1700s and early 1800s, several European hunters and explorers ventured into the Lowveld in search of game, gold and/or glory (see 'The Hunters'). However, the first white men to really leave their mark on the region were the Voortrekkers. Literally meaning 'forward pullers' (but more often translated as 'pioneers') this is the name given to a group of disgruntled farmers of Dutch origin who left the Cape colony because they resented paying tax to their new British overlords (who had finally taken control of the Cape from Holland in 1806). The Voortrekkers were also incensed by the recently imposed imperial ban on slavery and vowed to establish their own land, where they could treat the blacks as they pleased.

As so, between 1834 and 1838, dozens of small groups (often consisting of several extended families and friends from the same district) packed up their ox-wagons and set off into the wild interior. This cumulative migration was subsequently called the 'Great Trek'.

Within a few years, the Boers (as the Dutch farmers were known) had displaced many black natives from their land and established several towns in the 'empty' interior of the country, which was still recovering from the depredations of the *Mfecane*. But the despite the lack of indigenous resistance, the Boers were fractious and quickly started squabbling amongst themselves about who was in charge and where the capital city should be.

Soon, there were several different Boer 'republics' all jockeying with each other for position. Yet, despite their disagreements, everyone acknowledged that they would need a harbour outside English control if they were ever to realise their dream of independence from the bloody Brits.

Consequently, several expeditions went forth from the Highveld into the Lowveld. These pioneers were trying to establish a road down the mountains and through the fever country to Lourenço Marques, which was then a Portuguese port (named after a Portuguese navigator who explored the upper reaches of the Baia da Lagoa – Bay of the Lagoon, later contracted to Delagoa Bay – in 1544). Both the Bay and the port city are now called Maputo and, although they share a common meaning, Delagoa Bay should not be confused with Algoa Bay, near Port Elizabeth, which is now called Nelson Mandela Bay.

The Disappearance of Van Rensburg

Finding a practical route from the Highveld to the coast at Delagoa Bay was essential for the Boers, but it would prove to be a very difficult task. Once down in the Lowveld, malaria stalked the white men and *nagana* (sleeping sickness, carried by tsetse flies) decimated their oxen and horses. This was indeed a deadly land, as the Boer's were about to discover.

The first Voortrekker party to try and cross the dreaded Lowveld was led by an ambitious and determined farmer named Johannes Van Rensburg. His party consisted of 9 wagons and they had been trekking since early 1836, alongside another party of wagons which was led by Louis Trigard (also spelled Trichardt). As they trekked north, past what later became Pretoria, the two parties separated and Van Rensburg pushed on to reach the Soutpansberg mountains in the winter of 1836.

Without waiting for Trigard, Van Rensburg headed east and plunged over the escarpment into the Lowveld, eager to blaze a wagon route to Delagoa Bay and thus become a hero of the Trek. Unfortunately, his haste was to prove fatal and his entire party disappeared into the northern part of the Kruger Park, vanishing without a trace.

No-one knows what happened to the Van Rensburg trek, but it was probably gruesome. Traditionally, it is held that they were massacred by local tribes. 30 years later, according to some accounts, a Swazi raiding party invaded the AmaGwamba and found a young white man and woman living with the tribe. They spoke only the local dialect and remembered nothing of their European past. They would have been infants at the time of the disappearance and it is possible that they were the only survivors of Van Rensburg's ill-fated expedition.

In any case, a few weeks after Van Rensburg met his maker, Louis Trigard arrived at the Soutpansberg mountains. He decided to set up camp and waited several months for news from Van Rensburg. But no word came.

Undeterred, Louis Trigard knew that it was his duty to try and find out what had happened to the hapless Van Rensburg party. A small party thus mounted up and rode off into the forbidding bush, following the fading tracks of Van Rensburg's wagons. The tribes they encountered only offered rumours and vague threats, so the group returned to the Soutpansberg to reconsider their options.

It was nearly a year later, in August 1837, that Trigard finally decided the time was right to try again. By this time, the trekkers had done some reconnaissance and were more circumspect. They therefore sent a coloured servant named Gabriel Buys to Lourenço Marques with a letter asking the authorities to open trade links with the land-locked Boers.

Buys completed the dangerous journey and the Portuguese responded by sending two coloured soldiers back through the bush to meet the Boers and guide them to Delagoa Bay. Despite the expert help, the journey was a nightmare for Trigard and his party of around 50 people from 8 families.

The first problem was getting their cumbersome ox-wagons down the mountains. Unfortunately, Trigard chose to descend a particularly difficult part of the escarpment and it took the trekkers more than two months to manhandle their wagons down the tortuous route.

When they finally arrived on the flat plains of the Lowveld, disease began stalking the party. Malaria-carrying mosquitoes mercilessly ravaged the humans, while nagana took a heavy toll on the oxen and other livestock. It soon became a race against time as the Boer wagons rattled across the treacherous 350 kilometres to the coast.

Against all odds, Trigard finally staggered into Lourenço Marques in April 1838. The greeting from the Portuguese commander was enthusiastic, but the journey had taken its toll. Within a short time of their arrival, most of the party went down with malaria and 27 of them died, including Louis Trigard and his wife. The 26 survivors were taken by ship to Durban, where they related their woeful tale to the other trekkers. It seemed that the fever belt was a no-go area for the fragile white man.

The Rivers of Joy and Sorrow

Later, another trekker leader named Hendrik Potgieter launched several attempts to forge a path to Delagoa Bay. On one of these excursions, in 1844, the expedition was on top of the escarpment looking for an easy route down. To speed things up, Potgieter took a few men and broke away from the main party for a little recce. Several days passed with no word from Potgieter and his people began to despair for his safety. Finally, they decided to leave their campsite on the banks of a river that they decided to name the *Treur* (Sorrow).

A few days later, however, Potgieter rejoined his party and there was much rejoicing. In a wonderful demonstration of the literal-minded nature of the trekkers, the river they were fording at the time of the reunion was named the *Blyde* (Joy).

Appropriately enough, the rivers of Sorrow and Joy merge at a remarkable geological formation known as Bourke's Luck Potholes – a popular attraction on the Panorama route. From this confluence, the joyful Blyde River continues through the stunning Blyde River Canyon – the third largest canyon on earth (according to some). Such is the power of emotions.

In the years that followed, the Voortrekkers' quest for independence became the stuff of legend in many other ways. Indeed, the leaders of the Trek were turned into folk heroes and the entire period was mythologized by the cult of Afrikaner Nationalism, which began to take root in the early 20th century. Later, the narrative of the Great Trek became part of the political justification for Grand Apartheid, and it seemed that every town in South Africa was centred at the intersection of Voortrekker Road and Kerk (Church) Street.

The Transport Riders

By the 1840s, the Boers had established two large territories: the Orange Free State and the Transvaal. The Free State was located between the Orange River (named after the Dutch Royal House) and the Vaal (tawny-coloured) River, while the Transvaal covered the region between the Vaal and Limpopo rivers. The vast Transvaal area, which at one point consisted of 5 competing 'republics', was unified as the Zuid-Afrikaansche Republiek (ZAR) in 1852, with its capital in Pretoria. The Free State was later declared an independent republic in 1854, with Bloemfontein as its capital.

Despite the terrible fate of Van Rensburg and Trigard, the establishment of a wagon route to Delagoa Bay was essential for the Boer Republics. Consequently, they were constantly working to find a safe passage through the wild and unhealthy Lowveld to Lourenço Marques. Clearly speed was of the essence, as humans and livestock were both vulnerable in the fever belt. A railway line was seen as the best solution.

Unfortunately, the Boer republics were badly run, argumentative and frequently broke. To make matters worse, they had a largely subsistence economy and couldn't raise any capital from wealthier nations. So, the dreams of a railroad to Delagoa Bay remained firmly piped.

In the meantime, a breed of hardy transport riders stepped into the breach and pioneered a wagon route through the southern part of the Kruger Park. By scampering through the Lowveld during the dry winter months, these rough and ready adventurers were able to complete the overland journey to the sea with a reasonable amount of safety, and they soon became a fixture in the region.

The transport riders ferried a wide variety of cargo from the town of Lydenburg to the Portuguese port, and back again. Animal skins, dried meat, fabric, ammunition, gunpowder, cooking utensils and other merchandise all made its way through the Lowveld in a series of lumbering wagon trains.

Since most of the actual work on these trips was done by native servants and porters, the white transport riders had plenty of free time on their hands. So, they amused themselves by drinking brandy, eating biltong and hunting the abundant game that bounded through the bush.

Despite these simple pleasures, it was a hot, dusty and solitary life. Only a hard-bitten character would be able to hack it, and the personality of a typical 'Lowvelder' was thus set; eccentric, grumpy and tough. The transport riders also developed a reputation for having a ready wit, a sharp eye and a knack for telling fireside tales. For many years, it would be these calloused old coots who defined the region in the minds of white people.

Jock of the Bushveld

Ironically, the most famous character of the 'transport-rider' era is not a human, but a dog: Jock of the Bushveld. This fictional account of life on the old wagon road from Lydenburg to Delagoa Bay was written by Percy Fitzpatrick in 1907.

Intended as a children's book, 'Jock' describes the colourful adventures of a young man and his courageous dog as they travel through the wild and dangerous Lowveld. The episodic narrative is based on Fitzpatrick's own experiences, and many locations on the old wagon road are accurately (if romantically) described.

By the time he wrote the novel, however, Fitzpatrick had made a fortune on the gold fields of the Witwatersrand and become a prominent 'Randlord'. He would go on to enjoy a long career in politics.

Upon its publication, Fitzpatrick's story of the plucky little runt touched the hearts of many. 'Jock' quickly became a classic and a staple of South African literature. It has never gone out of print. Accordingly, starting in 1951, several historical plaques were erected along the old Transport Road in the KNP. These markers pinpoint various spots where significant events in Jock's narrative took place. Fans of the novel will thus be delighted to associate specific physical locations with exciting episodes in the book.

However, before you go out and purchase a copy of 'Jock' for yourself, I must sound a note of warning. I had never read the book, even though an old copy has been sitting on my bookshelf since I was a kid. So, as part of my research for this volume, I decided that it was time to fill that literary gap. Well, I can honestly say that I was horrified. Rarely have I ever read such a nasty, violent, racist and thoroughly repellent 'children's book' as *Jock of the Bushveld*.

Although the descriptions of the Lowveld are vivid and engaging, and the reader gets an excellent sense of what life was like on the old Transport Road, the general attitude of the author is simply appalling.

Natives are dismissed as inferior, drunken, lazy and warlike. In one passage, blacks are explicitly condemned for lacking in breeding and culture.

The attitude to wildlife is not much better. Kudu are admired as noble, but only for a moment before they are gunned down triumphantly by the heroic hunter. An impala stampede is described in marvellous detail, only to be spoiled by the narrator's frantic effort to shoot as many animals as possible before walking away and leaving a pile of carcasses to rot in the sun. In fact, the book is little more than a series of hunts and kills, which are all described in loving, gory detail, without the slightest trace of irony. Eventually I got so repelled that I put the book down and refused to read any further.

Now, I know that it is futile to apply modern standards to de facto old-fashioned attitudes. However, I have read many other books written 100 years ago, or more, and I can safely say that Percy Fitzpatrick's attitudes and references are offensive, even by the low standards of the day. Furthermore, the writing style is condescending, overwrought and pretentious.

The fact that such a book has been a regular feature of the school syllabus over the years is, frankly, terrifying. I would even go further to say that this novel may have played a not-so-minor part in the brain-washing of young minds that took place during the days of apartheid education. I strongly advise you to approach the book with extreme caution!

Thankfully, the modern edition that is now available has been revised and most of the egregious material has presumably been removed. I have not read this expurgated edition but one hopes that it is a less offensive tome.

The Old Transport Road

By 1874, the main wagon road to the coast had been well established. It began at the regional capital of Lydenburg (now officially called Mashishing), located high on the grassy plateau, well beyond the reach of the deadly malaria-carrying mosquitoes. From here, the road headed east across the mountain tops, through the gold-rush town of Pilgrims Rest, to the village of Sabie, a centre of the lumber trade. The road then tumbled over the escarpment in a rather haphazard cutting down the side of the Berg and headed out across the undulating plains of the Lowveld.

On the banks of the Phabeni River, near the modern-day rest camp of Pretoriuskop, a European trader named Joao Albasini had his trading post. This little shop did a brisk business with the passing wagons.

From Albasini's store, the transport road headed diagonally, in a south-easterly direction, past a line of distinctive ridges and koppies that made for easy navigation. The most visible of these landmarks is Ship Mountain, so named because it looks like the keel of an upside-down sailing vessel. This strange, tilted cap of red sandstone is still a prominent feature of the road.

By keeping to this convenient line of mountains, wagon drivers had little trouble in finding their way down to a drift across the Crocodile River, quite close to the present-day Crocodile River Bridge and gate. Once across the river, the road continued east to Komatipoort, a convenient gap in the Lubombo mountain range that was carved out of the rock by the confluence of the Crocodile and Komati Rivers. From here it is about 100 kilometres to Lourenço Marques.

In the 1890s, an entrepreneur named Alois Nellmapius secured a contract with the Transvaal government to make a permanent road along the route. As his price, he received several farms in the area.

This untarred road still runs through the KNP, more or less as described above. It was later rehabilitated and became known as the Old Voortrekker Road, in accordance with the general trend of the day.

The old Transport Route now offers a delightful drive through the southern part of the Kruger, leading from Pretoriuskop towards Crocodile Bridge. Despite the dramatic events that played out along its length, it is a quiet gravel road that offers modern visitors a picturesque and evocative experience, as well as the opportunity for some excellent game viewing. There are several historical plaques along this portion of road, and a number of significant events in the novel 'Jock of the Bushveld' played out along the route.

In addition to the wagon road described above, several other paths through the KNP were pioneered by the late 1800s. The northern route ran from the Zoutpansberg (near the modern-day town of Louis Trichardt / Makhado), through Venda territory, and into the Pafuri region of the KNP. From here, it passed through Modiakune to reach Inhambane on the coast. It was first described by Father Rita Montanha in 1856.

Another route ran from the Venda lands to the coast by crossing the Lubombo Mountains at the Shingwedzi Gorge. The Lobedu people (ruled over by the famous rain queen Modjadji) used a route further to the south, which crossed the Lubombo Mountains at Shilowa. Other routes in the south traversed the formidable Lubombo range through poorts created by the lower Limpopo and the Sabie rivers.

Joao Albasini's Store

Albasini was born in 1813 on board a ship in the bay of Oporto. His father was Italian and his mother was Spanish, but Joao became a Portuguese citizen by birth. He travelled to Portuguese East Africa (Mozambique) with his father when he was 19, and he was left there to establish trade routes from Delagoa Bay into the interior.

Joao travelled widely and became famous among the local people for his hunting prowess. He also became active in politics and was, at various times, a Vice-Consul for the Portuguese authorities and Native Commissioner of the Schoemansdal district (near modern-day Makhado/Louis Trichardt).

But it was as a trader that he won the widest renown.

Albasini's main trading post was situated within the borders of the modern KNP, on the banks of the Phabeni River. The land for this store was 'purchased' from Chief Magashula in exchange for about 22 head of cattle, and the store became known as Magashulaskraal (or Villa Albasini by the Portuguese).

From here, Albasini developed his lucrative trade network whereby African porters would carry goods on foot when the nagana disease was at its most virulent and oxen couldn't traverse the Lowveld safely. He also knew of a path through the bush that almost bypassed the tsetse fly belt, with only a short stretch of a few hours in the danger zone, and this was similarly exploited as an ox-wagon route. Several satellite camps were established to support his various enterprises.

With all the traffic going and coming from the coast, his trading store became a busy commercial hub. Sportsmen eager for a spot of elephant hunting would also use the store as a convenient base. To feed his guests and the native porters, Albasini started cultivating crops and hunted lots of game. He lived at Magashula's Kraal for only two years, from 1845 to 1847, but this was enough to make it a contender for the first European settlement in the Lowveld.

He then left the Lowveld and moved to the farm, Goedewensch, at the foot of the Soutpansberg mountains. From here, he continued to supervise his little empire. He also organised a monthly mail run to Lourenco Marques as part of his vice-consular duties.

As a major employer, Albasini soon became a well-known figure among the local people. They called him 'Juwawa', in imitation of his Christian name, Joao.

Despite his once-considerable wealth, Juwawa died in poverty in 1888 and his Phabeni store fell into disrepair. The ruin was stabilised and somewhat restored in 1979. The remains of Albasini's store, along with several information boards and displays, are located a short distance from Phabeni Gate.

The Hunters

Historically, the Lowveld has always contained a healthy supply of wildlife but not significantly more than the rest of South Africa. Indeed, in the years before well-armed white men began a centuries-long love affair with the hunt, wild animals abounded across the grasslands and plains of the sub-continent. The rivers were full of hippos and crocs, herds of buck, buffalo and rhino grazed on the rolling hillsides, and predators stalked the abundant prey in a happy, carnivorous game of cat and mouse.

By and large, native African tribes from the Bushmen to the more recent Bantu migrants integrated themselves with this natural order, utilising the herds of game efficiently and sustainably. Even the pastoral Bantu, who arrived with flocks of domesticated goats and cattle, managed to balance their need for pasture with the wild animals' need for space.

It was only when the Europeans arrived from 1500 onwards that the game of southern Africa started taking a hammering. This is because, rather than utilise wildlife for subsistence, the white men brought with them a commercial perspective that saw game as a valuable commodity. Animal products such as leather, fat, meat and ivory soon became monetary objects and were widely used as a form of currency.

The consequences of this exploitation were immediate. Within two years of the first permanent European settlement at the Cape of Good Hope in 1652, the forests around Table Mountain had disappeared, and the penguins and seals which lived on Robben Island were virtually wiped out.

The decrease of penguin numbers was so severe that Jan van Riebeeck was forced to issue a *placaat* (proclamation) which limited the number of penguins that could be harvested each day. This, ironically, was the first 'conservation' order issued by white people in South Africa (see next section).

The African tribes, for their part, were already used to the concept of conservation. The hunting of certain species was often restricted during certain seasons, and 'Royal Game Reserves' were occasionally established for the exclusive use of the king and his guests.

The European's obeyed no such niceties. The Dutch East India Company, who controlled the Cape as a corporate fiefdom, were happy to exploit the commercial value of any natural resources that they could lay their hands on.

Seals from Dassen Island were harvested for their valuable fat. Whales were harpooned in Table Bay for their blubber. Lions, elephants, buck and many other animals were hunted for their meat and hides. In each case, the rampant exploitation of the animals led to sharp drops in their numbers.

This wouldn't have mattered but, as the game disappeared, the Company noticed a consequent decline in its profits. Several restrictive decrees were thus issued. These limited the number of seals that could be harvested, or proscribed which types of trees could be felled, or protected certain species of antelope. However, in every case, it was matter of shutting the gate after the horse had been shot. Soon, there were no trees within a day's ride of the Fort, the seals had abandoned Robben Island altogether, and the big game had been pushed out of the Cape Peninsula by both hunters and the Company's burgeoning herds of cattle.

Things did not get any better when the white farmers began to spread out from the Cape in search of new farmlands. As they went, the white men merrily shot out the game, let their cattle loose on the tender native grasses and generally upset the natural order of things. To be fair, this situation was not unique to South Africa. The same process had already denuded Europe of its native wildlife and similar activities would take place in most territories colonised by the locust-like white settlers.

It didn't help matters that early explorers of the South African interior gleefully reported back that the plains were filled with innumerable herds of exotic animals that would look marvellous when stuffed and mounted on a Duke's wall. The hunt was on!

Throughout the eighteenth and nineteenth centuries, dozens of large-scale game expeditions were organised in which tens of thousands of animals were slaughtered for fun and profit. At the time, this was not seen as a problem because there was thought to be plenty of game around the next bend. But the African horn of plenty was a delusion. As the years passed, hunters began to report fewer and fewer herds, and shooting parties had to travel further inland to find enough game to satisfy their blood lust.

Probably the greatest hunt in South African history took place in 1858, on the farm *Bainsvlei,* west of Bloemfontein. It was a royal hunt, organised in honour of 16-year old Prince Alfred, second son of Queen Victoria, who was visiting his mum's colony. Nothing was left to chance and trackers were sent into the bush to chase the animals towards the royal party.

A local newspaper described the event in glorious detail: *"Masses of game kept breaking through as the pressure of the coming streams of antelopes, quaggas, zebras, blesbok, elands, ostriches, wildebeests, koedoo etc. etc. came pouring on towards us and checked by our fire commenced to whirl. The plain in which we were was of vast extent – I dare say nearly a hundred miles in circumference – and the whole of this extent was one moving mass of game. Prince fired as fast as guns could be handed to him. The circle of natives was closing in and the mass of game became so pressed together at last that the Prince and Currie took to their hunting spears and charged into the midst, driving home the blades into the infuriated animals. The slaughter was tremendous, considering that it did not endure beyond an hour. How many fell on the spot or died afterwards of wounds, it would be difficult to tell. The Prince shot 24. Most of the sportsmen looked more like butchers than sportsmen from being so covered with blood. His Royal Highness and Currie were red up to the shoulders from using the spear."*

Within a hundred years of Van Riebeeck's landing at the Cape, much of the Cape colony was stripped of its wildlife. Within 200 years, two major mammals had become extinct, the Bloubok and the Quagga – although it would be several decades before anyone realised it (see 'The Sad Tale of the Quagga').

After the Cape, it was the turn of the Orange Free State as, slowly but surely, the region between the Orange and Vaal rivers was emptied of its wildlife. Then the game-rich Highveld between the Vaal and Limpopo rivers was similarly drained.

Eventually, the hunters noticed that even the Transvaal's game supplies were drying up and they began to complain to the government. Several laws were passed to try and stem the tide of decimation. Hunting seasons were proclaimed, prohibitions on certain species of game were instituted, hunting licences and quotas were imposed but, without proper enforcement or legal consequences, it was a case of too little, too late.

Even the disease-ridden lowlands that would one day become the Kruger Park were heavily frequented by hunters. These hardy souls were drawn to the Lowveld by the plentiful herds of game and, each winter, several dozen hunting parties would trek into the area. These expeditions lasted for several months at a time and thousands of dead animals were hauled out of the bush every year. The once-plentiful herds of were subsequently shot out to such an extent that the area was virtually devoid of buck and large mammals by the late 1890s.

Nevertheless, the successful hunter was seen as a hero in the Lowveld. A man could win wide renown for his sharp eyes and steady hands, and several hunters became celebrities. This hunting elite included Henry Glynn and his two sons, Henry and Arthur, Bill Sanderson, David Schoeman, Stephanus Cecil 'Bvakenya' Barnard and Abel Erasmus (the fearsome Native Commissioner of the region).

Strangely, the hunting of lions was not very popular at this time. The big cats were difficult to kill and they had no real value, other than providing material for a good campfire story and a throw-rug. Instead, hunters preferred antelope with impressive horns and other grazers with the potential for either meat or display.

Faced with the collapse of the hunting economy due to a lack of game, it was decided that something had to be done to protect and preserve the wildlife that was still left. Not to avoid the local extinction of dozens of species, you understand, but to ensure that future generations would have something left to hunt! And in this incongruous manner began South Africa's modern conservation movement.

The First Conservation Order in South Africa

The following entry was made in Jan Van Riebeeck's journal on 14 April 1654:

"As within two or three days at the most we shall have no penguins left [in the Fort's stores]... we once again sent the boat with five casks to Robben Island, giving instructions to the bookkeeper Verburgh... to salt enough penguins to fill the casks and bring back alive as many as could conveniently be conveyed here. In view of the heavy consumption and the scantiness of our victuals, and to prevent the islands from being devoid of these birds, we gave orders that instead of thrice daily, food should be served only twice... and in the evening only half a penguin per person."

Just to put this order into perspective, the penguin population on Robben Island probably totalled tens of thousands when the Dutch first landed at the Cape. Within two years, a European population of a couple of hundred people had virtually wiped out the island's colony. Furthermore, the settlers were also hunting hippos, seals, buck and other wildlife in the mountains around the Cape, and they were also trying (rather unsuccessfully) to cultivate a vegetable garden on the slopes of Table Mountain. Clearly, the poor penguins of Robben Island were no match for the voracious appetites of the Europeans.

The Big Five

In the nineteenth century, the hunter epitomised bravery and pluck. The popular press was filled with exciting stories of life in the African bush, and the public lionised famous Big Game hunters, such as Frederick Courtney Selous, Denys Finch Hatton (who was portrayed by Robert Redford in *Out of Africa)* and William Cornwallis Harris. It was the latter who said "[I have been accused of having] 'shooting madness' and truly a most delightful mania I have ever found it."

It was during this time that the hunting fraternity in Africa coined the term 'Big Five Game'. Today, this is best understood as a tourism term for the five animals you have to spot before you can go home. The original concept, however, refers to the five species of African game that were considered the most dangerous to hunt. In no particular order, these were determined to be lion, rhino, leopard, buffalo and elephant.

The entrance criterion for the Big Five was evidently quite strict. Hippos, for example, were not included because it's easy to shoot a hippo – just go down to the river and fire away. Large mammals such as giraffes, wildebeest and antelope were also excluded, as were lesser predators such as cheetahs, hyenas and wild dog.

The list was so exclusive only the aggressive black rhino (which is prone to charge when cornered) made the cut. The more passive white rhino was not originally part of the Big Five. In South Africa, however, we don't like to judge things on the basis of colour, so we just refer to 'rhino'.

Whatever its origins, the Big Five concept plays an enormously important role in the popularity and marketing of wildlife reserves in South Africa. It is a keystone of our tourism industry; a convenient (if vague) label which has come to sum up the game viewing experience. The Big Five are so central to the South African culture, they used to have pride of place on our currency – until the new 'Randelas' replaced them with an image of our beloved Madiba.

From a game viewing perspective, however, the Big Five are not particularly rare and not particularly big. Some say that they are not even that interesting. They are simply five species grouped together by a bunch of hunters over a century ago. And yet we still have an obsession with them. Ask anyone who has visited the KNP what game they spotted and their answer will inevitably start with, 'I saw four of the Big Five'.

I think this is a bit of a pity. It takes attention away from many other, equally worthy species and causes tourists to get tunnel vision. But it's all about marketing and there are few brands bigger than the Big Five.

So, for the moment, any self-respecting game park simply has to contain the Big Five. It's almost a prerequisite, a badge of authenticity, a vital accreditation. Basically, if your reserve doesn't contain this cantankerous quintet, you'd better have something very special, like tap-dancing zebras, to have any chance of pulling in the crowds.

The Big Five (actually six) are:
- Lion: *Panthera leo*
- African or Cape Buffalo: *Syncerus caffer*
- Leopard: *Panthera pardus*
- Black Rhino: *Diceros bicornis*
- White Rhino: *Ceratotherium simum*
- Elephant: *Loxodonta cyclotis*

Theodore Roosevelt and the Great Safari

Subconsciously, many game reserves and lodges hark back to the era of the Great White Hunter for their styling cues and narratives. This is usually expressed in a colonial theme that manifests itself in many ways: the uniformed staff in pith helmets, the luxurious tented camps, the overstuffed leather armchairs, extravagant meals on crisp linen served under the stars, etc. It all seems to evoke an earlier time when tea was served in the morning and gin was served at night.

The prototype for this kind of safari experience was established by the long line of British hunter-gentlemen who ventured into Africa during the Victorian era. Yet, arguably, the most famous safari of the modern age was undertaken by the American president Theodore (Teddy) Roosevelt in 1909.

This expedition was organised by the Smithsonian Institution and the National Geographic Society, which were keen to collect African specimens for their natural history collections. Thus, armed with both guns and scientific fervour, the party was led into the wilds of British East Africa (Kenya) by none other than the legendary hunter Frederick Courtney Selous.

It was a very successful trip. In total, they shot or trapped 11,397 animals, ranging from insects to reptiles to mammals. Tons of preserved animal carcasses and skins were shipped back to the States, where they were duly stuffed and mounted. The task took years, but the zoos and museums of America were grateful for all their new exhibits.

Roosevelt felt proud of this contribution to science and wrote glowingly of his exploits in the popular book *African Game Trails*. He also paid tribute to Selous who, he said, was "the last of the mighty hunters whose experience lay in the greatest hunting ground which this world has seen."

Selous, for his part, would eventually grow weary of hunting and began to appreciate game while it was alive, as opposed to when it lay bleeding on the ground. In his later life, he would apply his considerable knowledge of the bush to more constructive uses and became a sincere supporter of conservation efforts. He was not alone, and several of the most voracious hunters became what were called 'penitent butchers'.

For his part, Roosevelt remained an enthusiastic hunter until the day he died but he was also a steadfast supporter of conservation efforts in America. As president, he set aside more federal lands, national parks, national forests, national monuments and nature preserves than all his predecessors combined. For more info about Roosevelt and his role in America's conservation journey, check out Ken Burns' epic 12-hour documentary series called 'The National Parks – America's Best Idea'.

The First to Go

The Blue Antelope, or Bloubok (*Hippotragus loncophaeus*) was a striking looking beast. It resembled a roan antelope in its size and in the shape of its horns, and its coat had a curious blue-grey hue. Van Riebeeck mentions the creature in his journal of 1653, when some of his men watched four hyenas attack a strange animal. The men chased off the hyenas and took the carcass back to the Fort for closer inspection.

The Bloubok's habitat was limited to the plains of the south-western Cape, and it was never very common. Within 150 years, it had been shot out of existence. The last Bloubok was probably shot in the Swellendam district in 1799.

Today there are four mounted Bloubok specimens housed in the museums of Stockholm, Vienna, Leiden and Paris. The South African Museum in Cape Town only has a couple of teeth.

The Sad Tale of the Quagga

The quagga *(Equus quagga)* was an odd-looking thing. Half horse and half zebra, it had brown stripes on its head, neck, shoulders and halfway down its torso. The bottom half of its trunk was an unbroken chestnut colour. Their name was an imitation of their 'shrill, barking neigh', and they were generally tame and easy to hunt.

The African tribes were very fond of eating quagga and used their skins to make bags and clothing. At one time, it was written that the plains of South Africa were "darkened as far as the eye can reach with a moving phalanx of gnoos [wildebeest] and quaggas whose numbers literally baffle computation."

Since quaggas were so acquiescent, the white hunters and farmers literally made a meal of them. Over the years, the quagga population dwindled but people didn't seem to notice. Then, quite suddenly, no-one could remember the last time they had seen one. The Cape Government gave it legal protection in 1888, but the last wild quagga had probably been shot during the early 1860s.

Several quaggas still lived in captivity, however, including a single female specimen that had been a resident of the Amsterdam Zoo in Holland since 1867. On the 12th of August 1883, this elderly creature – the last of its kind – died in its cage. The quagga species had ceased to exist.

Today, there are some physical remains of the quagga stored in several museums around the world. In total, this collection consists of 22 skins, 13 skulls and 8 mounted specimens. There is also an ambitious attempt to re-create a real, live quagga through selective breeding. For more information on this genetic experiment, check out the 'Quagga Project' online.

The Kruger Declaration

During the later 19th century, the government of the Zuid-Afrikaanse Republiek (ZAR) had a lot on its mind. The territory, also known as the Transvaal, was short of cash and many of the farmers were struggling to make ends meet. Furthermore, the British were poking their nose into Boer affairs from their adjacent Cape and Natal colonies, and the threat of annexation was looming.

In the 1870s and 1880s, however, alluvial gold was found in the ZAR; first near Pietersburg (now Polokwane), then in Pilgrim's Rest, and then in the rivers around nearby Barberton. In 1886, the stakes were dramatically increased when the world's richest gold reef was discovered on the Witwatersrand, halfway between the towns of Heidelberg and Pretoria.

The discovery of gold was a mixed blessing for President Paul Kruger. It was certainly a welcome source of income, but it also gave the British another reason to try and take over the troublesome Boer republic. With all of this going on, it is surprising that anyone in government had the time to worry about the vanishing herds of game.

Nevertheless, the economy of the ZAR was largely rural, based around hunting, and wild game supplied much of the electorate with meat, ivory, leather, biltong and sport. It was therefore a major cause for concern when, year after year, hunting parties reported smaller hauls and fewer animals to kill.

The problem was first mooted back in 1846 when the Volksraad (parliament) of the then-independent republic of Andries-Ohrigstad passed a proclamation urging its citizens to kill only as many animals as could be used at any one time, or an amount 'sufficient for one's own consumption'. This decree was the first conservation ordinance in the Transvaal. It also prohibited any 'foreigners' from hunting in the Ohrigstad region, under threat of banishment.

The proclamation had little effect, however. In 1855 alone, more than 90 000 kilograms of ivory was exported from the Transvaal, along with the usual heaps of skin and bone. By 1858, the game had become so scarce, even the most hard-headed hunter had to face facts or face ruin.

A new regulation was thus passed, a 'law for the improved regulation of the hunting of elephant and other wild animals in the South African Republic'. Unfortunately, this rather useless piece of legislation was skewed towards a specific political agenda and the majority of its clauses were designed to restrict the local African tribes' access to wild animals. The act stipulated that black people either had to be an authorised servant of a white man or have a 'pass' before they would be allowed to hunt.

Clearly, this restriction had little to do with game and more to do with making the black people less self-sufficient and therefore a more reliable source of labour.

It was also a heavy-handed way to disarm the black people, who had become proficient shots and were thought to present a threat to their white masters. Besides, the native tribes had been sustainably hunting wild animals for generations without denuding game at any noticeable degree.

In any case, the new law was impossible to enforce. Most of the white hunters were largely reliant on their 'zwarteskutters' (black shooters) and 'jagtkaffers' (hunting niggers) when out in the bush, and the white people couldn't really afford to disarm the hands that fed them. Nevertheless, in 1870, another law was passed to entrench and extend the 'preservationist' clauses from 1858.

But it was to no avail and in 1884, the Volksraad of the Zuid Afrikaanse Republiek heard representations from various parties about the 'rapid extermination' of the Transvaal's game stocks. Several people appealed to the new President, Paul Kruger, to restrict hunting and protect the game before it was exterminated altogether. The motion was turned down.

What followed this dismissal has now become quite controversial and historically contentious – in fact, much of the conservation history of South Africa is disputed or at least contradictory, so you will have to bear with me as we navigate our way through the dimly-lit past together.

Most traditional histories of conservation in South Africa hold that 'Oom Paul' (Uncle Paul) was always a committed conservationist at heart. They hold that, even though the 1884 motion was not passed by the Volksraad, Kruger remained a committed supporter of the concept and worked to create a reserve in which wild animals could be protected.

However, environmental historian Jane Carruthers challenges this version of events and points out that Kruger and his executive committee refused to take any action in this regard. Instead, they explicitly stated that the old game laws were good enough. Carruthers further suggests that this misapprehension about Kruger's motives stems from a typo in the book *South African Eden* by James Stevenson-Hamilton, and that the idea for a government reserve only began to take shape in 1889.

Be that as it may, nothing was done and the hunting continued unabated. By the late 1880s, the local extinction of several large mammal species was becoming likely and concerned private citizens started taking matters into their own hands.

For example, in the Bredasdorp region near Cape Agulhas, a number of farmers got together to protect a small herd of Bontebok, which had become extinct elsewhere. In the Kroonstad district, one farmer decided to establish a sanctuary for the rapidly disappearing black wildebeest. A similar haven was secured for the endangered Mountain Zebra in the mountains near Cradock. It is largely thanks to the efforts of these far-thinking farmers that we still have living specimens of these three species today.

Likewise, back in the Transvaal, a farmer in the Wakkerstroom district was busy with an experiment of his own. His name was Alexander Robertson and he was tired of his horses roaming over the countryside. So, he erected a wire fence along his property - the first enclosure of its kind in the Transvaal. Soon, Robertson noticed that a number of buck were slipping under the fence to graze in the relative safety of his sanctuary.

Although the buck came and went with the seasons, Robertson was encouraged to erect several additional enclosures which eventually encompassed an area of 9400 hectares. Robertson's son later recalled, "Blesbok and springbok were far in the majority though there were also considerable numbers of rooi and vaal rhebok, oribi, steenbok and duikers. Wildebeest, zebra and eland were a nuisance as they damaged the fences and were not encouraged. However, many farmers agreed to stop all unnecessary shooting and hunting."

Soon, news of this remarkable enclosure reached the ears of Albert Stoop, member of the Volksraad for Wakkerstroom. Stoop happened to be a friend of President Paul Kruger and a relative through marriage, and he passed on news of the enclosure to Oom Paul. Accordingly, the next time Kruger toured the country in his mule cart, he popped in at Robertson's farm to check out the little game sanctuary for himself.

Duly impressed by the astonishing difference a bit of fencing could make, Kruger and his Secretary of State, WJ Leyds, put a motion before the Volksraad which would forbid hunting on certain portions of state land, at least until the game stocks could recover. There were only two objections to the scheme and, in 1889, Article 1244 was passed making provision for the establishment of game reserves in the Transvaal for the first time.

It is important to note, however, that these were not game reserves as we know them today, i.e. animal sanctuaries where hunting was banned in perpetuity. Instead, they were considered 'preserves' where hunting was forbidden for a number of years so that the game would have a chance to recover before the hunters were allowed back in.

The Pongola Reserve

One of the opponents of the game reserves scheme, a certain Meneer De Beer, demanded to know the location of the government's proposed wildlife park. At the suggestion of JC Krogh, the landdrost (magistrate) of Wakkerstroom, Kruger identified a site on the banks of the Pongola River, in the south-eastern part of the Transvaal (now located in northern KwaZulu-Natal).

This area was eminently unsuitable for a game reserve. It was too small, too mountainous and didn't contain any significant stocks of game, but it was strategically important. Squeezed between the southern boundary of Swaziland

and the northern border of British-controlled Zululand, the Pongola reserve gave the Transvaal an access point from which they could conceivably reach the sea. Thus, by proclaiming the Pongola Game Reserve, the Transvaal Republic could entrench themselves in this ambiguous border area and potentially gain some valuable territory.

Despite the apparent urgency with which the law of 1889 was passed, it took several years before any concrete steps were taken. Eventually, the Pongola Reserve was declared in 1894. The services of a ranger, HF Van Oordt, were secured and the necessary farms were purchased.

The following announcement appeared in the *Staatscourant der Zuid-Afrikaansche Republiek* (Government Gazette of the South African Republic):

Proclamation R8009/89

"*I, Stephanus Johannes Paulus Kruger, State President of the South African Republic, acting on the advice and with the consent of the Executive Council and authorised hereto by the Honourable Volksraad by resolution of 2 August 1889 Article 1244, herewith make known and proclaim the following farms in the bushveld of the District Piet Retief between the Pongola, Swaziland and Lebombo as Government Game Reserve...*"

The Pongola Game Reserve, with a total area of 17400 hectares, was now official. Sadly, the history of the Pongola Reserve would prove to be ignominious. The reserve was simply too small to support any significant herds of game and the entire enterprise was neglected from its very inception. It was deproclaimed in 1921.

The Delagoa Bay Railway Line

The Boer republics, disorganised as they were, sought one thing above all else – to avoid any form of British interference in their affairs. The problem was that Boer goods still had to pass through the British ports of Cape Town and Durban, where they were heavily taxed.

The only other suitable harbour was located at Lourenço Marques (Maputo), which was under Portuguese control. Unfortunately, as we have seen, the transport route from the Transvaal to Lourenço Marques traversed the dangerous malaria and tsetse fly belt of the Lowveld. Mass transportation of goods was therefore impractical.

In the past, Joao Albasini had proposed using steam tractors to pull wagons through the dangerous region, and other people had suggested using river transport that wasn't reliant on oxen. However, it was clear that a railway line was the only sustainable solution. This scheme was first presented to the Volksraad by George Moodie in 1872, and was supported by then-President Burgers of the Transvaal.

Over the next 10 years, several attempts were made to raise enough capital to construct the line. A number of Boer representatives (including Burghers himself) went to Europe to drum up financing, but the unsettled political situation in the ZAR turned many investors away. Then, a low-grade war broke out between the Boers and Sekukhune of the Pedi. It was the final straw as far as investors were concerned and the dream of a railway line to Delagoa Bay began to fade.

By 1883, however, the government was once again talking up a rail link to Lourenço Marques. Major Joachim Machado was sent out to select a route, which he determined should run from Pretoria, across the Highveld, down the Eland's Spruit valley, and along the Crocodile River valley to Komatipoort. From here it was an easy chug to the sea at Delagoa Bay, making a total journey of 352 miles each way.

Both the Portuguese and Transvaal authorities were encouraged by this survey and it was agreed that each side would be responsible for financing and constructing their side of the line. The Portuguese granted the construction concession to the Delagoa Bay and East African Railway Company, and the Transvaal (now under the formidable Paul Kruger) granted their concession to a Holland-based consortium called the *Nederlandsche Zuit-Afrikaansche Spoorweg Maatschappij* (NZASM). After all the negotiations and paperwork had been settled, work on the line finally began on the Portuguese side in 1887.

A period of great activity now gripped the sleepy towns of Lourenço Marques and Komatipoort. Hundreds of white overseers and thousands of black workers swept into the area, and everyone indulged in their usual pastimes of drinking, fighting and arguing. Nevertheless, work continued apace.

By May 1891, the line was open from Lourenço Marques to the South African border at Komatipoort. By December, it had reached Malelane, on the southern border of the KNP. By 1892, it had reached Kaapmuiden, which gave the miners on the Barberton gold fields access to the railway.

A number of hills and difficult inclines along the Upper Crocodile River Valley now slowed construction of the line. During this time many men succumbed to malaria (the fatality rate was estimated at around 15%) and thousands of oxen and donkeys were taken down, either by *nagana* or the various predators which still roamed free. The line only reached present-day Nelspruit in June 1892 and, exhausted, the construction team took a break for several months.

By 1894, the line had reached Waterval Onder (Below the Waterfall). Here, the land rose sharply and a number of ingenious engineering solutions were required to conquer the slopes. A 213 metre tunnel was bored through the side of the mountain and a 914 metre cutting was made through the rock face. Once on top of the massif, the railway finally attained the high ground of the plateau and, from here, it was a relatively easy ride over the rolling grasslands to Pretoria.

The so-called Eastern Line linking Pretoria to the sea was finally opened in July 1895. Unfortunately, the Second Anglo-Boer War (or South African War) broke out just a few years later, in 1899. After several years of bitter fighting, the British finally resorted to starving the Boers into submission through a 'scorched earth' policy and, when the war ended in 1902, the British victors re-directed trade to its ports at the Cape and Natal. The much vaunted rail link to Delagoa Bay thus proved to be of little use, although it did much to open up the eastern Transvaal and Lowveld for development.

The Selati Rail Scandal

In 1890, while the Eastern Line was being built, a member of the Volksraad introduced a petition from the Soutpansberg district requesting the construction of a branch line from Komatipoort to the rich farmlands of the north-eastern Transvaal. This railway was to be run along the Selati River and would also service the booming goldfields around the Murchison range, based at the towns of Leydsdorp and Gravelotte.

The concession to build and operate this line was awarded to a dodgy French entrepreneur named Eugene Oppenheim. He had secured the contract with the help of thousands of pounds of bribes that were paid to various members of the Volksraad in exchange for their support. After several months of haggling, it was agreed that Oppenheim and his investors would put up about one quarter of the two-million-pound construction budget and the Transvaal government would put up the rest.

Work on the Selati Line began in 1892 and earthworks up to the Sabie River were completed by the middle of 1893. During this time, the Oppenheim consortium was busy with a number of fraudulent deals that made them huge profits at the expense of the Transvaal government. Books were cooked, false expense claims were made and the company, based in Brussels, signed a bewildering series of agreements with sub-contractors to obfuscate their financial mismanagement.

By 1895, however, the Selati scandal broke wide open when JS Smit (the government Railway Commissioner) began to investigate the whole controversial affair. Consequently, a series of legal suits and counter-suits were initiated by the Transvaal Government, the Oppenheim consortium, outraged shareholders and the Brussels authorities.

As a result, work on the Selati line was abruptly halted. Sub-contractors and labourers were cut loose in the Bushveld with no pay and they indignantly downed their tools and left. Hundreds of construction implements and stocks of building material were thus abandoned in the veld and this impromptu stockpile lay undisturbed for the next ten years.

At the end of the whole Selati affair, the Transvaal government was left with 74 miles of useless track that ended in the middle of nowhere. Over one million pounds had disappeared into the pockets of unscrupulous businessmen and just about every politician in the Transvaal was revealed as greedy and corrupt.

The Oppenheim brothers were sentenced to three years in a Brussels prison, but no action was taken against any members of the Volksraad who were complicit in the fraud. The Zuid-Afrikaanse Republiek became the laughing stock of the financial community and it was said that you couldn't find a single honest man in the whole of the Transvaal. Just think of the Selati Line as South Africa's original gravy train.

But the Selati Line did eventually prove it's worth – as we shall see in the pages that follow...

Birth of the Sabi Game Reserve

During the 1890s, things grew increasingly chaotic in the ramshackle republic of the Transvaal. Since the discovery of the Main Reef, Johannesburg had been growing in leaps and bounds as people from all over the world flooded into the golden city in search of their fortune. But these foreigners (called 'uitlanders' by the Boers) did not have a vote in the Republic and soon began clamouring for a political voice.

At the same time, the British were stepping up their plans to annex the newly wealthy Transvaal territory along with the rather shabby Orange Free State. Their plan was to unite the two Boer republics with the Cape and Natal colonies to create a fancy new confederation that would be under imperial control. Clearly, there was a major conflict brewing.

It was in this environment of xenophobia and mistrust that the first concrete proposal for a wildlife preserve in the Lowveld was put forward to the Volksraad of the Transvaal, in 1895. The two men who tabled the motion were RK Loveday and JL Van Wyk, members of the Volksraad for Barberton and Krugersdorp respectively.

They believed that "seeing that nearly all the big game in this republic has been exterminated and that those animals still remaining are becoming less day by day so that there is danger of their becoming extinct altogether, [we] request permission to discuss the desirability of authorising the government to proclaim a Government Game Sanctuary, where the killing of game shall be prohibited altogether." They further suggested a suitable area for this reserve, "a certain portion of the District Lydenburg, being Government land, where most of the big game species are still to be found."

To support their proposal, Loveday and Van Wyk pointed out that the Lowveld area was disease-ridden, unsuitable for agriculture, mineralogically insignificant and inhabited by only a couple of thousand tribal denizens and a handful of nutty Europeans. It seemed like a no-brainer.

Nevertheless, the initial vote on whether or not to discuss the proposal in parliament was a close one. It passed with a tiny majority of twelve to eleven. The actual debate (which took place on the 17th of September 1895) went much better and no significant opposition was recorded. The resolution passed comfortably, but the final vote was not unanimous.

However, as is often the way with politics, this resolution was not the end of the matter. Indeed, what followed proved to be an abject lesson in procrastination, bureaucracy and political expedience.

The problem was that the Volksraad did not have the power to proclaim a game reserve. That authority rested with President Kruger and his executive. The

Volksraad could only make a request to the supreme council, asking it to proclaim a reserve by putting the necessary notice in the government papers. Unfortunately, the council did nothing of the sort and the 'game preserve' failed to materialise.

In 1896, Loveday wrote to WJ Leyds, the State Secretary of the Transvaal, and enquired why nothing had been done about the Volksraad's request. Hunting was continuing within the proposed preserve and the game was diminishing every season. Once again, nothing happened.

Part of this inactivity is understandable. These were turbulent times in the Transvaal, with the British actively agitating to overthrow the Boer government. It is also likely that the Kruger regime did not want to alienate their electorate, which still considered hunting a basic right and a major source of income.

Loveday, however, was not about to be deterred. In November 1897, he again wrote to the Executive Council and demanded to know why the wishes of the Volksraad in this regard had been ignored for more than two years. Finally, the lugubrious politicians discussed the matter and, three months later, the Sabi Game Reserve was proclaimed. The date was now March 1898.

And it was still not a done deal. The Executive considered that the proclamation was only the first step towards declaring a reserve. Opinions had to be sought, surveys had to be done, time had to be wasted. Eventually, Loveday lost his patience and stood up in the Volksraad to openly criticise the inactivity of Kruger and his cronies.

Faced with such naked hostility, the Executive Committee relented and, in September 1898, the council announced that the new reserve would cover the region bounded by the Crocodile River in the South, the Sabi River in the north and the Lubombo mountains in the East. The Western boundary, however, was poorly defined as it lacked any distinctive natural markers.

A white warden was appointed at an annual salary of £250 and it would be his duty, along with four native policemen, to prevent hunting and poaching within the conservation area. The first official warden was WM Walker, but he proved to be a disappointment. Several successive wardens were quickly hired and fired, but none seemed a good match for the job.

Nevertheless, the wheels had begun to turn. The champion of the Lowveld game reserve, RK Loveday, had seen his plans come to fruition through vision, dedication and sheer bloody-mindedness. His role in the establishment of what would become the world-famous Kruger National Park has largely been forgotten, and this is not fair. Much later, the estimable James Stevenson-Hamilton confessed in his journal that the national park would have been better named in Loveday's honour rather than Kruger's.

A Bellicose Interruption

But then, just when things were getting going, the Second Anglo-Boer War broke out. Also known as the South African War, the conflict was largely instigated by the British, who thought that the conflict would be a short, sharp affair in which their army would sweep aside the backward Boers and usher in a glorious era of imperial rule over most of the sub-continent.

But it was not to be. The war lasted for 3 gruelling years and, after several early British victories, it quickly degenerated into a 'war of attrition'; a series of skirmishes and raids that proved impossible to stop – not unlike the present-day conflicts in Iraq or Afghanistan. The problem, for the British, was that the enemy refused to mount a massed force that could be defeated in a single battle. Instead, the rebarbative Boers formed themselves into small fighting units, which harried the British troops and then melted away – a model that came to be known as a 'guerrilla war'.

Understandably, the issue of the game reserves paled into insignificance and the early wardens of the Sabi Reserve were regularly released from their duties in order to contribute to the war effort. But even after the British took control of Pretoria, causing Kruger and his cabinet to flee, the war continued to drag on.

Eventually, the British resorted to a 'scorched earth' policy, in which the imperial forces burnt all the Boer farmlands in an attempt to starve out the Boer commandos. They also incarcerated thousands of woman, children and black farm workers in concentration camps, where disease and malnutrition took an appalling toll. This drastic action finally brought the festering guerrilla war to a bitter and inconclusive close in 1902, when the Boers reluctantly sued for peace.

By this time, however, the mighty Queen Victoria was dead and the British Empire was entering its period of terminal decline. Kruger also died two years later (in Clarens, Switzerland) while still in exile.

Meanwhile, in the Lowveld, an irregular force of British soldiers known as Steinaecker's Horse had taken it upon themselves to patrol the border with Mozambique, and the entire region was nominally under the control of the self-proclaimed suzerain, General FCL von Steinaecker.

Once again, it seemed that the issue of a wildlife protection in the wastes of the Lowveld was going to be forgotten and the nascent game reserve seemed likely to be de-proclaimed just as soon as the new British authorities got around to it.

The Sabi Reserve Resurrected

Once the trauma of the Second Anglo-Boer War ended, the entire country was in a state of uncertainty. The British Lord Milner was now in control and political negotiations with the defeated Boers were underway to hammer out a workable system of government. This eventually took the form of 'responsible government' by local politicians, as supervised by the colonial authorities in Britain. Eventually, in 1910, the new setup was formalised when the Union of South Africa was declared under prime minister Louis Botha (a Boer War general), and the new country became part of the British Dominions – later known as the Commonwealth.

For the purposes of our story, however, two important new figures entered the picture immediately after the war ended: Sir Godfrey Lagden and James Stevenson-Hamilton.

Lagden was appointed by Lord Milner to head the Department of Native Affairs, which had rather strangely inherited the administration of game reserves from the republican government.

By this time, several game protection agencies had been formed, both in Britain and in South Africa. Among these, the 'Society for the Preservation of the Wild Fauna of the Empire' and the 'Transvaal Game Protection Association' were two of the most prominent and they lobbied hard for various restrictions on hunting.

Oddly enough, these organisations had no problem with 'sports' hunting, in which well-equipped hunters went out to pit their shooting skills against any hapless antelope who crossed their path. They did object, however, to hunters who shot animals for commercial gain and found it appalling that anyone would kill magnificent wild animals for the measly value of their hides or flesh. Similarly, they deplored the native African hunters who trapped or stalked the game on foot, as this was seen as barbaric.

In fact, this was the one thing both Briton and Boer agreed on: the black hunters were deemed responsible for the rapid decrease in game numbers, despite the fact that African hunters had been going about their business for hundreds of years without any noticeable decline in game populations. It has been suggested, however, that since the members of these game organizations tended to be powerful landowners and businessmen, the real motive behind this stance was to deprive the native populations of their traditional source of sustenance and thus force them to seek work in the cities, farms and on the mines.

In any case, these pressure groups did convince the newly appointed British authorities to re-proclaim three of the Transvaal's game reserves: Pongola, Sabi and Groenkloof (a small enclave on the outskirts of Pretoria). The purpose of the game reserves was also explicitly declared for the first time.

Previously, the function of the wildlife preserves was ill-defined and they were thought of as little more than emergency measures to protect the few specimens of game that were left. Now, as was the British way, all the confusion was cleared up and a statement of intent was issued.

Henceforth, the game reserves would become reservoirs for game; places where hunting would be forbidden for several years so that the game numbers could increase. Thereafter, gentlemen hunters would be allowed into the reserves (for a suitable fee) and the shooting would recommence in an orderly and supposedly sustainable manner. Basically, the game reserves would be protected as breeding grounds for antelope and other big game so that the hunters of the future would have something left to kill.

It should also be noted that, at this time, the term 'game' applied mainly to the various antelope species that the hunters were so keen on shooting. Any predatory animals which stalked the buck (including lion, leopards, wild dogs, cheetah and crocodiles) were considered vermin and were thought to be only worthy of extermination. Hippo, giraffe, elephant, buffalo, wildebeest and other large ruminants were thought to be exotic and exciting to hunt, but remained secondary considerations. It was all about getting horned trophies to mount in one's manor house.

As soon as the hunting fraternity heard of the re-proclamation of the Sabi Game Reserve, several hopefuls (most of whom were keen hunters themselves) quickly applied to Sir Godfrey for the post of warden. A couple of unsuitable candidates were duly appointed but soon left or were dismissed. Then, in 1902, Lagden met a rather taciturn Scottish military officer named James Stevenson-Hamilton. The two men hit it off and Lagden offered Stevenson-Hamilton the warden's job at Sabi.

An aristocrat by birth and an iconoclast by nature, there could have been few candidates less likely for this tough and lonely position. But upon due consideration, James Stevenson-Hamilton accepted the post. He would stay on as head warden of the park from 1902 until his retirement in 1946. In many ways, he would become both father and mother of the Kruger National Park, and helped it grow from a dusty little orphan into the belle of the ball.

James Stevenson-Hamilton meets his 'Cinderella'

James Stevenson-Hamilton, or JSH as I will now call him, is both an iconic and iconoclastic figure in the history of the Kruger National Park. He was an altogether remarkable man and it is due in no small part to his redoubtable strength and passion that we have the financially healthy and biologically wealthy Kruger Park of today. But at the outset, he was certainly an unlikely saviour for an unloved game sanctuary in the wild South African Lowveld.

JSH was born in 1867 to Hilda Hamilton and James Stevenson. When he was still in his teens, his uncle (on his mother's side) died without leaving an heir and the young James inherited the Hamilton family estate, a substantial affair called Fairholm in Western Scotland. One condition of his inheritance was that he adopt the family name 'Hamilton' and thus he gained a rather cumbersome surname along with his title of Laird.

Although he was born into the landed gentry of the Victorian Age, JSH did not always have a happy childhood. His father was distant (as Victorian fathers were wont to be, apparently) and his mother died a few days after giving birth to her third child. James' father remarried in time, but his second wife also died as a result of complications arising from childbirth. The twice-widowed James Senior was thus left with several children and an expensive estate to run. A third marriage proved to be very unhappy and a source of constant tension within the family.

For the most part, JSH received a pretty standard education for his class. He attended several suitably prominent private schools (such as Rugby – which he hated) and military academies (Sandhurst – which he also hated). He performed adequately during his studies but was not inspired to excel. Nevertheless, the personal journals which he kept from a young age are filled with expressions of ambition and a desire to make a difference in the world.

As he headed into his twenties, the young JSH began spending time in London. Here he developed a reputation as a playboy and man-about-town; acquiring several expensive habits and enjoying many of the luxuries of late-Victorian life. He attended theatre, went carousing at all the popular watering holes and dated a number of attractive young females. Yet for all his apparent frivolity and extravagance, JSH seemed to want more.

Whatever happened, there was little doubt that James would one day enter the military. His father's family were all military men of good standing and reputation, and being an officer in the army was one of the most honourable things a member of the otherwise unemployable aristocracy could do. So, despite his rather short stature (he was only 5 feet 4 inches tall), JSH studied hard and, after several unsuccessful examinations, finally passed out of Sandhurst. Then he began the difficult business of shopping around for a military commission in the cavalry which, in those days, had to be purchased for a considerable sum of money.

To make matters worse, JSH was something of an individualist. He did not like the mindless routine of army life and often rebelled against the authority of his superiors, especially if he thought they were being stupid or incompetent. His penchant for speaking his mind would get him into trouble throughout his life.

As a result of his rather challenging personality (which would later turn downright cantankerous) James did not thrive in the military. He eventually secured a post in the 6th (Inniskilling) Dragoons, thanks to his family connections, and he tried his utmost to be a cavalry officer in the best Victorian tradition. But it was a hard slog. The self-reliant and often solitary young man was at his best when he was let loose in the field and left to his own devices. He was at his worst when he was cooped up with the troops and forced to perform endless drills on the parade ground.

Unfortunately, at that time, the old-fashioned British army was all about drilling. In fact, the entire 'art' of British warfare was based on rigid battlefield manoeuvres and military discipline required unquestioning obedience to one's superior officers. This was not to JSH's taste.

Furthermore, he was frustrated by the lack of good wars. In previous decades, the British Empire was full of battles and campaigns in which a good officer could impress the generals and win promotion. During James' tenure, however, all the juicy conflicts had been resolved and the cavalry as a fighting force was fast becoming obsolete. James' prospects were thus bleak and his military career stalled.

Things began to look up during the 1880s, however, when his platoon was sent to South Africa to subdue a native rebellion in Zululand. James thrived in the warm African climate and thoroughly enjoyed his time in the colonies, but the fun was quickly over and the 6th Dragoons were sent back to Britain. A dejected James then spent nine tortuous years, from 1890 to 1898, killing time with his division in various training camps around the UK.

The boredom mounted and the numbing routine soon became anathema to the strong-willed James. He grew restless, then frustrated and then depressed as his ambitions were constantly thwarted by the stodgy military hierarchy. Furthermore, he had an expensive estate to look after and income from the family land was decreasing every year. It was clear to the young James that he had to do something to improve his position, but he confided in his journal that he simply didn't know what.

Desperate for a change of pace, JSH took a risk and applied for leave from his platoon so that he could join an exploratory expedition to Barotseland (now Zambia). This trip, organised by the rather ambiguous figure of Alfred Gibbons, lasted from 1898 to 1899 and was intended to show that the upper stretches of the Zambezi River were navigable by boat.

Regrettably for the sponsors, the expedition proved just the opposite and the entire enterprise was a bit of a bust. Nevertheless, the journey proved to be a turning point for the young James who, much to his surprise, found that he loved Africa and thoroughly enjoyed roughing it through the unexplored wilderness.

He especially excelled when he was out on his own, making his own decisions and using his own initiative. He was clearly a person who preferred to operate under his own authority and was quite prepared to bear the consequences of his actions. He also experienced his first bout of malaria during this trip but he pulled through and was thus 'salted' for future exposure to the disease – even though he suffered from recurring bouts of malaria throughout his life.

When the expedition ended, James was unsure of his next step. Fortuitously (for him) by this time the Second Anglo-Boer War had broken out and JSH decided to rejoin his platoon, which had conveniently been posted to South Africa to support the imperial war effort. Eager for recognition and newly versed in the ways of the African continent, James was quite excited about his prospects in this new war and he served with moderate distinction, seeing action in several arenas. Unfortunately, he also fought with his commanding officers and did not win any major promotions.

At the end of the war, James was once again at a loose end. He didn't relish the thought of returning to cold, dreary England and shuddered at the prospect of tramping around the parade ground in a dead-end military career. He was no longer a young man and was beginning to feel like he was wasting his life.

To add to his melancholic state of mind: JSH was unmarried, his financial position was precarious, and his journal entries show that he still wanted to leave his mark on the world but was despairing of ever getting the chance. James was also having family problems back home, as his sister was becoming increasingly erratic and would eventually be institutionalised. All in all, JSH was a forlorn figure, caught between the devil and deep blue sea.

Conveniently, at this crucial point in his life, JSH met Sir Godfrey Lagden – the newly appointed authority in charge of native affairs and game reserves in South Africa. Lagden was impressed with the forthright military officer who had shown so much initiative and independence during the war, and he offered JSH the post of warden in the re-proclaimed Sabi Game Reserve.

JSH couldn't make up his mind. He was torn between his ancestral estate in Scotland, his military responsibilities and his instinctual attraction to Africa. This vacillation was a recurring theme in his life and just about every major decision he made was prefaced with several weeks of soul-searching.

After a period of prevarication, however, JSH finally resigned from his military post and agreed to give the Sabi Reserve a go. At the time, he had no experience of wildlife, nor could he speak Afrikaans or any of the local languages, but these shortcomings didn't seem to deter him and he looked forward to his new adventure.

It would prove be a momentous decision, both for JSH and for South Africa. For the first time, the restless Laird from Scotland found himself wholly responsible for a task that was both challenging and potentially important.

Upon arrival in the Lowveld, JSH quickly fell in love with the reserve. He would devote the rest of his life to protecting and nursing his new charge, often referring to it as his 'creation' and his 'Cinderella'. Despite his considerable interests back in Scotland, JSH was officially hooked and he remained the park's custodian, through thick and thin, for the next 44 years.

Getting Down to Business

As JSH wrote in his autobiography of the Kruger Park, *South African Eden,* "I was on the point of entering a country of which I knew practically nothing, with instructions to convert it as soon as possible from its time-honoured status of a hunter's paradise into an inviolable game sanctuary. My mandate had been vague, general, and verbally conveyed to me by people who were nearly as ignorant of the conditions prevailing as I was myself. Except for a brief notice in the Government Gazette, unlikely to have been seen by any of the local inhabitants, I had no visible authority behind me; no special regulations for the game reserve had been drafted; even the new game laws were not yet in being."

His first foray into the new reserve on the 6th of August 1902 proved equally disheartening: "Viewed as a game reserve the country was disappointing; even allowing for the time of year, and the consequent lack of much water in the veld, one would have expected to see at least some indication of larger wild life, yet there was not even an old spoor to indicate that anything of the kind had ever existed there. Indeed it was not until the fourth day...that we came across a few tracks of zebra, waterbuck and impala. The following morning I saw, in the flesh, a reedbuck ewe, a duiker and two jackals, and in the evening was much heartened by the appearance of a herd of nearly thirty impala."

Undeterred, the 35-year-old JSH set about his task methodically, consistently and pragmatically, as befits a military man. He split the reserve into a number of sections and slowly recruited suitable white rangers who were placed in charge of each station. Native 'police' were also employed and stationed at small posts to assist with patrolling the reserve.

The native workforce was allowed to "keep their wives and families, and to raise crops, but not to have any other relations or friends as guests. Neither guns nor traps would be allowed. Certain routes through the reserve would be set aside and proclaimed, by which alone natives going to and from work at the mines and elsewhere would be allowed to travel."

At first, reactions were understandably hostile. Many white hunters continued with their activities in defiance of the new laws, no doubt confident that the chances of being caught were slim given the vast size of the reserve with only a handful of people on patrol. Besides, they could always plead ignorance.

But news slowly got around, as did the native police, and JSH and his rangers proved implacable. Even military patrols monitoring the border with Mozambique were forbidden from hunting game and several criminal cases were mounted against transgressors in which fines were successfully imposed. And so, every winter, Boer hunters were firmly shooed out of the reserve and any poachers, black or white, were diligently sought out and prosecuted.

The black tribes living within the reserve proved to be a thornier problem. Before the white men had taken over the land, the locals had hunted freely and therefore found it difficult to accept the new legislation, which suddenly forbade killing of the animals that had sustained them for generations. JSH even acknowledged that "the damage they do in a year will not equal that done by a few Boers in a week."

Nevertheless, he was there to enforce the law and he didn't shirk from his duties. It was the policy of the reserve to remove as many native residents as was possible and, by 1903, several thousand African villagers had been evicted and relocated to land west of the protected area.

Within a few years, the diminutive James Stevenson-Hamilton had ushered in a new era in the Lowveld and become a force to be reckoned with. He had even been given a new name by the local African tribes, 'Skukuza' – the one who sweeps away. JSH's own translation of his nickname is a little bit gentler and is explained as "implying that I came along and turned everything upside down".

Skukuza and the 'Natives'

While JSH was certainly a product of his times, he showed an unusual even-handedness in his attitude to black people. He rarely refers to them as 'kaffers' and demonstrates an admiration for and understanding of their culture, despite his occasional lapse into offensive anthropology.

But then JSH was clearly a man who considered every person as an individual, each with their own particular merits and flaws. He was often scathing about the various white men in positions of power and had no problem is siding with the black people of the country when he felt that they were being exploited. He also showed a remarkably prescient understanding of the 'native problem' in South Africa and wrote in his journal that "in everything connected with the native, every single white man wants to have a finger in the exploitation pie!"

He even expressed an 'unofficial sympathy' with some of the native poachers who were "simple, straight-forward souls, and one knows where one stands with them. If caught red-handed, they cheerfully admit their guilt, and take what comes to them without complaint or malice. They display, in fact, 'a sporting spirit'."

In comparison, he showed a marked dislike of the natives who had become familiar with white people and their ways, claiming that they were tainted by the white man's cunning. He also expressed sadness that many of the old African customs were falling out of practice, saying that "in the safety of personal property and life, the native has benefited greatly by the rule of the white man, but it seems a pity that this protection should imply the complete destruction of all his time-honoured and interesting social organization, without giving him anything suitable in its place."

JSH also publicly acknowledged the difficulties faced by the native 'police' under his employ. Their job was to enforce the unpopular game laws within their own communities and, in his way, he found their dedication immensely impressive. As he puts it: "These poachers belong in most cases to the same tribes from which our own native rangers are recruited, and sometimes are even their blood relations. It is high tribute, therefore, to the natural courage, loyalty and instinctive obedience to authority which is characteristic of the Lowveld Bantu, that few of our police have ever hesitated to carry out their duties even at considerable personal risk to themselves."

JSH also expressed scorn for those 'less-educated' white people who treated the native people harshly. "It is a fact," he wrote in 1929, "that the more a certain type of white man owes to the native, including, in many cases, his entire livelihood, and the more deeply he has degraded himself in the past by intimate associations with native women, the louder he declaims against 'the lazy, cheeky nigger'." Although he was unquestionably the boss in his domain, JSH believed that good treatment of people got good results, and he felt respect had to be earned on both sides.

In his book *The Lowveld: its people and animals,* written in 1929, JSH devotes several chapters to the 'Natives'. His opinions on the subject are interesting and enlightening. While he was certainly a racist in that he feels comfortable comparing one race with another and tends to generalize tribal characteristics to an alarming extent, he never makes the mistake of judging the black man from a white man's perspective.

As he astutely points out: "In South Africa, few white men have either the time, the patience, the understanding, or the sympathy even to attempt to regard things from the native's point of view, and this failure is the source of general popular misunderstanding of his character and temperament."

JSH also debunks the myth that black people have a limited brain capacity and dares to suggest that they are eager and able to learn. He even goes on to state that literacy and education among the black people would be greatly improved if they were presented with relevant teaching material instead of the old European textbooks filled with snow and castles, which were foisted on them by well-meaning missionaries.

That having been said, however, JSH does repeat some well-worn racial stereotypes. Among other things, he describes the natives as superstitious, cruel to animals, unable to think on their feet and inherently sexual in nature. Well, nobody's perfect.

In short, JSH was both a prophet and a perpetrator. He forcibly removed many Africans from their homes, but he had the decency to wait until their crops had been harvested before he did so. He also had an acute understanding of what the future would hold for South Africa in terms of race relations.

As he pointed out in 1929, "There are signs that the more intelligent among the white people of South Africa are beginning to reconsider their ideas in regard to the native races, even if there be still a tendency to regard them as for ever hewers of wood and drawers of water, and to label all efforts towards their intellectual development as 'dangerous'. A policy of attempted perpetual repression would, however, ultimately be still more dangerous." He ends this unconventional opinion with a strange little verse that carries an eerie echo:

"By all ye cry and whisper
By all ye leave and do
The silent, sullen people
Shall weigh their Gods on you."

Labour Routes through the KNP

The discovery of the world's richest gold reef on the Witwatersrand in 1886 signalled a sea-change in the economic development of the Transvaal. Dozens of gold mines sprang up around the boom town of Johannesburg and hundreds of outsiders flooded into the region, eager to make their fortunes.

However, the proliferation of gold mines required a substantial force of cheap black labour to keep them operational, and suitably cheap workers were in short supply. African natives, at this stage, still had their own lands and operated under their traditional leaders. As such, they enjoyed a relatively independent lifestyle and had no need to travel to the mines in search of work.

To remedy this situation, mining companies sent touts out into the villages of the Transvaal, Mozambique and beyond to recruit workers for the mines. These touts received a fee for each worker they signed up, so it is unsurprising that many of them used unscrupulous means to convince the naïve tribesmen to join their work gangs.

In 1902, an organisation was set up by the Chamber of Mines to co-ordinate the recruitment of unskilled labour for the mines. This was named the Witwatersrand Native Labour Association (the WNLA or Wenela) and it operated several labour routes across the northern part of the KNP. In 1918, Wenela was even allowed to build a road through the Shingwedzi district to expedite their labour caravans from Mozambique. Additional recruitment stations were subsequently set up in present-day Namibia, Botswana, Zimbabwe, Zambia, Malawi, Lesotho and Swaziland.

Thus, tempted by often-specious promises of wealth and luxury, large groups of labourers were rounded up and sent to Theba Station – the Wenela base camp on the Limpopo River, near the present day Pafuri border post. From here they were transported through the wild Shingwedzi region on foot, donkey cart or ox-wagon.

The first outspan was located at the foot of a prominent baobab tree that grew on top of a rocky rise, just south of the Luvuvhu River. This tree still stands alongside the modern tar H1-8 road and is identified with a memorial plaque. From here, the procession continued to the south-west until they arrived at the WNLA terminus of Soekmekaar (now called Morebeng) in the Soutpansberg district. There were also Wenela camps in the vicinity of Satara and Letaba.

This entire process was carefully controlled and Wenela paid the Portuguese £1 for every worker they recruited. They then charged the mines a finder's fee for every worker they supplied. Wenela and its affiliates (such as the Native Recruiting Company, or NRC) continued operating in this fashion across southern Africa for decades, eventually building a 1500km road linking its stations in Namibia and Botswana and even launching its own airline (at one time the busiest in Africa). In

1977, Wenela and the NRC were amalgamated to become The Employment Bureau of Africa (TEBA), which continues to operate to this day.

Despite the harsh conditions on the mines, many Mozambican labourers were keen to join the ranks of their brethren working in the cities. As a result, the WNLA system became over-subscribed and many job-seekers resolved to find their own way through the park. However, following the Wenela model, any native Mozambican who wished to work in South Africa of their own accord also had to pay the Portuguese £1 for a labour pass that allowed them to cross the border.

This sum of money was out of reach for most of the prospective workers, so JSH helped facilitate a clever system whereby everybody got what they wanted. This is how it worked: illegal Mozambican immigrants would cross the border and present themselves to the park authorities as trespassers. They would then be sentenced to a fine of £1 or 14 days imprisonment, as was the law.

These 'prisoners' were then sent to work off their sentence on various projects within the park (road works, camp construction etc.). The conditions of their imprisonment were very liberal and, after their two weeks of labour were up, each prisoner was released and given a permit to seek work in the Transvaal.

The immigrants thus got their pass without having to fork over hard currency, and the park got a steady supply of free labour. This nifty little arrangement became so popular that groups of up to 40 or 50 people would arrive at a time and humbly present themselves to the warden. In this way, much of the park's infrastructure was developed and maintained by the steady stream of voluntary prisoners.

In 1926, however, the Portuguese became aware of this loophole and protested that they were losing out on the deal. A new convention was subsequently drawn up and, henceforth, all illegal immigrants had to be handed over to a Portuguese agent. JSH records the demise of his 'free labour' with sadness and states that after the supply of workers from Mozambique dried up, the salary bill for native labour increased considerably.

Expanding Horizons

What had begun as a rather temporary job soon turned into a passion for James Stevenson-Hamilton. He quickly became enchanted by the reserve, which he would sometimes refer to as his child, and proved to be a tireless champion of the unloved and often unwanted Sabi wildlife refuge.

That isn't to say that the job was cushy. Living conditions in the wholly undeveloped tracts of the game reserve were very basic. There were no roads, no communications, no irrigation for water. But you gotta start somewhere and JSH chose General Steinaecker's old base at Sabi Bridge as his headquarters. This was located on the south bank of the Sabie River, close to the old Selati railway line that had been abandoned in the 1890s.

Today, Sabi Bridge has been transformed into the bustling Skukuza rest camp. But back in 1902, it consisted only of a couple of ramshackle buildings, left over from the railroad days. The nearest town was about 70 miles to the south-east, at Komatipoort, and that wasn't much of a town. Luckily, the rusted Selati line ran unbroken from Sabi Bridge to Komatipoort and this rail link was an invaluable lifeline.

All in all, it was an isolated, lonely and difficult life, but the privation seemed to appeal to the tough Scot. He liked the landscape and he liked the work. Accordingly, he soon organised a railway trolley to shuttle the necessary supplies to Sabi Bridge. Then he sourced donkeys, wagons and good, 'salted' horses that could survive in the disease-ridden Lowveld.

There was little time and less money available, but a ranger station slowly began to take shape. Helping himself to the materials abandoned by the Selati Line construction crews ten years previously, JSH fashioned a rough but comfortable base for himself on the banks of the Sabie and here he spent many happy evenings sitting alone on his stoep, allowing the peculiar beauty of the bushveld to seep into his soul.

The incongruity of his situation was not lost on a man who had previously lived his life as an elegant London gadabout. As he wrote in *South African Eden,* "No doubt it is only congenital idiots who deliberately and unnecessarily seek hardship and discomfort. So I am driven to the unwilling conclusion that those of us who deliberately invite the austerities of life, must, in some way or another, be mentally deficient." Not only was JSH a self-confessed idiot, he was also incredibly stubborn and 'began to develop a certain hitherto unsuspected strain of obstinacy'.

Strangely, these seemed to be the ideal qualities for the job of warden, which he took very seriously. Confident and combative by nature, JSH was ready and willing to deal with the various opponents of the game reserve, and this was just as well. Over the years, he would do battle with the government, hunters, farmers,

71

veterinarians, tribal leaders, the military, mining interests, development planners and land owners. But first he needed some power!

When JSH arrived in the reserve, he had little to no authority. He couldn't try cases, he couldn't impose fines and he had to rely on the courts of Lydenburg and Barberton for any legal matters. He was also afraid that the police would send a force in to patrol the Lubombo border with Mozambique, which would introduce an autonomous element into his domain. Negotiations with Pretoria followed and JSH was duly declared a Special Justice of the Peace with the power to try all legal cases within the Sabi Reserve.

Later, in 1910, he would also become a Native Commissioner so that the tribal communities still living within the borders of the reserve would only have to deal with a single white authority. This was for the best, thought Hamilton, because "natives [are] accustomed...to the undivided authority of a single chief and dislike nothing more than being responsible to two masters at the same time". His duties amounted to collecting the government poll tax from the 5000 or so 'citizens' of the reserve and supervising their general administration.

As the new warden applied himself to the tasks at hand, he also began to explore his new domain in a more tangible sense. He started by travelling through the bush around Sabi Bridge, using either a donkey and cart or a good, 'salted' horse. These short trips soon grew into long expeditions that roamed the length and breadth of the Sabi reserve.

While he travelled, JSH took the opportunity to learn about the plants and animals of the Lowveld. He was an acute observer of the natural world and sought to supplement his knowledge by speaking to everyone, from naturalists to hunters to tribal elders. He also read widely and was particularly interested by the interactions between animals and the environment.

He would eventually amass an amazing store of bushlore and later published several books and articles that proved to be seminal texts in the field of what came to be called 'ecology'. Some of his most well-known titles in this genre include *Animal Life in Africa* (1912), *Wild Life in South Africa* (1947) and *The Lowveld: its wildlife and people* (1929).

As JSH's awareness of the wild grew, he began to realize that the Sabi Game Reserve simply wasn't big enough to restore the natural balance of game and nature. Within a few months after taking up the post of warden, he boldly proposed that the reserve should be extended northwards to the Olifants River and 12 miles to the west, to include the foothills of the Drakensberg and the Klaserie River.

To justify this expansion, JSH pointed out that the land he wanted was "unfit for the ordinary white man to live in during the greater part of the year" and "it was much the finest game district in the Transvaal". Eventually, he predicted, "We shall have a reserve which cannot be beaten, if not in the world, at all events in South Africa." On the down side, however, half of the land he wanted to incorporate was owned by private land speculators who had bought the farms cheaply from the government in the hope that they would one day prove valuable.

Undaunted, JSH ascertained who owned each of the hundreds of farms in the area and personally approached every landowner with an unusual deal. As JSH explained in *South African Eden*: "In return for the safe-guarding by the reserve staff of the flora and fauna, the prevention of prospecting, and the collection on their behalf of any rents due from native tenants, the companies undertook to hand over, for a period of five years, to government control, all their land in the Sabi-Olifants area, and within that period, neither themselves to make any use of it, nor to sell, let, or give any rights to third parties."

Remarkably, within a few months, JSH had signed agreements with all the relevant landowners. This task was made easier by the fact many of the farms were owned by one of several larger companies, such as the Transvaal Land and Exploration Company, so there weren't that many people with which to negotiate. Furthermore, many of the landlords had never visited the farms and the land was seen as practically worthless, apart from the meagre rents that the native 'tenants' were forced to pay for the privilege of living on their traditional land. This practice, which JSH considered 'indefensible', was crudely known as 'kaffir farming'.

When JSH submitted the agreements to Lagden, the wheels began to turn and the land between the Sabi and Olifants rivers was duly incorporated into the Sabi Reserve in late 1903. Around this time, the reserve also got its first official visit from Lagden and several other dignitaries.

Amazingly enough, the government party arrived eager for a spot of shooting in what they thought of as an exclusive hunting reserve. JSH had to use all his diplomacy and a good deal of disingenuous misdirection to prevent them from killing the game he was so assiduously protecting. Nevertheless, the party was impressed by what they saw and continued to support the reserve.

The Kruger Millions

One of the most bizarre manias to sweep the Lowveld was the search for the Kruger Millions. The legend goes like this: During the Second Anglo-Boer War, the British were advancing on Pretoria and the government of Paul Kruger was forced to take flight. The Boer refugees piled into a special train and headed east along the Delagoa Bay Railway line, putting up a spirited resistance as they retreated. Kruger was eventually forced all the way to Lourenço Marques, where he boarded a Dutch ship bound for Marseilles. Upon his arrival in Europe, he began to protest against the war and tried to drum up some support from anti-

British interests. But nothing came of his entreaties and he died in 1904 in Clarens, a small town in Switzerland.

This much is historical fact. But rumour has it that, before they left Pretoria, the Republican Government managed to clear out two million pounds in gold bars from the treasury and loaded the bullion on board their getaway train. This treasure was then secretly buried somewhere in the Lowveld.

Two million pounds of gold would have weighed several tons, but the implausible story of the Kruger Millions persisted. Lowvelders all seemed to have their own ideas about where, how and by whom the gold was buried. Over the years, many attempts were made to find the treasure, and a mildly amused JSH granted several permits to treasure hunting expeditions who wished to search in the Game Reserve (on condition that they carried no guns).

JSH remained dubious. As he said, "Little can be done by white men in the wilder parts of Africa without the ubiquitous, and, in his own sphere, omniscient native learning all about it practically at once." Nevertheless, several expeditions (some with government backing) went into the reserve full of hope, only to emerge empty-handed. Some of the more enterprising Lowvelders even hired themselves out as treasure-guides, claiming to have intimate knowledge of the elusive Kruger Millions.

Most of these expeditions met with nothing but disappointment. Then, in 1903, something incredible happened. A group of treasure seekers in the KNP dug up a length of steel cable. They followed the cable until they uncovered a locked iron safe. The elusive hoard had been found!

Supervising authorities were quickly informed and a train full of armed police arrived to transport the safe to a secure location. Finally, in a room filled with eager spectators, the safe was ceremoniously opened...

It contained piles of consignment notes connected to the Selati railway scandal.

After this public fiasco, the gleam of the Kruger Millions began to fade. And yet, over the years, the legend would continue to flare up from time to time, sparking off another fruitless treasure hunt. Today, the story is a quaint piece of trivia and permits for treasure hunting in the Kruger Park are not likely to be approved.

The Shingwedzi Reserve

In May 1903, the government proclaimed a new game reserve in the far north-east of the Transvaal. Initially proposed by Leonard Ledeboer, a resident of the Soutpansberg district, this large reserve was located between the Letaba and Limpopo rivers, on the international border between South Africa, Mozambique and Rhodesia (Zimbabwe). The new protected area was called the Singwitsi (now known as Shingwedzi).

The Shingwedzi region was (and is) very remote and very beautiful. Unlike the south and central parts of the reserve, Shingwedzi is quite mountainous, boasting several dramatic gorges (such as Lanner's Gorge) and lush river courses. The vegetation is also distinctive, with impenetrable stands of mopane trees, tropical ilala palms, garish fever trees and lofty baobabs.

Furthermore, Shingwedzi contained relatively few native settlements, and white hunters had not invaded the dense bush in great numbers, so it still carried a fair supply of game. All in all, it was an ideal candidate for preservation and, after a successful vote in the legislature, it was placed under the control of the warden.

JSH now found himself in charge of a huge area that extended several hundred kilometres, from the Sabi Reserve in the south to the Shingwedzi Reserve in the north. He was also officially in charge of the old Pongola Reserve, a relic of the former Transvaal Republic, which was located on the other side of Swaziland. The time had come, he decided, to visit both the Shingwedzi and the Pongola regions to better gauge their condition.

The trip to Pongola proved pleasant, but JSH quickly realised that the reserve was too small to be an effective refuge for game. As such, he placed it on the back burner and re-assigned its eccentric warden, Major AA Fraser, to the vast and remote Singwitsi Reserve. Only two native rangers remained at Pongola, which slowly deteriorated until it was deproclaimed in 1921. The eccentric Fraser would remain as the sole authority figure in Shingwedzi for many years, with only tobacco, whisky and a baying pack of dogs to keep him company.

Crooks' Corner and the Ivory Trail

The Shingwedzi was a wild place, far from any form of civilisation. The northern part of the reserve, between the Luvuvhu and Limpopo rivers, was particularly isolated – and infamous.

Known as Crooks' Corner, this slice of land was frequented by a procession of poachers, smugglers, labour recruiters, gun runners, prospectors, runaways and hunters; most of whom were up to no good. It was also part of the famous Ivory Trail, an elephant-rich hunting route that stretched in an arc across the northern part of South Africa. It is now remembered as a tourism route with a series of intriguing camps across the Limpopo province.

In the late 1800s and early 1900s, many well-known hunters made their mark on Crooks' Corner, such as the legendary Stephanus Cecil 'Bvekenya' Barnard – the one who swaggers when he walks. Other unique characters included 'Only Jones', who never told the truth, and Pat Fray, an Irishman who ate himself to death and was buried in a coffin made of canned-meat tins. A small trading post, built by Alec Thompson and William Pye, was the only permanent building in the area. Apparently, the two men couldn't stand each other.

The resident tribal authority in Crooks' Corner was the Makuleke. In 1912, Crooks' Corner was excised from the park as a result of the burgeoning Makuleke community, and it was only re-incorporated in 1969 after the Makuleke were forcibly removed. Recently, after a successful land claim, the Makuleke regained ownership of their territory and have chosen to keep it as part of the wider KNP (as will be discussed in due course).

The Game Rangers

In South African mythology, there seems to be a special place reserved for game rangers. Their exploits are legendary as is their bravery, and stories of their derring-do abound. In fact, it seems that just about every ranger who lived in the KNP has published a memoir about their exploits, and most of these have been best-sellers.

It must have been an extraordinary life; riding through the brooding bush, facing charging elephants, confronting man-eating lions and dodging grumpy hippos. Several of these encounters have ended badly and a number of rangers have lost their lives in the park, but that only serves to enhance their status. And there are many sides to the profession which goes beyond thrilling anecdotes and chilling fireside tales.

In the beginning, certainly, the rangers were a tough and hardy bunch of loners, recruited by JSH for their ability to survive in the wild. They were also expected to shoot straight, manage their staff effectively and patrol vast areas of bush for poachers. Knowledge of what became known as 'conservation science' was not a priority. All in all, they were a pretty mangy lot and JSH seems to have held most of them in some disdain.

The first intake of rangers was assembled on an ad-hoc basis during the first few years of the park's existence. They were all English-speaking and most had some hunting experience in the Lowveld. The first to be employed was the loyal Harry Wolhuter, based at Pretoriuskop. He would remain in the park for the next 40 years (retiring at the same time as JSH). Others included Thomas Duke (stationed at Lower Sabie), CR de la Porte (Crocodile River), GR Healy (Wanetzi, later named Satara), Leonard Ledeboer (Letaba) and the obstreperous Major Fraser who held court in Shingwedzi. This was the so-called 'First Guard' and they, along with JSH and their 'native police', can legitimately claim to be the park's founding fathers. Their original rangers' stations also live on as today's tourist rest camps.

But this was not an all-male environment. Although it was preferable for rangers to be unmarried, several had wives and children who had to cope with very trying circumstances.

There is one touching story of the ranger William Lloyd's young wife, who was living with her husband and three young boys at the remote Satara station. One summer, Lloyd went down with a severe case of malaria. Mrs. Lloyd did her best but, with few medical supplies at her disposal, he died a few days later. Mrs. Lloyd sent word to Sabi Bridge and then quietly buried her husband under a nearby tree.

Disease, old age and the various world wars took their toll on the First Guard, and new rangers were constantly being appointed to new stations. Over time, their character would change from English hunter-heroes into Afrikaner Bush warriors. Their focus would also shift from mere law enforcers to being ecologically-minded guardians of nature.

Today, game ranging is an exacting and demanding job. It requires several years of study and apprenticeship before the qualification is attained. This is necessary because a modern ranger needs to be able to juggle the needs of administration, tourism management, guiding and nature conservation.

Yet, for all the technical demands of the job, the call of the bush is probably still the main reason why people want to become rangers. It's like a drug; once it gets into your system, it's very hard to keep away. Even retired rangers can't seem to get enough of the bush and, in 1961, an Honorary Rangers association was set up. This worthy organisation allows members the opportunity to remain involved in the promotion and development of the park.

We should also take a moment to remember all the black rangers who worked alongside the white rangers. Their stories are not often told, as they were traditionally made to sit outside the light of the campfire. But the black rangers did much of the real work in the KNP and, no doubt, also enjoyed their fair share of adventures.

One famous black ranger was Nombolo Mdluli who worked in the park for 52 years, starting in 1919. He survived several lion attacks and saved the lives of more than one ranger. Thankfully, there is now a research programme in place to document the stories of these under-appreciated pioneers of conservation so that we may accord them their appropriate place in the park's mythology.

Native Nicknames

African people have a special gift for giving people nicknames. Their language is often idiomatic, succinct and marvellously expressive, saying in a single word what English can only convey in several.

We have already heard about JSH's nickname 'Skukuza' – he who sweeps away or scrapes clean – but most of the white rangers received vernacular monikers and appellations that reflect the staff's opinions about their superiors. Nombolo Mdluli worked in the park for many years and later recalled some of the ranger's African names for the benefit of researchers.

Ranger Lloyd was either *Kukuzele* (looks as though he is stalking you) or *Nwashibeyilana* (he who carries a little axe). H MacDonald was *Mahahalane* (scolds much). Tomlinson was *Rivalo* (awe-inspiring). JAB Sanderbergh, the unsuccessful successor to JSH, was derisively known as *Mashayimhala* (rode over an impala). And Anna Ledeboer, wife of a prominent ranger, was called *Nwashihubutane* (she always wanted to storm and rage).

A Day in the Life of the Warden

As the years wore on, JSH developed a regular routine of inspection and maintenance to keep his reserve in order. It was, as he describes it in *South African Eden*, a very pleasant task; part colonial safari and part adventurous expedition. Indeed, when describing this annual odyssey, JSH often speaks as if he is a country lord making a tour of his estate, which in many respects is exactly what he was.

From *South African Eden:*

"For my part, I gradually fell into a more or less regular annual routine. About mid-May, the rain was practically over for the season, and it became possible to camp with a reasonable likelihood of keeping dry. Since, however, there was still plenty of water remaining in the veld, this was the most suitable time of year in which to explore, with the aid of pack donkeys, the drier portions of the Reserve between the Sabi and the Crocodile Rivers. About June, I would start on my annual inspection tour of the north; Shingwedsi, Letaba or round the northern part of the Sabi Reserve along the Olifants River. For such a trek, the ox wagon, as well as the pack donkeys, and perhaps a couple of horses would be taken, with as much as two months' supplies of food and horse fodder. Arrangements would be made for mails to follow by runner to agreed places. It was a delightfully free and easy method of getting about and offered the widest opportunities of seeing the country.

"When the distance travelled seemed sufficient, and a pleasant shady spot was reached, with water at hand, one could decide to stay there for the rest of the day and the night, or as long as might appear desirable, and so would dismount, offsaddle, and sit down under an inviting tree to await the caravan. After a time, the donkeys would come trotting in; shortly afterwards the ear would catch faintly the pistol-like cracks of the wagon whip, and, ever drawing nearer, the raucous shouts of the driver, Tom, or Ntutu, or Seventeen, as the case may be. 'Ah Witpens! Ah Steenbok! Ah Bles, jou skelm, trek.' [Hey White Belly! Hey Steenbok! Hey Bles, you scoundrel, pull]

"The horses and donkeys roll [up] luxuriously in the dust, and from the recesses of the wagon appear camp table, chair, bottle, glasses, all the things tending to mitigate the asperities of life. The cook boy quickly has a fire underway, the kettle boils anon, and tea is ready. If it be intended to spend the night in this place, there is a general scattering to carry out well-accustomed duties. Some gather firewood, others set about, with axes and bill-hooks, the making of the essential zeriba [perimeter fence], tents are pitched, water fetched, and oneself may take a solitary stroll to explore the environs, returning at sundown to see the animals tethered, fed, and all snug for the night, before settling down to one's own excellent dinner by the camp fire, eaten amid the slowly swelling sounds of the night.

"After returning from the annual tour, perhaps about the middle of August, I generally established myself at a permanent camp for about three months, surrounded by all the domestic animals because grazing at Sabi Bridge ceased to exist after July. From 1910 onwards, I made regular practice of going to Tshokwane [now a popular picnic site], some 25 miles north of Sabi Bridge.

"Having eventually built a commodious camp at this place, I usually stayed on until the rains in November made it possible to take the animals back to Sabi Bridge. The summer months from December to the end of April were devoted to the arrears of office work, to visiting rangers at their different stations, and, so far as the weather allowed, hunting Carnivora in the neighbourhood of my station.

"It was a good and full year; there never was a moment when time hung heavy, and it was all one's own, to do with as one would without any outside interference. This last was perhaps the greatest charm, apart from the life itself and the nature of the work; it is impossible to imagine anyone having a freer hand than I had during all those years with regard to matters within the reserve. I could make or mar it as I pleased, and alas, nobody was likely either to praise or blame me whatever happened! It is better to crow alone on a little midden, than to form a mere unit of the chorus on a bigger one. Only when I thought of the future, did doubt and despondency creep in; so I thought about it as little as possible, and talked at great length about national parks – when I could get anyone to listen to me."

Shooting Lions

When JSH first arrived in the Sabi Reserve, his priority was to bolster the numbers of antelope and other large grazers, as these were the most popular animals to hunt. The carnivorous predators were therefore seen as a threat to the reserve and not an asset.

Furthermore, it was deemed that the numbers of Carnivora were too high when compared to the decimated herbivorous herds. The only solution was to shoot as many of the meat-eaters as possible. This may sound amazing today when these noble predators are considered to be the stars of the wildlife experience. However, back then, lions were seen as dangerous and useless creatures.

This anti-predator attitude was well entrenched. Early farmers and settlers were constantly tormented by lions, which used to hunt freely throughout Southern Africa. In the Lowveld, this fear verged on hysteria and, throughout the first (unfenced) decades of the park's existence, local farmers complained bitterly that the unpopular Sabi Reserve was nothing more than a breeding ground for hungry killers that attacked their cattle and stalked their children.

For these reasons, the warden and his rangers followed a committed policy of Carnivora culling. Lions, wild dog, leopard, cheetah and crocs were all shot as part of every ranger's daily activities. In this way, it was thought, the balance of nature would be encouraged to restore itself, and the neighbouring farmers would be placated. JSH even recounts several proud stories in which he stalks a vicious beast through the bush and triumphantly shoots it down, just like the stereotypical great white hunter he so despised.

We now know that this culling policy was severely misguided and that nature restores itself best when left more or less alone. Nevertheless, the policy remained in force until the reserve became a National Park in 1926. The reason for this about-face was that the tourists couldn't get enough of the lions and would not have tolerated their destruction. Nevertheless, the lion culling campaign was resurrected by the KNP research department during the drought years of 1953 to 1958.

Wolhuter and the Lion

One of the most enduring ranger stories about the Kruger Park involves the redoubtable Harry Wolhuter and his thrilling encounter with a determined lion.

Back in August of 1903, Wolhuter was returning from a research trip to the Olifants River. After camping near N'wanesti (now a picnic site), Wolhuter awoke on the morning of the 26th and struck camp. His destination was Metsimetsi (now a camp site), about 20 miles to south. He was travelling with several donkeys and a small staff of African police, but they were moving slowly and it was getting late, so he decided to ride on ahead with only his dog and a horse for company.

As the sun started to sink, Wolhuter found himself in the darkling bush, several miles away from his destination. The bush is a dangerous place at dusk, as this is the time when predators are at their most active and the land is full of shadows. Nevertheless, he pushed on through the twilight. Then, as he was crossing a dry river bed, his dog began barking at a black shape lurking in the vegetation. At first, Wolhuter thought it was a reedbuck but then it started moving towards him, approaching on the right flank.

This was pretty strange behaviour for a reedbuck and, just as he was pondering the peculiarity of nature, the animal broke from its cover and revealed itself to be a lion. The lion charged at Wolhuter, who sharply pulled his horse to the left. The lion leaped and caught the horse's hindquarters in its sharp claws. The horse bolted and Wolhuter fell heavily to the ground.

He was dazed for a moment, but looked up in time to see the lion chasing off after his frantic horse, with the dog in hot pursuit. Wolhuter then noticed a second lion, sneaking up on him from behind.

Before he had a chance to think, the lion sprang on the defenceless man and sunk its teeth into Wolhuter's right shoulder. It then started dragging him away to a dark spot where the feeding would begin. Wolhuter, still conscious, found his face pressed into the lion's musky chest. His feet were under its belly, heels bumping across the stony ground.

Wolhuter remembered his sheath knife, which he always carried in his belt. He reached around with his left hand and blindly fumbled for the knife, hoping that it had not been dislodged when he fell from his horse. After a few breathless moments, his fingers closed around the shaft and he clung to the knife as "a drowning man grasps a floating plank".

Eager not to waste his only chance at survival, Wolhuter carefully estimated the position of the lion's heart. He could not struggle, or the lion would have shaken him and broken his neck.

Finally, after a distance of about 90 yards, the lion reached a small tree and let go of its prey. Wolhuter grabbed the opportunity and plunged the knife into the lion, stabbing it twice in the torso and once in the neck. The lion leapt back and the two creatures, prey and predator, stood starting at each other for a breathless moment. Wolhuter let out a yell at the lion, which slowly turned around and limped into the bush.

Without thinking, Wolhuter scrambled up the tree. He was bleeding heavily and, fearful of losing consciousness, he took out a 'neckerchief' and tied himself to the high branch on which he sat.

No sooner had he done this, when the first lion re-appeared. It had given up the wild horse chase, discouraged by the barking of Wolhuter's plucky pooch, and followed the blood spoor back to the tree which housed a very vulnerable Wolhuter. The lion started circling the tree, as Wolhuter's dog kept up a spirited defence of its master. From the bushes, he could hear the other lion groaning as it succumbed to its wounds.

Time seemed to stand still. Then, finally, Wolhuter heard the sound of his men coming along the path. He began shouting to get their attention and the lion slid away into the dark bush.

The men quickly helped Wolhuter down from the tree and supported him as he walked the eight long, dark miles to the camp at Metsimetsi. The lion kept up with the party for some distance, and they could all hear it creeping through the tall grass as it kept pace with the group.

Eventually, a bleeding and exhausted Wolhuter stumbled into camp. But there was little relief. Metsimetsi contained no medical supplies and little could be done to clean the festering wound on his shoulder.

The next morning, Wolhuter was running a fever and he ordered his men to construct a rough stretcher from branches, which they used to carry him to Komatipoort. The journey took two days. When he arrived in town, the district surgeon was away, and a delirious Wolhuter was sent by train to Barberton.

He finally arrived at a hospital nearly three days after the attack. His shoulder was lacerated and his arm was black and swollen from blood poisoning. The doctors dressed his wounds but didn't think that he would survive for much longer.

But never underestimate a game ranger! The hardy Wolhuter pulled through and made a full recovery. He later returned to his post and continued to work in the park for the next 40 years. The only physical reminder of the encounter was a stiff shoulder (with matching upper lip). For his fortitude, he earned the nickname *Lindanda* – referring to his penchant for wearing a Swazi-style loincloth, called 'lihiya'.

The site of Wolhuter's attack can be found on the S35 gravel road, a short distance from the Tshokwane picnic site. The tree that he climbed is still there, although it is long dead with only a small remnant of the trunk propped up in a concrete plinth remaining. A memorial plaque has been erected on the site which describes the dramatic events of a century ago. The lion's skin and Wolhuter's trusty knife are on display in the Skukuza library.

Moving Towards a National Park

Under the effective leadership of James Stevenson-Hamilton, the Sabi and Shingwedzi Reserves were doing well. They had grown exponentially in size and the game was slowly recuperating after decades of untrammelled hunting. According to JSH's estimates, as quoted in Jane Carruthers' book on the history of the Kruger Park, "In 1902 there were no black rhinos, elephant, eland, hartebeest or ostrich in the area; there were about 15 hippos, 5 giraffe, 8 buffalo, 12 sable antelope, 2 roan antelope, 5 tsessebe, 40 blue wildebeest, 100 waterbuck, 35 kudu and numerous impala, reedbuck, steenbok and duiker. By 1909 he recorded 25 elephant, 7 or 8 rhinos, 50 or 60 buffalo, numerous hippos and eland, and large herds of roan antelope, hartebeest, kudu and many other species."

However, one question still haunted JSH – what would become of his beloved Cinderella and the wild animals that he was so carefully nurturing? In other words, as more than one critic asked the warden, "But what is the use of keeping the things?"

Typically, JSH had a realistic grasp of the situation and did not labour under any idealistic misapprehensions about the fate of the Reserve. In *South African Eden* he relates a conversation he had with an old-time Lowvelder named Hannemann in 1905, which crystallised both his hopes and his fears. "'When is this reserve of yours going to be thrown open for shooting?' [Hannemann asked]. I said I did not know, but I hoped never. 'What!' he exclaimed. 'Do you mean to tell me that the government is going to spend thousands of pounds every year just to keep game? What is the use of it anyhow? And even if the Government does so, you mark me, the public won't stand it! Someday this low-veld will be opened up, and then where will you be?'"

"Although I had heard a great deal of the same kind of thing before, somehow on this particular occasion it gave me deeply to think. After all, what goal were we striving for? In common with everyone else in the country... I had hazily accepted the idea that someday, I hoped a long way ahead, part at least of the Reserve when fully stocked, would be hired out for some kind of controlled shooting. In those days, to be shot was the sole end for which wild animals were supposed to exist. On the other hand, it did seem a waste of time and money if all the labour and care of the last three years, not to speak of the £15 000 or so which already had been spent, was merely to provide hides and biltong for a section of the local public, with the result that in two or three years we should be back where we were at the beginning.

"What then exactly was I working for, beyond the mere enjoyment of the life itself? Would it be possible to wean the South African public from its present attitude towards the wild animals of its own country, which was that of regarding them either as a convenient source of exploitation, or as an incubus hindering the progress of civilisation? It seemed pretty hopeless. There was no money for development, nor likely to be; in fact, at the start of each financial year I gave a sigh of relief when I found our small grant of £5000 still on the estimates."

It was around this time that JSH began reading up on the American National Parks system and was amazed to find that the Federal government (despite some opposition) was prepared to protect their natural landscapes and wilderness areas from the depredations of development (the world's first 'national park' was Yellowstone, declared in 1872). At the same time, he noted, they made this heritage accessible to the public for its edification and to bolster national pride. It was a uniquely democratic approach to land ownership and use, quite unlike the aristocrats and private landowners who controlled the beauty spots of Europe.

He also read texts by the influential naturalist and writer Aldo Leopold who believed that wilderness areas were an irreplaceable resource that had to be preserved for the physical and spiritual health of future generations. Furthermore, JSH was in touch with the Society for the Preservation of the Wild Fauna of the Empire, the Zoological Society and the Royal Geographic Society, all of whom offered their advice and support.

And so it was that JSH began to consider that the best course of action was to have the Sabi Reserve declared a National Park in which the wildlife and flora of the Lowveld would be protected in perpetuity. Unfortunately, the government had other things on its mind and the general public was far from supportive of the scheme. It would take over twenty years of constant campaigning and nagging before JSH's dream finally came true, and there would be many setbacks along the way.

The Storm Clouds Gather

From the outset, the odds were stacked against the Sabi Reserve. One of these challenges concerned the political infighting between governmental departments as to who controlled the reserves. Initially, the reserves were the property of the Native Affairs Department under Godfrey Lagden, but they were transferred to the Office of the Colonial Secretary in 1905, without Lagden's knowledge or permission. Then, after Union in 1910, the reserves were transferred again to the Transvaal Provincial Administration, under the authority of Johan Rissik.

JSH therefore had to meet and convince a succession of new bosses about the value and viability of the Sabi Reserve. Luckily, in most cases, he found the authorities to be sympathetic to the cause, despite some outspoken opposition from the electorate. Nevertheless, his position was always precarious as it would have taken nothing more than a notice in the Government Gazette to deproclaim the reserve and open it up for hunting and settlement.

Another problem concerned the Selati railway line, which had been abandoned some distance north of Sabi Bridge due to the embezzlement of funds by the original contractors back in 1893. Although only 75 miles of track had been completed, this ramshackle railway line ran from Komatipoort over the Crocodile River Bridge to the Sabi River, and it had proved to be a useful link between JSH's HQ and the outside world.

Then, in 1909 after years of neglect, the government suddenly announced that the Selati line would be refurbished and extended northwards to the town of Tzaneen, in the hope that it would one day reach through the northern Transvaal and into Rhodesia. In his journals, JSH offered the opinion that the funds for this rather ambitious project were freed up because the Transvaal administration wanted to spend its surplus cash before South Africa became a Union in 1910.

You see, under the upcoming dispensation, the Transvaal would have had to surrender its money to the new national government, so it was decided to splurge on several public works, which were quickly initiated before anyone could stop them. The Union Buildings in Pretoria were also commissioned as part of this free-spending campaign.

Accordingly, the firm of Pauling and Co. was awarded the construction contract and work on the new Selati line commenced in 1909. It would continue until 1912. All told, the 150 miles of new track was completed for the princely sum of £200 000, which is quite cheap when you consider that the old Transvaal authorities wasted more than £1 000 000 on the abortive 75 miles of original track.

Unfortunately, the Selati extension proved to be a major headache for JSH. The first problem was to prevent the construction crews from shooting his game for food. This proved to be a minor hassle as, once the situation was explained to the foremen in charge, orders were given forbidding the hunting of any animals within the reserve.

But that solution didn't mitigate what JSH saw as the biggest concern: his pristine wildlife sanctuary was now ruptured by a bloody great railway line that ran right through its heart. Furthermore, the railway line would open up the previously inaccessible Lowveld to development, and JSH was afraid that the coming of the railway might spell the end of Cinderella's splendid isolation.

Initially, JSH's fears proved to be well founded. By 1912, the once-reviled Lowveld was no longer considered a pestilential backwater. The Tsetse fly threat had been largely eliminated by the Rinderpest epidemic of 1896, which killed vast numbers of domestic and wild animals thus depriving the fly of its host. A campaign of DDT spraying did the rest and the dreaded *nagana* (or sleeping sickness) was no longer a hindrance for cattle farmers.

Malaria was still a problem in the summer months, but it had now been proven that white men could live with the disease if they used certain precautions, such as medication and mosquito netting. So, after Union, several interested parties began to appeal to the government to deproclaim the reserve and open it up to human development. The re-opening of the Selati Line certainly fuelled these initiatives.

Then JSH received a serious blow. In 1903, the land companies who owned a large number of farms in the central part of the park had signed over control of their private land to JSH for a period of 5 years, mainly because they believed the land was dangerous and worthless. In 1908, this agreement was renewed for another 5 years. However, by 1912, the Transvaal was becoming more prosperous and there was a pressing need for land. The land companies therefore refused to renew their contract with the Sabi Reserve and began to demand that they be allowed to utilise their farms in any way that they saw fit.

JSH leapt into action and began negotiating with the major land companies, proposing a land exchange, whereby the private farms would be swapped for government land lying to the west of the reserve. He found some support for this idea, but the land companies were playing hard to get. They demanded inflated prices for their land, which the government was unable or unwilling to meet, and several years of haggling ensued.

To make matters worse, farmers from the White River area had approached the Transvaal Provincial Administration demanding grazing rights within the reserve during the winter months, as was the case in the previous century. The authorities conceded and Johan Rissik explained the situation to an anxious JSH.

Ever the pragmatist, JSH agreed but with several conditions. As he puts it, "The only course was to make the best bargain possible. I insisted that, if this permission were given, it should be on a proper basis; that the ground be divided into areas and a fee charged; while it must be impressed on all that no shooting was be allowed and that the regulations would be strictly enforced."

In the first year, about a dozen farmers duly paid the £5 fee and 9000 sheep were led into the south-western part of the reserve, around the Pretoriuskop area. As it turned out, the grazing wasn't all it was cracked up to be and many sheep were killed by carnivora. The following year, few farmers returned and the threat of a domestic livestock invasion proved to be a minor concern.

Nevertheless, faced with opposition from all sides, JSH had to think of ways to make the reserve pay its own way. His first attempt at sustainability was to propose a scheme whereby wild animals would be captured and sold to zoos around the world. After all, in London, the price of kudu is very dear. Unfortunately, it proved to be unworkable and the scheme was abandoned after an unsuccessful pilot project.

Then, in 1914, World War One inconveniently broke out. As a reserve officer, JSH was appointed to the 2nd Cavalry Division by the War Office and, ever the military man, he felt compelled to abandon his Cinderella in order to fight for Britain. JSH thus installed a caretaker warden at Sabi Bridge (first De La Porte, then the eccentric Fraser) and sailed off to England. Several other game rangers also enlisted and, with only half the staff available, the reserve went into a form of hibernation for several years.

Back in Blighty, the newly appointed Brigade-Major James Stevenson-Hamilton's first port of call was with the Notts and Derby Mounted Regiment, stationed at Holt in Norfolk. Unfortunately, it did not take long for the old frustrations to manifest themselves and JSH did not enjoy practising military manoeuvres under his stuffy commanding officer. He then moved onto Egypt as part of the Mediterranean Expeditionary Force. Once again, he felt that his talents were being wasted and soon asked for another posting. This time he found himself stationed with the Lowland Division at Cape Helles on the Gallipoli Peninsula of Turkey, where he arrived in July 1915.

The infamous Gallipoli campaign was one of the most controversial and deadly arenas of World War 1. Living conditions were atrocious and the Turkish forces kept up a constant barrage of artillery shells that went on for months on end. Between the fighting and the dysentery, casualties were high but JSH carried out his duties competently in very difficult conditions. After several months, the War Office realised that the position of the troops was hopeless and ordered a general evacuation.

In 1916, JSH returned to Egypt with the rank of Lieutenant-Colonel and took charge of the General Headquarters at Ismalia. Ever the iconoclast, JSH found his duties to be unpleasant and tedious. He once again applied for a transfer to the civil service of the Sudan, which was granted in November. During this time, he also suffered the loss of his youngest brother Olmar, who died of cholera in India.

JSH would spend nearly three years in the Sudan. With little direct supervision and a largely unexplored region to administer, JSH once again found himself in a satisfying position. He enjoyed his time in the Sudan and quickly got to grips with the new tribes and wildlife that he encountered. He also got involved with wildlife preservation efforts and was encouraged to stay in Sudan when the war ended.

By this time, JSH had been away from South Africa for four years and he had just turned 50. Reports of Fraser's mismanagement of the Sabi Reserve disheartened him and his letters to the Transvaal administrators regarding the future of the park seemed to be coolly received. After much indecision, he decided to stay in the Sudan. Then, in early 1919, he changed his mind, resigned from the Sudan Government Service and returned to England.

Once back in cold and dreary Britain, he soon grew depressed. His sister was becoming increasingly difficult, the country had changed into a proletarian state, the Fairholm Estate was only just solvent, and he didn't have any immediate job prospects. His thoughts naturally turned to South Africa where the weather was good and the living was cheaper.

More importantly, the pull of the Lowveld was strong. And so was his determination to see things through with the Sabi Reserve. After several more letters to the Transvaal administration, 'Skukuza' returned to South Africa in March 1920 and hurried back at Sabi Bridge, which "does take hold of me more than anywhere I have ever been".

But there was much work to be done. Fraser had left the place in a shambles. Poaching was on the rise. Several rangers had either retired or been killed in the war and new rangers had to be employed (several of whom were Afrikaners, a first for the park). JSH was depressed and felt that he was back where he started in 1902.

The Game Reserves Commission

After the war, the political climate of South Africa changed. In 1919, the first prime minister of South Africa, Louis Botha, died of heart failure and was replaced by his fellow Boer War colleague, Jan Smuts. Under Smuts, the ruling South African Party came to be considered pro-British by the opposition and the old dream of establishing an independent Boer republic began to take root once again.

With the rise of Afrikaner Nationalism, spearheaded by the National Party of JBM Herzog, the battle lines were clearly drawn and the game reserves found themselves caught in the middle of a political tussle. Smuts himself was a staunch supporter of nature conservation but many other opposition politicians (especially those with electorates based in rural areas) were rabidly opposed to the 'useless' and 'sentimental' reserves.

This ideological conflict had become apparent as early as 1912, when the Witwatersrand branch of the Transvaal Game Protection Association urged the government to 'nationalise the Sabi and Shingwedsi Game Reserves' – the first time that such a notion had been formally placed on the agenda. In 1913, TJ Kleinenberg of the Soutpansberg made a similar proposal. Nothing came of these entreaties, despite the urging of Jan Smuts to "appoint an impartial commission to go over the ground [of establishing a National Sanctuary]".

Then, in 1915, a contrary motion was tabled by SJ Coetzee, the member for Lydenburg, who asked the Union Government to reduce the area of the Sabi Reserve. At the time, the First World War was raging in Europe but the issue was deemed important enough to demand an answer.

And so, in June 1916, a Game Reserves Commission was duly appointed with JF Ludorf as chairman. Upon meeting, the commission decided that the members should visit the reserve and see the Sabi for themselves. A visit was duly arranged and, in the absence of JSH, Ranger Wolhuter escorted the party around the Pretoriuskop and Sabi Bridge areas.

Whatever preconceptions they may have had prior to their arrival, the commission was very impressed with what they saw. As JSH puts it, "Few can sojourn long within the unspoilt wilderness of a game sanctuary, surrounded on all sides by its confiding animals, without absorbing its atmosphere; the Spirit of the Wild is quick to assert her supremacy, and no man of any sensibility can resist her."

The commission returned to Pretoria and sat at intervals throughout 1917 and 1918. It eventually issued its report at the end of that year, and there was good news. The report was very complimentary of the reserve and paid high praise to the rangers who had carried out their duties so admirably.

They went on to say: "In the course of our investigations we were not a little struck by the uselessness of having these magnificent reserves merely for the *preservation* of the fauna – in an area practically unknown and made to a great extent inaccessible to the bulk of the people... for these and other reasons we recommend that the policy of the Administration should be directed toward the creation of the area ultimately as a great national park where the natural and prehistoric conditions of our country can be preserved for all time."

Despite the commission's stipulation that winter grazing be allowed to continue, it was a great victory for the Sabi Reserve. Unfortunately, the commission was only mandated with writing up a report and no practical steps were taken for implementing their recommendations for several years. When JSH returned to his post in 1920, the commission's findings were still lying dormant.

'Round in Nine'

Even though the Game Reserves Commission had issued a very favourable report, Stevenson-Hamilton had a torrid time when he returned to his post in 1920. Across the country, opinions were turning on the notion of game reserves as a sanctuary for wild animals. Already several reserves had been deproclaimed as a result of pressure from the agricultural, mining and/or housing lobbies. These included the forlorn Pongola reserve (1921), the Rustenburg Game Reserve (1914), Namaqualand (1919), Gordonia-Kuruman (1924) and the Umfolozi (1920).

Back at the Sabi Reserve, things were looking equally bleak. A coal mining syndicate had secured a concession along the Selati Line north of Sabi Bridge. The railway company wanted to deproclaim the land around the line to the south, to be sold off in lots for timber cutting and farming. The winter grazers were pushing to be allowed further into the reserve. And the farmers to the south of the Crocodile River were clamouring to get their hands on the 'unrivalled farming land' on the north bank.

And things only got worse. There were plans to prospect for gold along the Luvuvhu River. The land companies were agitating about their unresolved rights to the farms within the reserve. Farmers stepped up their complaints about lions breeding in the unfenced reserve. The press railed against the menace that carnivorous 'vermin' presented to peaceful citizens. Citrus farmers wanted to carve up the reserve. The Department of Native Affairs wanted the land for native settlements. The Department of Lands also wanted a chunk of the reserve for additional white settlements. Everywhere he looked, JSH saw only trouble ahead.

Then the storm broke. The Transvaal Consolidated Land Company, which had by now bought out most of the private farms within the reserve, resolved to bring matters to a head and, in 1922, they sent out their manager, Percy Greathead, to visit the reserve and complete a tour of inspection. On his return, it was announced that the Company would establish a cattle ranch in the middle of the Sabi Reserve, a little to the north of Sabi Bridge.

The aim was to force the government's hand. Either they would be compelled to pay the inflated prices the Company was demanding for its properties, or they would deproclaim a large chunk, if not the entire reserve. JSH knew that the government wouldn't pay a "penny piece to save the Sabi" and feared that the entire affair would cause the authorities to abandon his Cinderella. With few options available to him, JSH decided to play nice for the moment and showed the manager of the new ranch, a Mr. Crosby, every courtesy.

After several nights of stoep talk, Crosby was turned and became an unofficial supporter of the reserve. JSH now had to sit back and wait for the land company's next move. It didn't take long. Crosby was soon instructed to shoot some game as a test of rights. Crosby informed JSH of his orders and JSH calmly replied that he should "get on with the good work".

Crosby duly shot a single wildebeest and immediately reported his actions to the warden. A summons was taken out against Crosby and the case was tried in court, where the verdict went against the land company. Various appeals went on for many months, but by the time the case was settled (in favour of the Sabi Reserve) other events had overtaken the matter.

You see, just when things were looking really grim, an ally appeared in the unlikely form of South African Railways. In 1923, the railways launched a new tourism product called the 'Round in Nine' tour. This was a circular, nine-day rail excursion through the scenic delights of the eastern Transvaal; the highlight being an overnight stay in the continental seaside town of Lourenço Marques (now Maputo).

With regular departures during the winter months, the Round In Nine tour proved popular with tourists. The route took passengers from Johannesburg to Pietersburg (now Polokwane) and onto Tzaneen. From here, it chugged across the Lowveld and through the Sabi on the Selati Line, crossing the bridges over the Sabi and Crocodile Rivers, to Komatipoort. The train then crossed into Mozambique and headed over the plains to Lourenço Marques, famous for its golden beaches and glittering European-style nightlife. On the way back to Johannesburg, the train passed through Nelspruit, with side trips to the beautiful mountains around Pilgrim's Rest.

At first, the train did not stop in the Sabi Reserve, much to JSH's dismay. But the itinerary was soon changed and the Sabi was transformed. But I'll let the inimitable James Stevenson-Hamilton relate the story in his own words.

From *South African Eden*:

"When the programme of the service was shown to me I was a little disappointed, though perhaps hardly surprised, to discover that these tourist trains were scheduled to pass through the reserve by night on every occasion, and, of course, without stopping. I called on the system manager, whom I knew, and mooted the idea of allowing each train to make a halt while passing through, or at least to make the journey in daylight. 'But why?' he asked me, with a surprised air. 'Well,' I said, 'perhaps some of the people might like to look at the game.' He looked at me steadily for a moment or two, as one does at a person of whose complete sanity one is not quite sure, then he leaned back in his chair and burst into a hearty laugh. 'What! Look at your old wildebeests! What on earth do you suppose anyone wants to see *them* for? But look here' - suddenly struck by an idea - 'I'll make a bargain with you. If you will allow us to stop and have a little shooting, I am sure that would amuse the passengers. We could put an expert shot on board, and some of them might like to have a go themselves.' Well, well! Twenty years work of building, and no more helpful suggestion at the end than to allow neophytes to practise with lethal weapons on semi-tame animals. But that was still the public attitude towards game even so recently as 1923.

"I did not allow myself to be discouraged, and ultimately it was settled that the train, without rifle and expert hunter, should stay the night at the siding opposite Sabi Bridge, where we would arrange a camp fire for the passengers, and next morning, very early, proceed to Newington [near Sabi Sands], to remain there for an hour in daylight. I don't think anyone was more surprised than the railway authorities when they discovered at the conclusion of the first tour that the short halt in the Game Reserve was, to the majority of passengers, mainly townspeople from Johannesburg, by far the most interesting and exciting part of the whole tour. Later, it was agreed that more time in the Reserve should be spent by the tourist train, and it was further arranged that a ranger should travel on it, and at each halt take the passengers for a little walk in the bush. The campfires too, became a great attraction; the people sat round the huge blaze, alternately singing choruses and shivering with delight at the idea of being watched, from the dark bush close at hand, by the hungry eyes of beasts of prey, though I am sure every wild beast within earshot had long fled headlong from the clamour.

"One of the stewards on the train, having possessed himself of a lion skin, would sometimes envelop himself in it, and would come crawling stealthily into the ring of firelight, to be greeted with shrieks from the more timid of the ladies, while the bolder of the men would assume protective attitudes. To add to the realism, our SAP sergeant at the bridge could give a very passable imitation of a lion's roar through a long glass tube, and while his confederate was approaching, would, from a place of concealment, provide the necessary vocal accompaniment.

"The interest betrayed by the public in the animals, and the remarks I overheard when mixing with the passengers, made me at last confident that, could only our national park scheme mature, it would become popular, and therefore an asset to the country. It was beyond measure encouraging to feel that the South African public, despite tradition, might be content to look at animals without wanting to kill them."

JSH was quick to realise that the power of tourism could be the salvation of his precious Sabi and was eager to capitalise on the reserve's rapidly spreading fame. But he still had to win over many opponents before he could get the legislative and financial power to nationalise the reserve.

Crucially, however, he no longer felt like a lone voice in the wilderness. He could now show that there was indeed a point to 'keeping the things' and was gratified to find that other people could appreciate wild animals as part of their natural heritage.

As for the Selati Line itself, it remained in regular use until the 1960s with as many as 250 trains a week shunting through the park. Obviously, many animals were taken out by the rolling stock and it was eventually decided to build a new line around the western edge of the reserve. The last train travelled through the reserve in September 1973.

Today, there are still several substantial relics of the railroad era standing in and around Skukuza rest camp. The Sabie railway bridge is clearly visible from the riverside promenade, often beautifully silhouetted against the bushveld sunrise, and then there's the old Skukuza passenger halt, complete with an SAR Class 24 stream locomotive (#3638) that actually used to ply the Kruger route. This is coupled to a wood-panelled lounge car that was released for use in 1929. There used to be two additional coaches, a dining car and kitchen car, but these were destroyed by a fire in 1995. Until recently, the carriages and platform were used as a restaurant but this facility is now dormant.

H. Stratford Caldecott

Within a few years, the 'Round in Nine' excursion was well-established and SA Railways began to appreciate the huge tourism potential of the Sabi Reserve. The SAR publicity department consequently embarked on an aggressive marketing campaign, supported by the general manager of the railways who was an ardent supporter of the reserve. And so, in 1925, a series of wildlife posters to promote the Sabi as a potential public asset was commissioned. The man chosen for the task was Harry Stratford Caldecott, a Kimberley-born and Paris-trained artist, then living in Cape Town.

Caldecott set off for the Sabi Reserve and spent two months travelling through the bush to sketch the wildlife. He proved to be a quick study and fell in love with the bush and its denizens. When Caldecott met JSH, the two hit it off immediately and they began to discuss appropriate ways to develop the reserve as a tourist attraction. JSH would later say of Caldecott that "Until his lamented and premature death in 1929, there was no single man in South Africa who worked more strenuously and successfully for the cause of wild life preservation in the sub-continent."

Caldecott returned to Cape Town and drew up a variety of marketing materials. His most famous advert is the stylish 'Giraffe' poster that was put up at every railway station in the country. The slogan read (in Afrikaans) "Come with South African Railways to the Transvaal Game Reserve – the most unique sanctuary for wildlife in the world. Visit your National Park."

His vivid illustrations and bold colours captured the public's eye, and his many enthusiastic articles appeared in periodicals and newspapers around the world. In every respect, Caldecott became a tireless campaigner for the reserve and, later, joined several wildlife preservation societies. He even gave JSH a rather good idea, but more on that in a moment.

It's interesting to note that it took a healthy dose of advertising to bring people round to the idea of nature conservation. Yet this is not surprising. We are a reactive species and often don't appreciate an object's value until someone else points it out. After all, every new idea has to be sold a little.

Caldecott and his posters were therefore a major catalyst for a shift in public opinion that would help turn the Game Reserve from a pariah into a source of national pride and personal aspiration. Who knew that by turning giraffes into celebrities, Stratford Caldecott would help save the Sabi?

Becoming Kruger

It was make or break time for the Sabi Reserve. Either it was going to be declared a national park, as per the recommendation of the Game Reserves Commission, or it was going to be deproclaimed and developed by various commercial interests.

On the one side stood JSH and his allies: Prime Minister Jan Smuts, the various Game Preservation Associations and a growing sector of the general public, won over by the Railways' publicity for their Round in Nine tours. On the other hand, several powerful groups still wanted the reserve carved up and the game destroyed.

It would require luck, diplomacy and timing to make Cinderella into an official National Park princess. However, as is the way with Government, the political endgame proved to be complicated, divisive and a little tedious.

By 1921, the central government had been drawn into the controversy, with the private land owners, the Department of Mining, the Department of Native Affairs and the Department of Lands all wanting their piece of the Reserve. It was clear that a round-table discussion was needed to settle the matter once and for all (again). This initial conference was held in February 1921 and, initially, it didn't appear that the outcome would be in the Reserve's favour.

However, JSH took the opportunity to meet with the Minister of Lands, Deneys Reitz, and used all his powers of persuasion to bring the ex-Boer commander round to his point of view. Surprisingly, Reitz proved receptive to the idea. He felt that a National Park could contribute to a newly awakened sense of national pride. Reitz also visited the park with some government representatives and was duly impressed (even though the steadfast warden refused the visitors' request to do a bit of hunting while they were there!).

The final decision of the conference was that the Sabi Reserve should indeed be declared a national park, but within smaller boundaries. Specifically, it was proposed that a large chunk of the western section of the reserve be deproclaimed and handed over to the Department of Native Affairs for the establishment of black settlements.

JSH grabbed the offer and reconciled himself to the loss of land in exchange for the promise of nationalisation. Today, this excised area is heavily-populated and includes sprawling communities such as Bushbuckridge, Acornhoek and Klaserie.

This excision also, conveniently, included many of the privately-owned farms that had been such a big obstacle to proclamation. The land owners were now an issue for the Native Affairs Department to deal with. The conference further mandated the Department of Lands to buy or swap out the remaining private farms that still remained within the reserve.

It all seemed to be coming together. Prime Minister Jan Smuts was openly talking about tabling the necessary legislation before parliament and, in 1923, the Sabi and Shingwedzi reserves were merged and renamed 'The Transvaal Game Reserve'.

However, the land companies still refused to co-operate and continued to haggle with the government over land valuations. Smuts was forced to postpone his legislation until the issue was settled. He could not risk the possibility that the draft bill would be thrown out of parliament, never to be re-tabled.

It was uncertain time for JSH and, during his annual summer leave, he returned to Britain to consider his options. If the reserve wasn't nationalised, it would surely be deproclaimed. If the bill was successful, however, there was a good chance that he would be replaced by a new warden; one who would be more acceptable to the forces of Afrikaner Nationalism that were sweeping through the halls of power.

Either way, it looked like JSH would be out of a job for the first time since 1902. He discussed employment opportunities with both the Zoological Society of London and the Society for the Protection of the Wild Fauna of the Empire. Understandably, he was reluctant to commit to anything until the fate of his beloved Sabi had been resolved.

But when he returned to South Africa in 1924, JSH was faced with a new challenge. There had just been a general election and, in a huge upset, dedicated conservationist Jan Smuts was ousted from office by the National Party of JBM Herzog (in coalition with the Labour Party, to create what became known as the Pact Government). With the new government came a new Minister of Lands, Piet Grobler, and JSH had to return to Pretoria to canvas the support of yet another politician.

JSH had reason to be nervous. The general Nationalist opinion was that Smuts, Stevenson-Hamilton and the Sabi Reserve were all unwelcome relics of British imperialism. Fortunately, Grobler was in favour of the National Parks scheme, for a number of reasons. Firstly, by a happy coincidence, Grobler was the grandnephew of Oom Paul Kruger himself, and was thus naturally inclined to realise the 'dream' of his famous ancestor. Furthermore, Grobler was an ardent Afrikaner Nationalist and believed that the establishment of a National Park would contribute to a proud, new (white) South African national identity.

As Jane Carruthers writes in her excellent book, *Wildlife and Warfare,* "National Parks in other parts of the world – the United States and Australia for example – also came into being for reasons related to the promotion of national feeling. Indeed, national parks appear to be connected to a certain stage in a country's cultural evolution and serve to weld together different groups within it."

Grobler accordingly took a firm line with the private land owners who had been a thorn in the side of the Sabi Reserve for so long. He found suitable land outside the reserve and proposed a land swap in late 1925. This time the land companies agreed, perhaps fearing that their land would simply be expropriated should they stall any longer.

By April 1926, the deal was signed. The land companies exchanged a total of 196 000 acres of land in the reserve for 135 000 acres on the outside. Several owners settled for financial restitution, which totalled £40 000. In addition, the triangular piece of government land between the Olifants and Letaba rivers was added to the reserve. The final hurdle was down and the road ahead seemed clear.

However, there was still the danger that the bill would be turned down by parliament so, around this time, JSH and his staunch supporter Stratford Caldecott hit on a sure-fire way to win support for the National Park. As JSH describes it, "We were talking of the early beginnings of the Reserve and I was showing him a copy of the first proclamation of 1898 signed by President Kruger. He looked hard at me, and catching on, I said at once 'Of course you are right, that is the obvious name – 'The Kruger National Park'! Few would be willing to oppose the founding of an institution linked with the name of the great president, and one felt that much of any possible opposition would thus automatically collapse."

In his private journal, JSH was more forthright. "The man who *really* was responsible was RK Loveday... but the 'Kruger stunt' is I think of priceless value to us, and I would not for the world do aught but whisper otherwise... I wonder what the old man, who *never in his life* thought of wild animals except as biltong. I wonder... what he would say could he see himself depicted as the *'Saviour of the South African game'!!!*"

With this little secret under his hat, JSH presented the 'Kruger' idea to Grobler, who was naturally thrilled with the opportunity to honour his illustrious forebear. In short order, the name was officially proposed by Judge JAJ de Villiers to the National Monuments Commission in December 1925, and it was immediately adopted.

Some English-speaking citizens didn't like the name, claiming that it was partisan and politically loaded. Alternative suggestions included 'The South African National Park' and even 'The National Milner Park', after Lord Milner who had re-proclaimed the Sabi and Shingwedzi reserves after the 2nd Anglo-Boer War. But these names were quickly brushed aside and the Kruger Park was born.

In what seemed like an instant, all the opponents of the reserves transformed themselves into avowed National Park supporters. It seemed that, in the scramble to get on the bandwagon, many people had conveniently lost their memories. The same kind of voluntary amnesia would strike the nation when apartheid collapsed in the 1990s and suddenly no-one could remember voting for the National Party.

And so, after the Kruger Park got its name, JSH was suddenly surrounded by supporters. This gave JSH considerable satisfaction and he would often smile inwardly when a former enemy "endeavoured to acquire credit for having been among the first to push on the scheme. Truly nothing succeeds like success!"

Grobler also had the good sense to propose that the management of the park should remain outside of politics, so that the protected area could not be used as a political pawn every time there was an election. He therefore set up a board of 10 unpaid trustees who would be devoted to the preservation of game above all else.

This 'National Parks Board' would be responsible for the Kruger Park and any other reserves subsequently declared in the Union. The Parks Board would continue to run the Kruger until it was transformed into a new organisation, South African National Parks (SANParks), after 1994.

With everyone on board, the time was right to prepare the necessary legislation and put it before parliament for a vote. Dr Schoch, legal advisor to the government, had already written up a draft National Parks Ordinance back in 1923, under instructions from Jan Smuts and Deneys Reitz (both of whom were subsequently excluded from the National Park narrative). This was revised in early 1926 into the National Parks Act.

Finally, on the 31ˢᵗ of May 1926, Piet Grobler introduced the Act to parliament. The bill was seconded by Jan Smuts, now the leader of the opposition, and several long-standing supporters of the reserve (including HB Papenfus and Deneys Reitz) also made some speeches. The Act was passed and drafted into law on 11ᵗʰ June 1926. Cinderella was safe at last!

Endless rounds of back-patting followed and JSH was swamped with congratulatory telegrams prompting him to quip that he "began to think I should have to buy a larger size in hats". Caldecott simply wrote a letter saying 'Finis Coronat Opus' – a Latin expression meaning 'the end justifies the work'. JSH would adopt this slogan as his personal motto.

In his private journal, however, he was a little more rueful: "[Piet Grobler] has got the excellent idea that the whole National Park emanated from him... In fact, all the people who have had anything to do with it, think 'they alone did it' and it is well it should be so. What a quaint old world it is. Between me and this page, I do believe that it is only my humble self and the way I have consistently worried everyone that has kept game preservation going in the Transvaal since 1902. But being only a damned foreign Scotchman, of course, the less one dwells on this, the better..."

Strangely, JSH also expressed a note of melancholy when describing this triumphant era. "I suppose," he wrote, "that a certain sensation of anti-climax is apt to follow the successful consummation of any kind of mundane effort."

Perhaps it was just the taciturn Scot talking, but he seemed almost disappointed that he no longer had any battles to fight. Later, when he was approaching the end of his life, he went further saying that there seemed to be "little benefit to living after one's work is done". There's just no pleasing some people!

The National Parks Board of Trustees

Following Grobler's exhortation to keep the National Parks out of the political arena, the first Parks Board was a robust mixture of men from various backgrounds. The chairman was Jack Brebner, a leading member of the National Party. Other staunchly Nationalist members included Oswald Pirow, a controversial figure who supported Nazi Germany during the Second World War, and Gustav Preller, an ardent promoter of Afrikaner culture and identity.

From the opposition parties came RA Hockly and the estimable Messrs. Deneys Reitz and HB Papenfus, both of whom were long-time friends of the reserve. Independent candidates included the mining tycoon Sir Abe Bailey, naturalist and land baron WA Campbell and Dr SK Haagner, head of the Pretoria Zoological Society. It was a good mix of people and it boded well for the future.

However, even though the newly-minted Kruger National Park was finally on a firm footing, it wasn't immune to the political turmoil that was about to unfold. Briefly put, in 1934, JB Herzog's ruling National Party joined with Jan Smuts' South African Party to create the United Party. This 'betrayal' was prompted by the economic hardships caused by the Great Depression, but resulted in hard-line politician, DF Malan, breaking away from the 'Nats' to form the *Gesuiwerde Nasionale Party* or Purified National Party. With the outbreak of World War II in 1939, however, Herzog refused to support the British cause and was pushed out in favour of Smuts, who began his second tenure as Prime Minister – serving with distinction for the duration of the war.

But then, in an eerie echo of the fate that befell Winston Churchill in Britain, Smuts lost the first post-war election of 1948 to DF Malan's *Herenigde Nasionale Party* (Reunited National Party). This new version of the National Party would go on to become the primary force behind the growth of Afrikaner Nationalism and the iniquitous system of Apartheid, ruling South Africa with an increasingly iron fist from 1948 until our peaceful democratic revolution of 1994.

Thus, as the political climate became more oppressive, the trustees changed and the Board became increasingly aligned with Nationalist policies. Afrikaans became the only language spoken at board meetings and the history of the park was re-written to emphasise the 'legacy' of Paul Kruger as creator of the park, while underplaying the contributions of such people as Smuts, Reitz, Loveday and even JSH himself.

Over the years, the National Party would continue to appropriate the status and imagery of the Kruger Park for their own propaganda; mixing it in with Voortrekker wagons and the church to create a holy trinity that justified and elevated the 'heroic' narrative of Afrikaners as God's chosen people.

The Changing Face of Kruger

In 1960, the massacre at Sharpeville galvanised the world to condemn the Nationalist government of South Africa. The next year, a characteristically unrepentant HF Verwoerd led South Africa out of the Commonwealth with a smug smile and declared the country a republic, ushering in the era of Grand Apartheid. Under the new dispensation, the culture of the Kruger National Park seemed to harden and change.

It was now administered and marketed as a playground for the white race, and its symbolism was subsumed into the Afrikaner psyche. One newspaper article declared as recently as 1993 that the KNP was "a Boere-paradys deluxe... [where] your card-carrying Seffrican Engels-sprekend could feel like an outsider, to say nothing of a Finn or a Japanese or – unthinkable – a Disenfranchised."

There is evidence of this cultural hegemony all over the KNP. Most of the historical sites commemorate the exploits of the white men. Memorial plaques to various members of the Parks Board are nailed up on various boulders. And at Skukuza, the faces of Paul Kruger, Piet Grobler and James Stevenson-Hamilton are carved into a large frieze next to the reception, labelled as 'Our Founders'.

To top it off, in 1974 the Paul Kruger Gate was opened near Skukuza. To commemorate the event, an imposing bust of Oom Paul was erected at the road side. This rather sombre sculpture, carved from pale sandstone, looks down disapprovingly on motorists as they drive past, reminding everyone of the park's supposed provenance.

Thankfully, the Kruger culture has changed considerably since the advent of democracy in 1994. It's now more inclusive and very cosmopolitan, attracting visitors from just about every nation on Earth. However, the 'paleness' of Kruger's heritage sites remain controversial.

The highly visible Kruger statue is a particular bugbear. There are periodic requests to have it torn down and replaced by a less offensive icon. There have even been suggestions to change the name of the Kruger National Park itself, as it is an affront to many South Africans. But this is unlikely to happen because the Kruger brand is simply too well known.

In the future, the KNP intends to update its heritage register and refresh some of the established historical sites. Bushman rock paintings are being surveyed and may be made accessible to the public. The lives of the black rangers are being documented, and research on the Wenela Labour Route through Shingwedzi is on-going. Histories of local tribes and their modern counterparts are also being compiled. This all adds up to a wealth of new history that will allow us to celebrate the wider Kruger community.

South Africa's Other National Parks

Over the years, a number of other conservation-worthy areas have been declared as national parks and placed under the administration of the Parks Board (now re-incorporated as South African National Parks, or SANParks).

With an annual operating budget of around R1.2 billion, SANParks is the custodian of 20 parks around the country, incorporating just over 4 million hectares (or 40 000 square kilometres). This covers around 4% of the total area of South Africa (1 220 000 square kilometres).

Combine this with the hundreds of provincial, regional and private reserves dotted all across the country and South Africa is well on its way to realising its goal of getting 10% of SA's land and around 20% of its coastline is under protection.

FYI, here is a list of the country's other magnificent national parks (each of which deserves a book of its own):

Addo Elephant National Park: proclaimed 1931, 163 297ha (to be expanded to 360 000ha including an adjoining 120 000ha marine reserve)

Agulhas National Park: proclaimed 1998, 20 415ha

Augrabies Falls National Park: proclaimed 1966, 58 699ha

Bontebok National Park: proclaimed 1931, 2432ha

Camdeboo National Park: proclaimed 2005, 18 946ha

Garden Route National Park: proclaimed 2009, 137 796ha, formerly the Tsitsikamma, Knysna and Wilderness reserves

Golden Gate Highlands National Park: proclaimed 1963, 34 062ha

Groenkloof National Park: SANParks headquarters, 7ha

Karoo National Park: proclaimed 1979, 84 082ha

Kalahari Gemsbok National Park: proclaimed 1931, 960 029ha (part of the Kgalagadi Transfrontier Park)

Mapungubwe National Park: proclaimed 1989 (as the Vhembe Dongola National Park), 15 311ha, part of Limpopo-Shashe Transfrontier Park

Marakele National Park: proclaimed 1994 (as the Kransberg National Park), 60 865ha

Mokala National Park: proclaimed 2007 (as Vaalbos National Park), 29 414ha

Mountain Zebra National Park: proclaimed 1937, 27 900ha

Namaqua National Park: proclaimed 2002, 130 641ha

Richtersveld National Park: proclaimed 1991, 162 445ha (part of |Ai-|Ais/Richtersveld Transfrontier Park, established 2003)

Table Mountain National Park: proclaimed 1998, 33 010ha

Tankwa Karoo National Park: proclaimed 1986, 138 570ha

West Coast National Park: proclaimed 1985, 47 026ha

JSH Ties the Knot

After 24 years of tribulation, James Stevenson-Hamilton had finally accomplished his mission – the Kruger National Park was a fact. He was now 60 years old and at a loose end.

Feeling that his job here was done, he considered his options. He didn't relish the thought of operating under a supervisory board, as this went against his individualistic nature. He also received word that his elderly father in Scotland was ailing. He notified the newly formed Parks Board that he was considering retirement and returned to Britain on long leave.

He arrived back at Fairholm just in time. Within a few days, his father was dead and JSH was faced with the task of getting the estate in order. It was not a pleasant task and the old warden felt, "I am a stranger to my own land and this is in no sense my home. I don't have one, except Sabi Bridge."

Several years of dithering followed. First, he took up a job as Secretary of the Fauna Society in London. He didn't enjoy the work and returned to the Kruger in a temporary capacity. Unfortunately, he had a bad relapse of malaria and had to be hospitalised.

Faced with apparently failing health, he began training up a successor, Elliot Howe, albeit with a heavy heart. "Everyone knows now about my going and who is taking my place. But I still eagerly and pathetically cling to the notion that I shall end my days here... now I have burnt my boats. They would have kept me another 10 years and I chuck the whole thing to go to England which I hate. I have done it this time and no mistake. I lie awake at night and wake before dawn, thinking 'what a fool'... Formerly I cherished the idea of getting married, but I am too old now."

Always indecisive about his personal choices, JSH wrote to the board saying that he would consider returning after a year's sick leave, but he did not really think that they would want him back. He returned to Britain and his post at the Fauna Society with foreboding. His fears proved to be well-founded and he soon became glum and frustrated with the dim, cold, boring streets of London.

However, fate had a pleasant surprise in store for JSH. In August 1928, he was visiting at a friend's house and was introduced to Hilda Cholmondeley. An aspiring artist and wildlife enthusiast, Hilda was only 27 (35 years younger than JSH) but the two made a connection. A few months later they met again in London and began regular communications about wildlife, Africa and the bush that JSH knew so well.

By the end of the year, JSH realised he had feelings for the girl, but acknowledged that he was "too old and now too unwell" for her. In early 1929, Hilda left for an extended trip to South Africa, but JSH remained in England.

Soon, his year-long leave was up and he had to make a decision. After the usual prevarication, JSH wrote to the Parks Board and expressed an interest in returning as warden of the Kruger Park – motivated, perhaps, by the proximity of his new lady friend. After several agonising weeks of silence, the Board accepted the offer and in June, JSH was back home at Sabi Bridge.

Hilda, for her part, had totally fallen in love with South Africa and resolved to stay as long as she could. Naturally, correspondence continued between JSH and his 'Chum', as he called her. She also visited Sabi Bridge, where she was jokingly introduced as JSH's great-niece.

Despite opposition from Hilda's mother, the unlikely couple decided to marry and on the 12ᵗʰ of August, they tied the knot. JSH was now 63 years old. Yet, despite his advancing years, he took well to married life and even contemplated the production of an heir, saying "It would be a bore if I pegged out at his juncture before I could get a family."

Hilda and James would eventually have three children together – Margaret (who died as a child), James and Anne. Buoyed up by his new family, the 'ailing' old man would stay on as head warden of the Kruger Park for another 17 years.

Opening the Gates

Now that the Kruger National Park was a reality, there was much work to be done. One of the stipulations of the National Park Act was that the park must become an asset to the nation and members of the public should be allowed into the reserve to experience their wonderful natural heritage. This meant that the park had to build roads, rest camps and all the other conveniences of contemporary tourism.

However, there wasn't any money for infrastructure development. Appeals to the public were made, which did not yield much of a response. Eventually, government coughed up some cash (an annual contribution of £7000 from the Union Government and £3000 from the Transvaal provincial coffers, plus a once-off gift of £7000 from the Treasury), but that wasn't enough for the vast public works that were required.

Never one to shirk a challenge, JSH set about with the limited funds available. He began by improving the rough roads that linked up the various ranger stations in the park. The first 'two-track' roads to be constructed included the route from Crocodile Bridge to Lower Sabie, from Acornhoek to the Mozambique border via Satara, from Gravellote to Makubas Kraal (near Letaba), and White River to Pretoriuskop. These thoroughfares were built with the help of migrant labourers in conjunction with the rangers.

Then, in 1927, it was decided that Pretoriuskop (the most accessible ranger station) would be opened for tourism. Several loop roads around the Pretoriuskop area were built, and day permits were introduced. They then enlarged the path from Sabi Bridge to the Olifants River, followed by the road from Sabi Bridge down to Pretoriuskop and the Crocodile River.

Initially, visitors were expected to make their own camps and bring everything they needed along with them. Early tourists were even permitted to carry one loaded firearm in their car, in case of attack by a rogue lion. However, these guns were secured by a piece of wire and a lead seal so that the rangers could tell if they had been fired.

Despite the rough roads, absence of facilities and relative remoteness of the reserve, visitors were enchanted by their new National Park. Tourist numbers grew exponentially. In 1927, the first year of operations, three cars carrying a dozen intrepid visitors entered the park through Pretoriuskop. The following year, there were 180 cars. In 1929, the number of cars had surpassed 850. Soon, the Parks Board began charging an entrance fee of £1 per car and this finally set the Kruger Park on the road to financial sustainability.

Every year, during the dry season, JSH and the Park staff continued to build additional roads and the network grew rapidly; from 122 miles in 1927 to 900 in

1936. Ferries and pontoons were constructed to transport cars across the major rivers (such as the Sabi, Crocodile and Olifants). Makeshift bridges of wooden poles anchored to the river bed were built across the smaller streams. In the summer, these primitive roadways were often washed away by floods, and maintenance of the network was a constant chore.

Once this construction process was underway, JSH turned his attention to the problem of where the tourists were going to sleep. By all accounts, early accommodation in the Kruger Park was a chaotic affair. There were no rest camps or shops in the reserve and guests needed to be entirely self-sufficient. But this was seldom the case.

The task of caring for the herds of tourists fell to the unfortunate rangers, who were forced to turn their humble field stations into guest houses. As JSH describes it, "The rangers were obliged to surrender their own quarters to the visitors, who camped out in every room and on the verandahs, the rightful owner having to sleep as best he could outside." As one ranger remarked, "I did not mind so much their using my soap, towels, plates, knives and forks, but I do wish they had not used my toothbrush!"

JSH realised that the situation was untenable. He simply could not have his rangers neglecting their wildlife duties in order to wrangle the unruly tourist hordes. Luckily, one of the members of the Parks Board was the manager of a Johannesburg gold mine and he donated surplus building material to the Park. Construction thus began on the first three tourist huts, located at Satara, Pretoriuskop and Sabi Bridge.

These simple 'rondawels' consisted of a circular concrete wall topped by a conical thatched roof and, by 1930, there were about 100 beds available located in Pretoriuskop, Lower Sabie, Balule, Olifants, Satara, Malelane, Letaba and Sabi Bridge. The latter had by this time been renamed *Skukuza,* after the Tsonga nickname for JSH – he who sweeps clean.

To ensure the smooth running of the Park, the management of the new rest camps was gradually handed over to contractors and supervisory staff, who provided petrol, catering and supplies to the tourists. Entry permits were issued at the entrance gates by 'tourist officers', who collected entrance fees on behalf of the park in exchange for a small percentage of the take. It was becoming a good little business.

The First Tourist Huts

The first rondawels in the KNP were built in the 'Selby' style (named after an American engineer who served on the Park Board). The design called for units without windows, as it was thought that lions would leap into the huts and devour the tourists. Instead, they were built with a small gap between the wall and the roof, to allow the breeze to blow through. A hole was also cut into the wooden door of the hut, so that the guests could check for wild animals before entering or exiting their accommodation.

Predictably, the rondawels were stifling in summer and frigid in winter. The lack of windows also made the huts very dark, and the peep holes were abused by passers-by, who couldn't help from looking into the huts in the hope of spotting a bit of human wildlife. In the mornings, the peep holes were often found stuffed up with socks and paper. From 1931 onwards, rondawels were built with windows.

A few of these original tourist huts have been preserved at Skukuza and Pretoriuskop, complete with period furnishings. They are open to the public and provide a fascinating frame of reference for the park's modern accommodation. The accommodation at Balule still utilises some of the original Selby huts.

In 1931, tents were supplied for the first time (at Skukuza and Satara) and the rest camps were fenced. A year later, the first ablution blocks with showers and baths were built at Skukuza. Hot water was also (controversially) supplied to Punda Maria and Letaba in 1933, with the other camps only receiving this decadent 'luxury' in 1939.

In other rest camps, such as Lower Sabie, old buildings were sometimes converted into larger guest houses but these structures were often dilapidated and fell out of use within a few years. More remote camps, such as Punda Maria, had to make do with traditional wattle and daub huts, as concrete was in short supply. A number of additional rest camps were also established around the reserve in these early years, but several were subsequently abandoned due to flooding, mosquitos or logistical reasons (such as Rabelais Gate, Malopene and Tsokwane – now a picnic site).

To compensate for the increasing demand for additional tourist accommodation, an appeal was made to government in 1935 and £30 000 was released for the construction of new facilities (including a spanking new rest camp at Lower Sabie), as well as improvements to water supplies for the game.

Well-known architects Gerard Moerdyk and Gordon Leith were commissioned to design and supervise the expansion of the various rest camps (often under considerable budgetary constraints). And slowly, the KNP that we know today began to take shape.

Teething Problems

Early visitors were given a relatively free hand in their new national park. Speeding motor vehicles kicked up huge clouds of dust as they hurtled through the reserve. Ignorant of the danger, many foolhardy people got out of their cars and approached sleeping lions, eager for a closer look or even a pat. Driving at night was allowed and cars would often get stuck in the middle of the dark wilderness, far from any human eyes. There were also many cases of animals being run down by speeding vehicles.

Back in the rest camps, things were hardly restful. In the evenings, camp fires were lit and gramophones were cranked up. Hours of singing, dancing and general merrymaking ensued, and one can only imagine what was going on in the windowless rondawels.

Within a few years, the warden had issued regulations which put an end to much of this rowdiness. It was also decided to close the park during the hot summer months, as the visitor numbers were low and the chances of contracting malaria were high. Furthermore, the heavy rains of summer made the road network unpredictable and the rangers grew tired of rescuing cars and trucks that were stuck in the mud.

Only the Pretoriuskop area remained open all year round, as it lay in the foothills of the Drakensberg where the threat of malaria is reduced. This was done for the benefit of overseas visitors who enjoyed travelling to sunny South Africa during their icy winters.

Whatever hassles may have been caused by rampant tourists, it was obvious that the park was a great success. News of the unique game viewing experience in the Lowveld spread like wildfire through the press and by word of mouth. Visitor numbers exploded; 6000 cars and lorries carrying 26 000 people trundled through the gates in 1935 alone. With so many curious holiday-makers clogging the bush, it is little wonder that JSH wrote "I had perhaps some excuse for feeling relieved when each season closed without someone or other having paid the penalty of folly."

In 1931, the remote and often neglected Shingwedzi section was opened to the public. Formerly a lonely outpost, manned by only a single ranger and handful of native police, the northern part of the park was now considered to be worthy of exploration. The animals were unusual (including nyala, eland and elephant) and the scenery was attractive, with lush valleys cut through the hilly landscape by rivers rushing towards the great Limpopo.

By 1933, 100 miles of road had been constructed in Shingwedzi and a low-level causeway had been built over the Letaba River. It was now possible to drive an ordinary car from Malelane at the bottom of the reserve to the Luvuvhu River at the top. The Kruger National Park was open for business!

Many things were learnt during the first 5 years of the park's existence. At first, it wasn't known how the game would react to the sudden appearance of noisy, smelly cars full of noisy, smelly people – all belching smoke and dust. Several authorities were particularly worried that ravenous lions would attack the vehicles and maul the tourists. To everyone's relief, the animals paid the cars very little heed and continued with their business, much as before.

Another surprise was that the lions quickly became the star attraction of the Kruger Park. Previously dismissed as vermin, the big cats proved to be of overwhelming interest to the city slickers – so much so that Piet Grobler issued JSH with an order to stop his programme of culling lions. Stories of lion spotting quickly came to dominate campfire discussions, and little has changed.

Then, as now, the standard Game Reserve question 'Did you see anything?' really translates as 'Spot any lion?'. This idolatry confounded JSH who thought of lion as somnolent beasts who were intelligent but rather boring. He preferred the various antelope species, the original 'game' for which the Sabi Reserve had been declared.

It many ways, the opening of the Kruger Park began a process whereby environmental awareness became part of popular culture in South Africa. Before the Kruger Park, perspectives of wildlife were limited to their commercial or sporting value. Today, we have moved from a culture of exploitation to a culture of appreciation, conservation and education. Wildlife is now part of our heritage, and integral to our identity as South Africans. The role of the Kruger Park in entrenching this attitude cannot be understated

To quote JSH: "It is hard to realise how deep was the ignorance of natural history prevalent among the townspeople even of South Africa, and I am sure that the Kruger National Park… has done more than all the zoos and natural history books put together to implant some knowledge of the habits and appearance of the various creatures, even though little but lukewarm interest be taken in anything but lions, with giraffe, elephant and hippo tying as bad seconds."

JSH Bids Farewell

By 1935, the Kruger National Park was firmly established in the iconography of South Africa. It was attracting tens of thousands of visitors every year, and the park was running smoothly. For JSH, however, it seemed to be a bittersweet victory.

When he first arrived, the reserve was untouched and unloved, a genuine wilderness in which he could roam for days without seeing any form of human civilisation. Now the park was full of tourist cars and busses, and the rest camps were packed with holiday-makers, nattering about the game they had seen. The solitude was gone and, in later years, JSH would look back on the old Sabi Reserve with considerable nostalgia.

"I could hardly recognise my beloved and once battered Cinderella in her new garb and surroundings, and, truth to tell, I did not admire her nearly so much in them. The whole atmosphere had changed. The Spirit of the Wild shunned the neighbourhood of crowded camps and roads... Civilisation had come to us, and was not to be shaken off.

"In moments of temporary depression... I would reflect that I had been to a considerable degree responsible for the transformation; forgetting for the moment that had she not found her way into the palace, she would inevitably have been swept into oblivion, unregretted and unrecorded."

JSH realised by opening the magnificent wilderness to the visitor, some part of its innate wildness was destroyed. This is true of most conservation efforts. It's an axiom; no matter how careful the visitor may be, the simple act of observation unavoidably changes the scene being observed. This situation is exacerbated when the accoutrements of civilisation (roads, rest camps, picnic sites) are added to the equation.

As JSH wrote, "A certain amount of artificiality is inevitable in any region where man is present, however firmly he may restrain his hand, and however honestly he may endeavour to leave nature to herself. But in the Kruger National Park there exists the opportunity of getting nearer the truth than is possible perhaps anywhere else in the world."

JSH's concerns were not just ideological, however. His new masters at the National Parks Board were more intrusive than his old bosses in the Department of Lands. The Board issued suggestions, questioned decisions and generally made themselves a nuisance to the venerable old warden. But JSH was never one to submit meekly to authority and, over the next 15 years, several battles and conflicts flared up.

Some of these disagreements arose because of the political differences between the Afrikaner-dominated Board and the stubborn old British warden.

Other disagreements were over principles of nature conservation, game management and the park's development.

JSH was of the firm opinion that the dilettante Board didn't know a damn thing about wildlife. He wanted to run things the way he had always run them, and resented input from the so-called scientists and committees that suggested otherwise. He also didn't want to over-civilise the park and resisted several development schemes. For example, he refused to replace the old coir sleeping mats with 'luxury' mattresses and refused to have electric lighting installed at Pretoriuskop in 1939.

Accordingly, power struggles were common and several attempts were made to replace JSH with a candidate who was more in keeping with the Nationalist sympathies of the Board. Of course, none of this behind the scenes intrigue was made public at the time. Yet, despite the mounting opposition of the Board, JSH hung in there and remained at his post until 1946.

At times, it seemed as if the old man simply refused to step down; clinging to power like an ageing dictator. Perhaps the role of warden had become part of his identity and he feared that without the Kruger Park, he would be nothing at all. Perhaps he didn't want to lose face with his young wife who adored the game reserve and probably enjoyed being the First Lady of the Kruger Park.

In any case, by 1939 JSH was over 70 and the Board made concrete recommendations that the warden be retired as soon as a suitable replacement was found. Fortunately for JSH, World War Two broke out shortly afterwards and he was given a stay of execution, as most of the potential candidates for the job were involved in the South African war effort. During the war, JSH fretted about the fate of Europe and vigilantly patrolled the park for any Germans who might have snuck in over the border from Mozambique.

When the war finally ended, in 1945, it was decided that JSH was simply too old to continue the good work. His memory was becoming unreliable and he was often bed-ridden by bouts of pneumonia and malaria. He was, after all, nearly 80.

And so, on the 30th of April 1946, Lieutenant-Colonel James Stevenson-Hamilton was officially retired from the Kruger Park with all the honours due to a great warrior for wildlife. Medals, accolades and honorariums poured in. JSH, however, felt as if he was being "pushed out" and wrote that he would have preferred to have "died in harness".

The weeks leading up to his retirement were tortuous for JSH. He spent many hours collecting his old notes and reports. He tidied up the desk he had inhabited for over 40 years. He wrote out detailed instructions for the new warden, to ensure that his Cinderella would be chaperoned in a suitable fashion. And he bade farewell to his faithful friend Harry Wolhuter, the only remaining ranger from the early days. Soon, Wolhuter would also retire. Indeed, the old guard was about to become extinct and it must have been a dreadful time for the doughty warden.

Leaving the KNP was so distressing to JSH, he requested that no party be held in his honour and asked that he be allowed to go quietly. When the fateful day finally arrived, JSH wrote in his journal, "Last day as warden. All intriguing and bad feeling lately. I had to make a speech of sorts but nearly wept."

After a heart-wrenching departure, JSH and Hilda bought a farm in White River, alongside Longmere Dam. They named their new home 'Gibraltar'. Money was tight but the couple had many friends in the area and the lifestyle was pleasant. JSH spent his time writing up his notes and playing with his children. He even became something of a celebrity and had to deal with many visitors, as well as written correspondence seeking his sage advice.

In his retirement, JSH was appointed to the National Parks Board but his membership was abruptly rescinded after only a year. He was also made *warden emeritus* of the Kruger National Park, but was frustrated that the position was only ceremonial. At least his replacement was considered suitable; a military man, Colonel JAB Sandenbergh, to whom JSH offered his rather begrudging mentorship.

Naturally, JSH kept up to speed with developments in the park and was dismayed to find that things were not going well. Sandenbergh was proving to be a bit of a disaster. There were also allegations of corruption and mismanagement in the Park, which were investigated by the Hoek Commission of 1952.

As a result of this commission, the Parks Board was overhauled and power was centralised in Pretoria, depriving the warden and rangers of much of their authority. Sandenbergh was replaced with Louis Steyn, an Afrikaner who had been first employed as a ranger back in 1929. Steyn would remain in the post for many years.

The Stevenson-Hamilton family visited Britain several times during these twilight years, and JSH reacquainted himself with the family estate of Fairholm in Scotland. Part of him wanted to return to his ancestral manor but, as usual, he could not make up his mind. Finally, in 1952, JSH finally decided that he was getting too old to travel and decided to remain in White River, close to his Cinderella.

The final years of his life were marked by a gentle decline. His health was failing and he was becoming frail. But he adored his son, Jamie, and his daughter Anne got married in 1954, which was cause for great celebration. Despite his infirmities, he kept up his regular journal entries and every morning he would walk outside and start up the generator. On the 2nd of October 1956, JSH turned 90.

He wrote in his journal: "Today I attained the unexpected age of 90 years. Two years older than my father when he died in 1926. So, I have beaten him, but

I don't expect to see another. In fact, for the past two months, I have been pretty ill, and on my back a lot, which I recognise as purely senile decay. My hearing is poor, my voice suffers from chronic laryngitis and I can barely hobble on two sticks and usually take Hilda's arm. In fact, I depend on her now for almost everything, and must give her a lot of trouble with my slow ways."

Two months later, on 10th December 1956, James Stevenson-Hamilton passed away. As he had predicted, the cause of death was 'nothing but old age'. It was a graceful end to a remarkable life. One can only be thankful that the Kruger Park had such a loyal and persistent champion.

Managing Kruger

The story I chose to tell in this book more-or-less ends with the departure of James Stevenson-Hamilton from his post as head warden of the Kruger National Park, in 1946. But that isn't to say the Kruger has spent the intervening 60-odd years resting on its laurels.

Since JSH's retirement, a ceaseless succession of wardens and rangers from all walks of life, each legendary in their own right, has stepped into the breach and contributed new chapters to the on-going saga of this captivating region. However, it is simply beyond my scope to offer an incremental breakdown of the Kruger's more recent history.

If you are interested, and I do hope you are, there is a wealth of material available, ranging from individual memoires to multi-volume histories by respected figures with whom I couldn't begin to compete. Comprehensive spotting guides and natural history books are also available covering the birds, game, plants, spoor and trees of the Lowveld.

So, rather than get in over my head, I offer instead this chapter featuring selected highlights of the park's development since the 1950s.

Rise of the Scientists

In the 1800s, game was seen as a commodity, to be exploited for commercial gain. In the early 1900s, attitudes became more romantic, thanks to the writings of various game rangers and naturalists (including JSH himself). The ideal of an untamed wilderness, left largely to its own devices, gained credence and the splendid isolation of the bush became an ideal to which some people aspired. This emotional response to nature grew stronger when the reserves were opened to tourism in the 1920s.

After the Sabi Game Reserve became the Kruger National Park in 1926, attitudes towards game conservation went through another metamorphosis. This time, it was the turn of enthusiastic amateurs on the National Parks Board who thought they could improve on nature, or at least give it a helping hand.

Their often ill-informed but well-intentioned ideas drove the warden crazy. These included: the introduction of alien animal species, such as the lechwe, springbok and blesbok, to make the wildlife more interesting; the importation of fruits and grasses from Kenya to bolster the park's food supply; and Gustav Preller's observation that the park didn't have enough birds. His solution: shoot all the jackals.

In the background of this struggle over the management of the KNP were the scientists, intent on studying the wildlife from an academic perspective. They wanted to know the habits of each species, how many there were, what they ate, how they lived. JSH, for his part, hated the scientists. He felt that they stripped the wilderness of its wonder. He also associated them with the veterinarians of old, who reviled the game reserve as a vector for livestock diseases.

After JSH retired in 1946, the scientists broke into the mainstream. Dr R Bigalke of the National Zoological Gardens in Pretoria was appointed to the board and he established a scientific division with a full-time zoologist. He also championed several other worthy programmes in the park: the removal of alien plant species, an ambitious education programme, the establishment of a scientific journal and a historical survey of the region.

Dozens of researchers thus invaded the wilderness every year, armed with clipboards and calculators. They darted animals, fitted radio collars, filmed from helicopters. Gradually, they decoded the manifold mysteries of the natural world, and delighted the world with their discoveries. By 1957, the Board's motto had become 'management by intervention'. By 1965, the University of Pretoria was offering a degree in wildlife management.

But, as the body of environmental knowledge grew, so did the researchers' boldness. Some began to think that they knew better than nature and developed methods which, they felt, would stimulate biodiversity. Over-populated species were culled, artificial watering holes were dug, and the park was divided into 400 blocks for rotational burning. Unfortunately, scientists don't always get it right first time and some of these interventions are now considered overly invasive.

The debate on the best way to handle conservation areas continues to this day. Should nature be left alone to establish its own balance, or should a threatened environment be actively managed to help it recover? The KNP has tried it both ways, and is now leaning towards a more organic approach that allows nature to take its course whenever possible.

This change of direction is quite recent and can be traced back to the transformation of the old National Parks Board into the more inclusive South African National Parks (SANParks) organisation, which followed SA's first democratic elections of 1994. After all, many members of the old Parks Board came from an agricultural background and wanted to run things the way they did on the farm. This involved active management of natural resources and suggestions to the contrary were usually ignored.

The new SANParks authorities, however, have a broader background and have sought input from various stakeholders. This has resulted in more holistic conservation strategies. Incidentally, the concept of 'holism' was first coined by that old fan of conservation, Jan Smuts, back in 1926 when he published a book called 'Holism and Evolution'. According to Smuts, the concept can be defined as "The tendency in nature to form wholes that are greater than the sum of the parts through creative evolution."

As such, the park is now divided into a number of usage zones, each with its own policies and restrictions. These range from well-developed tourist nodes to pristine 'wilderness' areas where visitors are not allowed.

The old controlled-burning policy has been replaced with a less intrusive mosaic or patch burning technique. Culling has largely been curtailed. Even the extensive network of windmills is being revised, and several superfluous watering holes are being decommissioned.

Furthermore, the KNP currently has over 150 active research projects involving scientists from all over the world. Everything from the biggest mammals to the smallest insects is studied, and a huge amount of invaluable information has been gathered within the great expanse of Kruger.

There are also several 'exclosures' located around the park. These are long running experiments that are designed to investigate things like climate, rainfall and vegetation. You can see one of these exclosures on the S10, near Pretoriuskop.

The 'Water for Game' Campaign

One of the first attempts to manage the natural environment of the KNP was instituted in the early 1930s. The problem was that, at the end of the dry season, the park was virtually without water. The few remaining pools therefore attracted a huge amount of game, which resulted in the destruction of all the grass and trees in the vicinity. To remedy this, Stevenson-Hamilton wanted to sink boreholes in the arid stretches of the park, which would encourage game to spread out and graze more evenly.

In 1933, JSH chatted with a regular visitor, Mr. Jearey, about the issue. Jearey offered to start a fundraising campaign where members of the public could contribute to the construction of dams and boreholes in the KNP. The first appeal went out in The Star newspaper in Johannesburg and the response was enthusiastic.

Within a few months, thousands of pounds had been raised and around 14 successful boreholes were sunk at various points in the park. The fundraising campaign continued for many years, operating under the inspirational banner, 'Water for Game'.

Subsequently, hundreds of windmills, reservoirs, drinking troughs and dams were built. Many of these were named after particularly generous benefactors, and several watering holes still have small plaques on the roadside which identify the relevant contributors. Today, however, some of the reservoirs are getting decommissioned because they are considered overly invasive.

Fencing the Reserve

The next big management challenge was to throw a fence around the entire game reserve. This needed to be done for two reasons: to keep the game in and to keep the humans out. But it was an enormous task, and one which would require a great deal of money. So, it remained a nice-to-have for many years.

In 1958, however, there was a severe outbreak of foot-and-mouth disease in the park. The state veterinary department was alarmed and wanted to erect a fence along the park's borders to prevent the infected wildlife from transferring the disease to domestic animals on nearby farms. The government duly issued a substantial grant for the construction of the 720km fence, which was completed in 1961.

At first, the game resisted the man-made barrier as it cut them off from their traditional seasonal migrations, which ran from east to west rather than north to south. After a number of years, however, the adaptable animals learnt that some things can't be overcome and changed their browsing patterns.

At this time, most of the rest camps were still largely unfenced, apart from basic screens and thorn barricades. This must have made things quite exciting for the visitors who had to keep an eye out for hungry carnivores. In 1966, however, a couple of tourists were badly bitten by hyenas and animal-proof fences were quickly erected around all the rest camps.

The Culling of the Elephants

Now here's a hot-button issue... The KNP has a problem with elephants. There are simply too many of them. They are destructive eaters and impact heavily on the environment. If something is not done, say SANParks, the Kruger's biodiversity will be threatened.

Thing is, everybody loves the elephants. They are one of the park's biggest drawcards and no-one wants to be part of a bloody culling campaign. After all, these are majestic and intelligent beasts. If you shoot them, do they not bleed?

However, the current elephant population of the KNP is 13 000 strong and growing. So, what's to be done?

This isn't a new issue. Research done in the late 1960s suggested that the ideal elephant density is 1 pachyderm per 1 square mile. This equation puts the optimum Kruger population at 7000. A culling campaign started in 1967 and continued until 1995. During this time 14 500 elephants were killed and 2500 elephants were relocated.

In 1996, a moratorium on elephant culling was declared and SANParks initiated a series of workshops to try and find an equitable solution to the emotional elephantine issue. This was followed by the 'Great Elephant Indaba' in

2004. After much argument, it was agreed that the elephant population had to be managed to avoid the destruction of the park. Now the question is, how?

Contraception is one alternative. But darts are expensive and the KNP is too large to make this practical. Relocation is another possibility, but elephants tend to migrate back to their old stomping grounds. It is also expensive and most reserves in Southern Africa are already fully stocked. Several Transfrontier mega-parks are being established, which should be able to hold greater numbers of elephant, but these might only come on-line in several years. SANParks, for its part, maintains that elephant culling is the only viable solution and is ready to take action.

And still the debate rages on. Some opponents of culling have questioned the validity of the old '7000 elephants' target. Others accuse SANParks of pushing the culling option because they profit from the sale of elephant hides and ivory. 'Mega-Park' proponents have urged the authorities to wait and see if the elephants spread naturally into the newly established Limpopo National Park in Mozambique. Then there are those who say that a natural elephant die-off occurs every couple of hundred years and any attempt to mess with one species will only cause imbalances in other parts of the ecosystem.

Amid all this talk, there is a sense that SANParks is running out both of patience and options. Several pro-culling advocates have even started sniping at international conservation organisations, the most vociferous opponents of culling. They say that the well-meaning foreigners have an overly sentimental reaction to the issue and no real understanding of the situation on the ground.

The great elephant debate remains unresolved for the moment, and it is not for me to suggest an outcome. SANParks is still circling around the moratorium, looking for a way to lift the ban without causing too much bad feeling. Their opponents are monitoring the situation intensely. It's a potentially explosive situation – especially during times of drought (the recent drought of 2016 has already resulted in the limited culling of hippo and, potentially, buffalo).

Whatever the outcome, to cull or not to cull remains a compelling question; one which does not have a simple answer.

The Magnificent Seven

Elephants are wonderful creatures with wise eyes and rumpled skin, which always reminds me of my father's face. But it's the tusks that count and, in 1980, chief warden Dr. Uwe 'Tol' Pienaar identified the 'Magnificent Seven' – a septet of elephant bulls with mighty tusks weighing more than 50kg each.

Thanks to some adroit publicity, the public responded enthusiastically and Pienaar (later Chief Director of SANParks) decided that, upon their death, each big tusker would be preserved in the Elephant Hall at Letaba rest camp. And so, today, you can still marvel at the skulls and tusks of Dzombo, Kambaku, Mafunyane, Ndlulamithi, Shawu and Shingwedzi (only João – the biggest of them all – is missing because he broke off his tusks in a fight and the remains were never found).

Eager to keep the legend going, the KNP has recently launched the Emerging Tuskers Project 'to identify all of the Park's large tuskers and clearly define their home ranges'. Visitors are all encouraged to participate by sending in photos of elephants with impressive tusks, with dates and location information.

The Rise of Poaching

By far the most tragic issue facing the Kruger (and many other conservation areas across Africa) is the dramatic increase in rhino poaching over the last few years. The main reason for this slaughter is mind-blowingly idiotic – men in the Far East can't seem to get it up without some ground-up rhino horn in their food! This benighted traditional remedy combined with a rising wave of prosperity sweeping across the region has pushed the demand for rhino horn through the roof.

Already, the Western Black Rhino was declared extinct by the International Union for Conservation of Nature (IUCN) in 2011. And the other 5 remaining rhino species are all listed in the IUCN Red List of threatened species.

In South Africa alone, the number of rhinos killed for their horns has skyrocketed to the point that, unless the trend is reversed, rhino deaths will outstrip births within the next couple of years. This is a huge issue because South Africa is home to over 80% of Africa's rhinos and 73% of the world's wild rhino population.

And the numbers certainly are alarming. After years of stable poaching rates ranging between 10 and 25 a year, things started deteriorating around 2008, when 83 rhinos were murdered. The following year, the number rose to 122 before leaping to 333 in 2010. And graph keeps rising: 448 in 2011, 668 in 2012, 1004 in 2013, 1215 in 2014 and about the same in 2015 and 2016.

Unsurprisingly, it's an issue that has provoked a passionate reaction in the general public who have rallied around their precious rhinos with increasing fervour. But it is a scourge that is proving hard to stop. With rising prices and a growing demand for the product, several international syndicates have established sophisticated poaching networks complete with helicopters, tranquiliser guns and smuggling routes.

To counter the poachers (many of whom are impoverished locals being exploited by their wealthy overlords), a number of anti-poaching initiatives have been launched. A variety of rhino conservation organisations have been established. Large donations have poured in from all over the world. Patrols in reserves have been stepped up. Arrests have been made (including several prominent vets and rangers). Anti-poaching legislation has been improved, with more severe penalties. And educational commercials starring Asian celebrities aimed at reducing the demand in Asia have been launched. But not even Jackie Chan can get the situation under control.

Other increasingly desperate remedies to the problem are being floated every day: poisoning rhino horns, injecting horns with dye, cutting off horns as a preventative measure, and legalising the trade in horn have all been discussed, but the daily press is still filled with terrible photos of butchered rhinos and the massacre continues unabated.

On a more positive note, in January 2017, SANParks launched their innovative 'Meerkat' wide-range surveillance units. Developed by SA's Council for Scientific and Industrial Research (CSIR) and supported by the Peace Parks Foundation with contributions from UK lottery funds, Meerkat uses radar to detect and map suspicious movements in the reserve. This compact system can fold up and fit in the back of a truck, with only a small team required for operations. Equally effective during the day and at night, the first Meerkat unit managed to stop five out of nine detected poaching incidents over the course of two weeks. Following this successful pilot project, it is hoped that an additional three or four units will be able to cover the entire park and finally bring the poachers to heel.

In any case, one can only hope that the cumulative effects of the anti-poaching lobby will eventually begin to take hold and the number of dead rhinos will start to fall. Until then, we can only contribute to the fight in any way we can...

Re-introduction of Species

When the KNP was originally proclaimed, several native species were on the verge of local extinction. Over the course of the next 50 years, some of these populations did indeed die out, either as a result of disease or because the breeding population was unsustainably small.

One of the first species to be re-introduced to the park was the Black (or Square-lipped) Rhino. This elusive and solitary animal became extinct in the Lowveld in the 1890s and, in 1961, several specimens were translocated from the Umfolozi reserve in Natal. A number of oribi were also moved from the Badplaas area to an enclosure at Pretoriuskop, with limited success.

In 1963, 14 white rhino were brought into the park, the first to live in the area since the 1930s. Four red duiker were also released into the thick bush around Pretoriuskop. Numerous other species have been periodically brought into the park, or relocated to different districts of the park, to bolster sagging populations.

In exchange, the KNP has been a generous supplier of game to zoos and game parks, both in South Africa and around the world. Zebra, hippo, elephant, white rhino and wildebeest are among the most common exports.

In addition to direct animal sales, regular wildlife auctions take place around the country. These are big business and generate crucial conservation revenue. Disease-free buffalo are particularly valuable and can fetch millions of rand each (the record price is R168 million for a single bull, paid by a consortium of investors in 2016). The members of the Big Five are also highly prized, as there is stiff competition between the various game reserves for the best specimens.

Surprisingly, the KNP also contains an animal abattoir. This unpleasant facility is actually located on the outskirts of Skukuza rest camp, but its activities are shrouded by an air of secrecy. In years past, when culling was more widespread, the abattoir was kept very busy processing the hides, tusks and meat from animals that were killed in the line of duty. Zebra, elephant, buffalo, wildebeest, impala and hippo all went on the chopping block at one time or another, and their by-products found their way into curio shops and dog food tins across the country.

In a way, perhaps, we have come full circle and returned to an idiom where wildlife is a commodity. But at least this time the animals are being accorded their proper value while still alive.

Managing the Tourists

In addition to conservation management, the KNP authorities also have a lot of human management to worry about. Roads, rest camps, electricity, sewerage and water supplies have to be maintained, and well over a million visitors must be fed and housed every year. The KNP is also the single largest employer in the area, with a staff of thousands.

All in all, it's a mammoth enterprise, especially when you consider that the KNP covers a vast expanse of wilderness, with few links to the outside world. I spoke to one Kruger-ite about the complexity of running such an enormous reserve. Her reply was, "It's even worse than that... OK. The KNP is the size of a small country. Now, imagine if every single person in that country had to be fed by the same company. And all the accommodation had to be organised by that same company too. It's huge."

To help them cope, SANParks has outsourced several aspects of the park's tourism activities. Shops are stocked by an external supplier and the restaurants are run on a concession basis. At one time, the rest camps were also outsourced, but SANParks has resumed control of this lucrative part of the business.

When you take into account all the challenges, you've got to admit that they do a helluva job. The park generally runs smoothly and its visitors want for nothing. All right, the catering is a bit unpredictable (especially when restaurant franchisees go rogue) and some of the rondawels are in need of an upgrade. But this is all part of the wilderness experience. I mean, who wants to see a Sheraton on the Shingwedzi?

Speaking of which, the debate about whether to allow the development of a large, full-service hotel within the boundaries of the park has been raging for decades. Recently, however, SANParks announced that following an extensive environmental impact assessment, the construction of a 240-bed hotel has been approved. The proposed Radisson Blu Safari Resort will be located on the periphery of the park, close to Malelane Gate.

Despite the howls of outrage from Kruger purists, the public has been assured that the new facility will not be a high-rise monstrosity but will blend into the environment and complement its surroundings, in line with existing SANParks guidelines. It will also offer an alternative to the self-catering accommodation currently available (apart from the super-expensive concession lodges that only rich foreigners can afford).

Furthermore, the new hotel will allow 24-hour access, so guests can arrive at any time (night driving within the park is forbidden unless you're on an official game drive). It will also offer all the resort-style services that appeal to both the international and emerging tourism markets. Time will tell if this new endeavour is successful...

Land Affairs

When the Sabi Reserve was proclaimed at the turn of the twentieth century, it was decided that the protected area should be cleared of all permanent human habitation. This meant that the several thousand African villagers living within the confines of the new reserve had to be relocated.

Never one to shirk from his responsibilities, James Stevenson-Hamilton swiftly arranged for the removal of "black squatters... settling them closer to their traditional tribal chiefs in adjacent areas". This prompted the natives to nickname the park warden 'Skukuza', derived from the Zulu 'sikhukhuza' – he who sweeps or scrapes clean. By 1905, however, this policy was reversed and around 3000 native inhabitants were allowed to stay in the reserve, as long as they obeyed the anti-hunting regulations.

The reasons for this about-face were not philanthropic. Rather, the Africans were now considered 'tenants' on Crown Land and, as such, they were liable for an annual rent that had to be paid to the white government. This fee could be paid either in cash or labour, and the 'squatters' became quite a valuable resource that could be exploited.

This meant that the warden and rangers were now responsible for the management and control of the black 'tenants' who lived in the reserve. To streamline administration, the warden was named the Native Commissioner for the entire area.

In addition to collecting taxes and/or labour commitments, the commissioner also had to handle native 'insubordination'. Any breaches of the law were dealt with decisively, with the most common being poaching and trespassing.

As a result, many Africans began to resent the new game reserve. To them, it was a place of exclusion; an unfair land grab that robbed them of their traditional homesteads and livelihoods. This attitude persisted for much of the 20th century and most of the country's national parks were shunned by the black populace as being a white man's playground.

This lingering resentment was entrenched in the 1950s when the remaining black population of the KNP was finally moved out for good. This time, however, the relocations were about more than conservation or financial considerations. Racial segregation had become the bedrock of South African society, and politics dictated that each racial group should be allowed to 'develop separately' in their own areas.

The first of these forced removals took place in 1956, when the KNP and Department of Bantu Affairs effected a land swap of 1000 morgen in the Numbi Gate area. The Africans were then re-settled in their new 'location' and the animals were chased over into the KNP. In the same year, some members of the

Makuleke community were also removed from their lands in the Pafuri district. Additional land (and people) exchanges were made in 1957, 1960 and 1969. Tellingly, the first boundary fences in the park were erected at these times, to prevent the relocated people from moving back into the reserve.

Today, SANParks is trying to reverse the low opinion that many black people have towards the national parks. Efforts are being made to bring more black visitors into the game reserves, and the indigenous people of the country are being encouraged to consider conservation areas as a source of national pride.

It is a slow process, but the tide is definitely turning. One park in particular, Mapungubwe, is proving to be very popular with black tourists and SANParks is trying to extend this model to their other reserves. However, turning our national parks into a more inclusive place may not be a simple matter of ideology.

Firstly, Mapungubwe is unusual. It contains the physical remains of a mighty African civilisation that resonates with the concept of an African Renaissance. As such, it is a source of pride for many African people who endured decades of denigration at the hands of colonial and apartheid historians. Secondly, tourism is not yet a well-developed activity within a black society that is still characterised by financial hardship.

Furthermore, statistics show that when black people do travel, it is usually to attend a funeral, a wedding or to visit relatives. Additionally, those middle-class black people who are wealthy enough to travel for leisure generally do not want to visit a game reserve. As more than one person has informally told me, many black tourists do not consider the wilderness to be an aspirational destination They would rather check into a comfortable hotel and indulge in some western-style luxury.

It should therefore be remembered that the ideal of an untouched natural environment, devoid of the trappings of civilisation, is not a concept shared by all cultures. For many people, the relatively basic conditions of a game reserve reminds them of a former life, when they were forced to live in rural areas without any infrastructure. As several black comedians have stated, candlelit dinners may be romantic to white people but to black people, it just reminds them of being poor.

Nevertheless, recent figures show that the percentage of black South Africans visiting national parks has increased to around 10% from an estimated 4% in 2003. Mapungubwe, Golden Gate and the Kruger National Park are the most popular destinations for this demographic. FYI, out of the total number of annual visitors to SANParks' reserves (nearly 6 million for the year ending February 2016) roughly 73.5% are South African, 1.5% are from SADC (Southern African Development Community) countries, and 25% are international tourists.

Community Spirit

SANParks is working hard to include black communities in their national parks. This is being done through marketing initiatives which encourage black visitors, educational campaigns that stimulate an awareness of conservation in children, and through programmes which seek to extend the financial benefits of the parks to the surrounding communities.

These community-involvement activities are getting a lot of attention from SANParks. Their aim is to bring the local people into the parks system by offering them direct benefits, such as employment, and indirect benefits gained by the financial spill-over from tourists visiting the KNP. They are also facilitating park visits for neighbouring communities who have never experienced the reserve for themselves. This good work is being done under the auspices of the People and Conservation Division of SANParks.

The long-term goal is to "build constituencies amongst people in support of the conservation of natural and cultural heritage efforts through: strengthening relationships with neighbouring park communities, cultural resource management and indigenous knowledge, environmental education, awareness and interpretation, social science research and youth outreach."

The old 'top-down' management model is also being supplanted by park forums, where various stakeholders in the wider community can get involved in the decision-making process. SANParks is also getting involved in developmental activities, such as craft workshops and training, and is helping nearby communities build and sustain much-needed infrastructure.

Balule Rest Camp

Obviously, in the old days, people of colour were not encouraged to visit the KNP. This might have resulted in immoral mingling of the races and the subsequent downfall of society. After all, one of the ostensible purposes of the game reserve was to protect the game from the depredations of the native populations – it wouldn't do to invite them back in!

And this didn't just apply to the blacks. In 1932, more than a decade before the National Party came to power, Gustav Preller complained that Indians were staying in the same rest camps as the white people. JSH countered the complaint with the cheeky defence that he thought they were Portuguese. Later, a Japanese ambassador visited the park and JSH grumbled in his journal: "Pray God these fatheads do not treat him as 'Asiatic'."

In order to keep things nice and separate, the first (and only) non-white rest camp was opened in 1932, at the suggestion of then-Minister of Lands and future prime minister, JG Strijdom. It was located on the south bank of the Olifants

River, after which it was named. But then, in 1961, the 'Olifants' name was given to the newly renovated whites-only camp on the other side of the river and the black camp changed its name to 'Balule', a contraction of the XiTsonga name for the Olifants River.

At Balule, a pontoon across the Olifants River was constructed. This floating platform carried vehicles across the wide watercourse from 1929 to 1937, when a permanent causeway was built a short distance upstream. A memorial plaque has been erected on the site, and it is one of the few historical markers that pays tribute to Deneys Reitz, an early supporter of the national park movement.

Although it may seem out of character for the apartheid regime to allow the existence of a camp for the darker races, it was hardly a place that encouraged visitors. Located in a remote part of the park, far from the nearest entrance gate, Balule was a pretty rudimentary affair. There was no shop, fuel or reception office. Accommodation consisted of a couple of basic rondawels and a handful of campsites. Electricity was never installed.

The token camp was also very small, only a few hundred metres from side to side, and was roughly fenced with thin wire. All in all, Balule was not an inviting place and was described as 'austere', even in the 1980s.

Surprisingly, Balule is now one of the most popular camps in the KNP, for people in the know. It's booked out months in advance and aficionados claim that it is the most peaceful and least intrusive rest camp in the entire park. There is still no electricity, nor is there a reception office, swimming pool, or restaurant. This lack of modern accoutrements allows the small camp to blend into the bushveld, integrating with the landscape in a way that the larger camps simply cannot do. It is a favourite haunt for happy campers and caravanners who pitch tents along the perimeter fence and gaze out happily into the bush, over a steaming mug of coffee.

Youth Development

One of the most exciting initiatives currently being developed by the KNP is *Taking Kruger to Kasie* (a slang term for a black township, taken from the Afrikaans word for 'location'). It's a great project that seeks to spread the message of conservation and environmental education to the communities living along the boundaries of the KNP.

Several busses have been donated, with the help of Shell SA and the Honorary Rangers, and kitted out with TV screens and multimedia equipment. These will assist the KNP's People and Conservation Department in its vital task of 'taking the park to the people'. The busses also transport school and community groups into the KNP so that the people can experience the park for themselves. This is all very much in line with SANParks mandate to make the park more accessible.

I would suggest that there is great potential for *Kruger to Kasie* to work the other way round too. Imagine if visitors to the KNP could take a guided tour through the bustling African communities adjacent to the park. This 'cultural exchange' will not only complement the visitors' wildlife experience, but will provide the neighbouring communities with a welcome source of income.

Kruger to Kasie is also part of a wider youth education programme that includes Kids in Parks, the Kudu Green School initiative and the Imbewu Youth Project.

The Makuleke Land Claim

As is often the case, the park authorities had to break a number of eggs to make the KNP omelette. This included the forced removal of many African communities that originally lived inside the park's borders. It is therefore no surprise that, under the new democratic dispensation, several of these displaced communities have lodged land claims against the KNP.

The consequences of these land claims could be catastrophic for the KNP. If successful, large chunks of land may have to be deproclaimed and handed back to the tribal authorities. The park would shrink, human development would encroach, and the sustainability of the eco-system would be threatened. It's a thorny problem – what do we do when something good has been created from something bad? How do we redress the wrongs without undoing the rights?

Fortunately, SANParks is actively participating in these negotiations and working to find mutually acceptable solutions for all the stakeholders. And it seems to be working. One claim has already been successfully settled, and it is being used as a blueprint for the others. To find out more, we must travel to the far north of the park to meet the Makuleke people.

The Makuleke are a Tsonga-Shangaan tribe who moved into the Pafuri region sometime during the 18th century. Their lands were located between the Luvuvhu and Limpopo Rivers, on the border between South Africa, Zimbabwe and Mozambique. Part of their domain included the lawless piece of land known as Crooks' Corner, and they were once active in the region's ivory trade.

In 1903, the land between the Letaba and Limpopo rivers was incorporated into the Shingwedzi game reserve. Overnight, the Makuleke had become 'tenant farmers'. As the population grew, however, it was decided to remove the Makuleke. The chief, Mhinga, refused to budge so the authorities decided to move the border of the reserve south to the Luvuvhu River, thus cutting the problematic villagers out of the protected area.

At this time, the borders of the reserve were not fenced and the vast Shingwedzi region did not have enough rangers and native 'police boys' to patrol effectively. So, the Makuleke soon began moving back and forth across the

Luvuvhu; causing the authorities a great deal of concern. In the 1930s, it was decided that the Makuleke had to go and a piece of KNP land to the south was earmarked for resettlement.

The community put up a spirited defence, and they found support from an unlikely source - the Department of Bantu Affairs. This was because the Department was constantly pushing for land on which they could establish native settlements and they resented all the good ground being taken up by the 'worthless' game reserve.

The Parks Board was determined, however, and they approached the Transvaal government for help. The provincial authorities obliged by declaring a new 'Pafuri Game Reserve', which surrounded (but did not include) the Makuleke land. Still, Bantu Affairs refused to authorise the relocation of the tribe. The Makuleke were literally caught in the middle and the stalemate lasted for years.

It was an impossible situation and deeply unfair to the Makuleke. Even one of the Parks Board secretaries pointed out, "It is obvious that Pafuri is better agriculturally than the dry piece of grazing land we offer in exchange... Frankly, I foresee in this gain of today, if we acquire the Pafuri, the future germ of destruction of the whole park."

Throughout the 1940s and 50s, the Makuleke lived in limbo. They were not allowed to keep cattle, goats or sheep; only donkeys were permitted. This was because domestic herds could bring anthrax and foot & mouth disease into the park. It was also a useful way to ensure that the Makuleke could not hunt game for the pot and claim it was beef. As a result, the Makuleke ate little meat and had to buy most of their supplies from a small store run by John Fernandez.

By the 1960s, everyone wanted the Makuleke to go, but they refused to budge. Finally, in 1969, the old chief died and the government moved in. According to Lambson Makuleke, "They came at gun point and they gave people matches to burn their own houses." Altogether, about 300 Makuleke living in ten villages were relocated to Ntlhaveni, to the south-west of Punda Maria gate. The Pafuri game reserve was then incorporated in the greater KNP. Ntlaveni later became part of the abortive 'homeland' of Gazankulu.

After the first democratic elections in 1994, the new government announced that any communities that had been forcibly moved from their traditional lands under apartheid could register a land claim. The Makuleke decided to do just that and lodged their claim in 1995.

At first the National Parks Board was resistant. As Lambson Makuleke says "It was still the board of yesterday. They objected to the claim and their attitude was very negative. It was one of the first and they didn't believe that we would achieve with our endeavours." Then, the old Parks Board was transformed into a new organisation, SANParks, and attitudes began to change.

Once their claim had been declared legitimate, the Makuleke community held a number of discussions to decide what to do with the land. The elders of the village still had strong emotional ties to the Pafuri and wanted to return. The younger people, however, had grown up in Ntlhaveni and didn't want to move back into the remote wilds.

Lambson Makuleke, an active participant in the process, describes it like this: "The whole community made a decision after several meetings of discussing the issue. We looked at the advantages and disadvantages, and at the end of the day, the whole community bought into the idea that we need to retain the status quo [of Pafuri] as a bio-diversity area or conservation area."

With the decision taken, SANParks entered into negotiations with the Makuleke to iron out the details. A Conservation Management Plan was drawn up and a joint-management board was established. The Makuleke community officially reclaimed their land in 1998. This strip of pristine bush between the Luvuvhu and Limpopo rivers is now known as the Makuleke Concession Park.

Technically, the land is owned by the Makuleke and managed in partnership with SANParks, as a contractual park. The Makuleke also have the sole right to operate hotels, lodges and game drives within their territory, and they have granted several concessions to tourism companies.

The money made from the concessions is paid over to a Communal Property Association, a registered legal entity, and the funds are then allocated by a committee to the three Makuleke villages around Ntlhaveni. New schools, improved electricity supplies and other developmental projects have already been started, and most members of the community seem pretty satisfied with the way things are going. There are also around 100 Makuleke being directly employed by the concessionaires and this contributes more money to the community.

Thankfully, the Makuleke decision makers have no intentions of over-developing their little piece of heaven. Only two luxury lodges, Pafuri Camp (formerly run by Wilderness Safaris, now run by ReturnAfrica) and The Outpost, have been established (with a total of 116 beds), and an upmarket eco-training camp operates in the concession area. ReturnAfrica also runs walking trails and the upmarket Baobab Hill Bush House in the Pafuri. The idea is to generate income from a small number of visitors who pay quite a bit for their accommodation, as opposed to creating a mass tourist product that would require lots of guests to make the same money.

Unfortunately, this means that an overnight stay in the Makuleke Concession Park is probably out of reach for most local visitors. Furthermore, KNP vehicles are not allowed to traverse the concession area, so game drives are only available to guests of the concession lodges. But don't despair. The tar road from Punda

Maria to Pafuri Gate is open to everyone, so you can still sample this remarkable landscape for yourself.

I asked Lambson if many Makuleke had visited their park. He replied, "lots". I then asked if they got a discount on overnight accommodation. He replied, "They don't stay here because this is a business. It is up to us to practise good governance."

And what about the future? Lambson replied, "I think that the process is under way and it's operating well. And we are growing. This is the heart of the new Great Limpopo Transfrontier Conservation Area, and we are waiting for the bridge to Gonarezhou [an adjacent reserve across the border in Zimbabwe]. We haven't yet achieved what we want. I think that will take another [few] years. But we are optimistic. Of course, the past was painful and it was a challenge to get where we are today. But now it's becoming a blessing in disguise."

Crossing Borders

Although the Kruger Park is famously the same size as Israel or Wales, it is still not big enough. More specifically, it is the wrong shape.

Before the invasion of modern civilisation, the game in the Lowveld migrated with the seasons, from the coastal plains in the east to the mountain foothills in the west. The KNP, however, runs from north to south and its width is quite narrow (averaging only 50km). As a consequence, the plants are overgrazed, species are over-populated and water is often in short supply.

The reason for this misalignment is that the orientation of the KNP corresponds to the old tsetse fly belt, which made the area unsuitable for domestic animals and human habitation. In fact, it was the threat of *nagana* (the tsetse-borne disease) that made the proclamation of the game reserve viable in the first place.

So, to fully restore the eco-system of the Lowveld, the KNP must expand laterally to give the animals freedom to re-establish their old migration routes. Happily, there are big plans to extend the reserve in the north, east, and west, and Kruger has already been united with the Limpopo National Park in Mozambique as part of a bigger Transfrontier Conservation Area.

Altogether, it is hoped to grow the size of the greater KNP protected area from around 2 million hectares to over 10 million! This will make it one of the largest unbroken conservation areas on the planet, and a site truly worthy of UNESCO (United Nations Educational, Scientific and Cultural Organisation) World Heritage status.

Eileen Orpen

One of the first extensions to the KNP was the result of a generous donation from a stern-eyed, old battle-axe named Eileen Orpen. She was part of the wealthy Barry family, a trading dynasty based in Swellendam. Together with her husband, James Havelock Orpen, Eileen became one of the KNP's most devoted benefactors.

The Orpens had a long history in the conservation movement of South Africa. James was involved with the construction of the Armstrong fence around the Addo Elephant Park and the establishment of the Mountain Zebra National Park. He also surveyed the western boundary of the Kruger Park, planned the Shingwedzi rest camp, and laid out the roads in the Pretoriuskop region, all without recompense. He was a member of the National Parks Board for 14 years, starting in 1939.

Eager to help, Eileen started buying up private farms that adjoined the KNP to ensure that no hunting took place on the reserve's boundary. Between 1935 and 1944, she purchased a total of seven properties, comprising 24 529 hectares. She then donated all the land to the Kruger Park. She also sponsored the construction of four rest camps, built the Orpen dam, and donated several windmills as part of the Water for Wildlife campaign. Orpen Gate is named in her honour.

James Orpen died only 4 days after his wife, on the 28th of May 1954. Several information boards with photographs of the Orpens can be found in the Rabelais Hut Museum, close to Orpen Gate.

Sabi Sands

The Sabi Sands Reserve is located in the south-west of the KNP, close to Skukuza. This 65 000ha piece of land, bordered by the Sabie and Sand rivers, was once part of the old Sabi Reserve but it was excised in 1926 and handed over to private landowners in exchange for their former properties inside the new national park.

Nineteen farms in the Sabi Sands area were subsequently surveyed and given incongruous European names, such as Toulon, Exeter and Eyrefield. Most of the new farm owners set up cattle ranching and hunting operation, but there were some exceptions. Two nature enthusiasts, Charles Varty and Frank Unger bought one of the farms, Sparta, and built a camp on the river banks. Then, there was a wealthy sugar baron named William Campbell who bought MalaMala ('sable' in XiTsonga) and built a private hunting lodge on the property.

Whatever their original plans, the beauty of the Lowveld soon won over the new residents, and in 1934, fourteen landowners met at MalaMala and decided to form the Sabi Sand Game Reserve. They appointed a ranger and committed themselves to preserving the balance of nature on their land. The reserve flourished and slowly opened itself up to visitors. MalaMala took its first guests in 1962 (and was bought two years later by the Rattray family, who run it to this day). Londolozi (run by the famous Varty's) opened in 1965, as did Sabi Sabi. Other luxurious lodges followed suit and, today, the Sabi Sand reserve is filled with some of the plushest bushveld retreats in South Africa.

At first, there were no fences between Sabi Sand and the KNP. In 1961, however, the threat of foot and mouth disease prompted the erection of a fence between the two reserves. Another fence was also built along the western border of Sabi Sand to prevent game moving into the native settlements, and vice versa. This greatly disrupted the normal east-west migration of the animals. After lengthy discussions, the internal fence between Sabi Sand and the KNP came down in 1993.

Manyeleti

North of Sabi Sands is the 23 000ha Manyeleti game reserve. This was originally the home of the Mnisi people, who were displaced when the land was divided up into 5 farms and sold off to white investors. In the 1960s, these farms were purchased by the Department of Bantu Affairs and turned into a game reserve for non-white nature lovers. It was named Manyeleti, meaning 'place of the stars' in XiTsonga.

After 1994, the Mnisi people initiated a successful land claim and won back rightful ownership of their ancestral land. Three exclusive concession lodges have now been established, offering guests a peaceful and luxurious stay. There is no fence between Manyeleti and the KNP, and the reserve is managed in collaboration with SANParks.

The Associated Private Nature Reserves

West of Manyeleti is a cluster of several large game reserves, including Klaserie, Umbabat, Balule, Thornybush, Kapama and Timbavati (home of the famous white lions). Originally consisting of dozens of privately owned farms (which were swapped out for farms located inside the KNP's boundaries in the 1920s), the entire area has now been incorporated into the Associated Private Nature Reserves (APNR), a non-profit organisation that co-ordinates conservation efforts between the various land-owners.

Altogether, the APNR covers 180 000ha of land. There are no longer any internal fences and the entire boundary with the KNP is open. There are more than a dozen lodges in the area and several private camps, such as Ingwelala where lucky people can purchase a private rondawel in the bush. However, there is no direct road access from the APNR into the greater Kruger Park and traversing rights on each individual farm must be respected.

Kruger to Canyons

One of the most exciting developments on the western boundary of the KNP is the Kruger to Canyons Biosphere Reserve, launched in 2001. This is a community-based initiative that seeks to create a large conservation area that will eventually link the Kruger Park with the Eastern Transvaal Drakensberg escarpment in a 'unique constellation of public, provincial, private reserves and natural resource areas'. The biosphere would also include the breathtaking Blyde River Canyon – said to be the third largest in the world.

It is an ambitious project. Over 1.5 million people live within the proposed biosphere, and the land belongs to dozens of different management authorities.

Land usage currently includes agriculture, forestry, mining, rural developments, urban developments, tourism and conservation. Out of a total of 2.5 million hectares, 1.4 million is already dedicated to long-term conservation (900 000ha of formally protected areas and 400 000ha of privately owned conservation land).

Whatever challenges may lie ahead, the organisers are committed to their vision and are focussed on engaging with the local communities and international organisations to realise their goals. Through a combination of audacious vision and responsible tourism, they hope to create an enormous biosphere reserve that embraces a truly remarkable bio-diversity. The potential is mouth-watering.

Transfrontier Conservation Areas

Animals have no respect for politics. They refuse to carry passports and simply cannot understand the invisible network of borders that dissect the land into nominal sovereign states. Instead, they prefer to move about as they please, following natural migration routes that were established many millennia before modern man stuck his oar in.

Conservationists have often noted this fact and it has been a long-standing goal of game preservation to transcend petty political boundaries. Now, this dream is coming true. Thanks in part to the revitalising effect of the tourism dollar on local economies, governments are getting together to declare large Transfrontier Conservation Areas (TFCAs) that extend, unbroken and unfenced, over several different countries.

These worthy endeavours are being driven by the Peace Parks Foundation, a non-profit organisation established in 1997. The three founding members of Peace Parks are the dearly beloved Nelson Mandela, the late tobacco baron Anton Rupert and the regal Prince Bernhard of the Netherlands, all of whom carry considerable cache. With that kind of backing, funds have been secured from several prominent institutions and Peace Parks has already made a real difference to the conservation landscape of southern Africa.

Their activities are numerous: funding research programmes, supporting educational initiatives, building facilities, spearheading fundraising campaigns and generally promoting a holistic approach to conservation practises and management. But their main aim is to help establish Transfrontier Conservation Areas (TFCAs) that vault over the old colonial borders of Africa.

The SADC Protocol on Wildlife Conservation and Law Enforcement of 1999 defines a TFCA as "the area or component of a large ecological region that straddles the boundaries of two or more countries, encompassing one or more protected areas as well as multiple resource use areas".

All in all, 18 potential TFCAs have been identified and, after years of painstaking negotiations, many of these 'mega parks' are well on the way to becoming a reality.

Multi-national treaties have already been signed for the establishment of:

|Ai-|Ais/Richtersveld Transfrontier Park: Namibia / South Africa, 5920km²

Great Limpopo Transfrontier Park (including the KNP): Mozambique / South Africa / Zimbabwe, 37 572km², phase two will enlarge the TFCA to almost 100 000km²

Kavango - Zambezi TFCA: Angola / Botswana / Namibia / Zambia / Zimbabwe, 520 000km²

Kgalagadi Transfrontier Park: Botswana / South Africa, 35 551km²

Malawi - Zambia TFCA: 31 792km²

Memoranda of Understanding (MoUs) have also been signed by the relevant state parties for the establishment of:

Chimanimani TFCA: Mozambique / Zimbabwe, 4091km²

Iona-Skeleton Coast TFCA: Angola / Namibia

Greater Mapungubwe TFCA: Botswana / South Africa / Zimbabwe, 5909km²

Lubombo Transfrontier Conservation and Resource Area: Mozambique / South Africa / Swaziland, 10 029km²

Maloti-Drakensberg Transfrontier Conservation and Development Area: Lesotho / South Africa, 14 740km²

Additionally, there are a number of TFCAs that are still in the conceptual phase. It is hoped that politics, war and economic depression will not derail these proto-parks, and one looks forward to their successful evolution. These nascent TFCAs include:

Kagera TFCA: Rwanda / Tanzania / Uganda

Liuwa Plains-Mussuma TFCA: Zambia / Angola

The Lower Zambezi – Mana Pools TFCA: Zambia / Zimbabwe

Maiombe Forest TFCA: Angola / DRC / Congo

Mnazi Bay - Quirimbas Transfrontier Marine Conservation Area: Comoros / France / Madagascar / Mauritius / Seychelles / Mozambique / Tanzania

Niassa - Selous TFCA: Mozambique / Tanzania

ZIMOZA TBNRMP: Mozambique / Zambia / Zimbabwe

The Great Limpopo Transfrontier Park (GLTP)

This mega-park will eventually straddle the borders of South Africa, Mozambique and Zimbabwe. It became a reality in December 2002 when an international treaty was signed at Xai-Xai by all three heads of state.

The idea for the GLTP began as early as 1932, when ecologist Gomes de Sousa proposed the idea of a Transfrontier park to the Portuguese colonial authorities. Nothing came of the idea until 1990, when the then-President of Mozambique, Joaquim Chissano, met with the president of the World Wildlife Fund at the urging of Anton Rupert's Transfrontier Park Foundation (forerunner of Peace Parks).

Feasibility studies were soon undertaken with the help of the World Bank and the Global Environment Facility. The time was not ripe, however, as Mozambique was still in the throes of a long civil war and South Africa was a much-hated pariah state.

Thankfully, political tensions largely dissolved after the Mozambique peace accord of 1992 and the democratic South African elections of 1994. So, in 2000, an initial MoU (Memorandum of Understanding) for the establishment of the TFCA was signed at Skukuza. A joint-management board and various management committees were subsequently set up to iron out the details, such as conservation practices, safety and security, finance, human resources, legislation and tourism – all the fun stuff.

After the official treaty signing in 2002, work on the new park began in earnest. The initial focus was on the consolidation and integration of the new 10 000 km² (1 000 000 hectare) Limpopo National Park, on the Mozambique side of the KNP.

Originally named Coutada 16, this area was first fenced off as a hunting concession area in 1969. No subsequent development took place until 2001, when the Parque Nacional do Limpopo (PNL) was declared and developed with the help of the German Federal Ministry for Economic Cooperation and Development. Park management is now busy with community development programmes, the training of rangers, conservation efforts, infrastructure development, the drafting of tourism plans and the removal of landmines left over from the civil war.

The 200km border fence that separated the KNP and PNL started coming down in 2003 and this process is on-going, although the scourge of rhino poaching has caused some to question the wisdom of dropping the barrier. Communities living on the Mozambique side of the park were moved (after due consultation) and more than 6000 animals from the KNP (including elephant and roan antelope) were relocated into the under-stocked Mozambican bush. Many other species, such as buffalo, are also starting to migrate across the border of their own volition.

On the Zimbabwe side, progress has been slowed down by the continuing political and economic problems of this once-great country. Nevertheless, all things shall pass – even Mugabe – and one looks forward to the day when the Gonarezhou Game Reserve (the home of the elephant), Manjinji Pan Sanctuary, Malipati Safari area and the Sengwe communal lands are incorporated into the GLTP. The first step in this process would be the construction of a bridge and border post over the Limpopo River into Zimbabwe.

When it's all done, the Great Limpopo Transfrontier Park will cover an area of over 30 000 square kilometres. And that's just the first phase. The second phase will see the park grow to include the Banhine and Zinave National Parks, the Massingir and Corumana areas and the interlinking lands. The result will be one of the world's largest conservation areas, extending over 100 000 square kilometres. When this great dream is realised, it seems certain that the Great Limpopo National Park will be declared a UNESCO World Heritage Site, signifying its global importance and value.

Visiting the Limpopo National Park

The Limpopo National Park (or Parque Nacional do Limpopo – PNL – in Portuguese) is a large reserve measuring 10 000 km² (1 000 000 hectares), which lies to the east of the KNP. It is part of Great Limpopo Transfrontier Park (GLTP) that will eventually unite the KNP, the Limpopo National Park and Gonarezhou National Park in Zimbabwe.

The PNL is still in the developmental stages, so road and accommodation infrastructure is rather basic. Visitors should also be aware that you cannot currently get fuel, food or water in the park, and the roads are all gravel, so you need to be self-sufficient (complete with breakdown equipment). Nevertheless, it's a wonderfully remote and rugged area that deserves to be explored.

At the moment, the information available online is a bit sketchy but accommodation options in and around the park seem to include:

Campsites: Campismo Aquia Pesqueira (Fish Eagle Camp) and Campismo Albuteira are both located on Massingir Dam and will appeal greatly to fishermen. Basic 2-bed Chalets are apparently available at Fish Eagle Camp. Rugged 'overlander' campsites for the 4x4 crowd are also operational in various locations around the park (e.g. Nhampfule, Sandalo, Giriyondo and Mbona Kaya).

Covane Community Lodge: located on the Massingir Dam, just outside the entrance gate, Covane offers luxury chalets, traditional Shangaan huts and a houseboat, all available on a bed and breakfast basis. Fishing is the big attraction (bring your own gear), along with boat-based game and bird watching. The headquarters of the PNL is also in the area. Check out the website: www.covanecommunitylodge.com.

Machampane Luxury Tented Camp: an intimate, luxurious camp located on a lush river bank, only 30kms from the Giriyondo border post. It offers 10 en-suite safari tents, fully furnished to a high standard, and rates include all meals (currently around R2000 pppn). Guided walks into the bush are also available. The website is www.machampane.com.

Other activities in the park include multi-day hiking trails, self-drive 4x4 eco-trails and the Rio Elefantes Canoe Trail – a guided three-day, 70km river excursion, fully catered, with overnight accommodation in rustic bush camps.

To access the PNL, you can use one of two international border posts located within the KNP. The older border post is located at Pafuri (about 70km from Punda Maria rest camp). To facilitate better access to this far-northern section of the reserve, SANParks' has recently opened the new Pafuri Border Camp, which offers overnight accommodation in converted Wenela / TEBA migrant-labour facilities. The remote Mapai Gate into northern Mozambique is about 80kms from the Pafuri border post, but it's only accessible with a capable 4x4 and you'll need a permit, obtainable from the PNL office at Massingir Gate.

In 2006, a second border gate between the Limpopo and Kruger national parks was opened at Giriyondo (located about 55kms from Letaba rest camp). All the Presidents attended the symbolic event: Guebuza from Mozambique, Mbeki from South Africa and Mugabe from Zimbabwe. Giriyondo is currently the most accessible way for KNP visitors to enter the vast, undeveloped wildness of the PNL. From the border post, it's about 70km to the PNL entrance gate at Massingir, in the south east. Massingir is, in turn, located about 330kms from Mozambique's capital city, Maputo.

Please note: Giriyondo and Pafuri are fully-functioning international border posts, so make sure that you have all the necessary documentation. South African citizens need to carry a valid passport, but do not need a visa. International guests should check with their embassies and arrange for the necessary visas before they arrive. And it's a good idea to check the border gate times before heading off into the wilderness.

Unfortunately, the various websites for the PNL/LNP are somewhat scattershot or outdated (or hacked) so Google around for the latest info and contact numbers.

Heritage Sites in the KNP

There are literally hundreds of natural and cultural heritage sites within the KNP. However, many of these sites are unmarked or far from established tourist routes. Those that have been identified were generally done so by the old National Monuments Council, reflecting their one-sided view of history. The choice of sites, and the wording on some of the commemorative plaques, therefore belongs very much to the Old South Africa.

SANParks is now working to update their heritage register. They want to make the KNP's history more inclusive and are investigating ways to make more sites accessible to the public.

Here is an alphabetical list of selected heritage sites, which you might find marked on your Kruger tourist map.

Afsaal Picnic Site: an old outspan on the Old Transport Road, this modern picnic site boasts an intact, if crumbling, ox-wagon on site. Food, drinks and snacks are usually available.

Albasini Ruins: partially restored remains of Joao Albasini's trading post, located near Phabeni Gate. Also known as Magashula's Kraal, info boards and displays at the site give an idea of life at the store. Most common comment in the guest book is *'interessant'.*

Albasini's Trading Post: trader Joao Albasini maintained a satellite store on the banks of the Sabie river for several years. It was part of the footpath that ran from his base at Magashula's Kraal to Delagoa Bay. The ruins of the store were destroyed in 1969 during construction of the tar road from Lower Sabie to Crocodile Bridge.

Alf Roberts' Store: site of Alf Roberts' trading store, Tengamanzi, operational during the 1880s. Located at Nellmapius Ford, where the Old Transport Road crossed the Crocodile River. Roberts was killed by unknown assailants while tending shop.

Anna Ledeboer's Grave: burial place of Ranger Leonard Ledeboer's wife, located near Letaba. Known for her bad temper (perhaps unfairly), she died suddenly of a heart attack or malaria and was interred at Hatani ranger post in 1921.

Baobab Hill: a distinctive landmark, this was the first outspan on the Witwatersrand Native Labour Association's route to the Soutpansberg, 1919-1937. Located between Pafuri border post and Punda Maria.

Baobab Tree: huge baobab tree with an enormous circumference, now sadly scarred by the initials of idiots with knives. Said to be the most southerly baobab in the KNP. Located between Tshokwane picnic site and Satara.

Ben Viljoen Attack Site: on 16 Sept 1900, at the height of the 2nd Anglo-Boer War, General Ben Viljoen destroyed his artillery and ammunition to prevent them from falling to the approaching British army under General Pole-Carew. Not sure why it's called an attack site. Sounds more like a retreat to me. Located east of Malelane.

Black Rangers Memorial: located at Kruger Gate, this long overdue memorial is an attempt to draw attention away from Oom Paul's brooding presence.

Borcher's Store: an old shop set up to service the nearby WNLA station at Thebe (now Pafuri border post).

Bowker's Kop: hill named after Miles Robert Bowker, a keen hunter who camped here. It is recorded that they 'returned with many trophies, including malaria'. Located near Boulders.

'Buck' Buchanan's Baobab: a big tree named after a Big Game hunter. Located near Crooks' Corner, in the far north.

Bushman Rock Art: there are about 130 documented Bushman rock art sites within the KNP, along with three rare rock engravings. None are easily accessible to the public at the moment, except as part of the three-night Bushman's walking trail, which departs from Berg-en-Dal.

'Bvekenya' Barnard Plaque: commemorating Stephanus Cecil Rutgert 'Bvekenya' Barnard – legendary elephant hunter and poacher who later turned conservationist. According to his son, Barnard had the change of heart after coming face to face with Ndlulamithi, a mighty tusker he had been stalking for years but didn't have the heart to kill. Located in Crooks' Corner.

Crocodile River Bridge: old railway bridge over the Crocodile river, constructed as part of the Selati Railway, now partially collapsed. Visible from Crocodile Bridge rest camp.

Crooks' Corner: the name given to a thin piece of land that juts out into the cross-border region between South Africa, Zimbabwe and Mozambique. It was a lawless place, frequented by unsavoury characters, and a well-known stop on the famous Ivory Trail. Located in the far north of the park.

Das Neves Cross: a Portuguese Cross carved into an old Leadwood tree. Of uncertain provenance, it is thought to have been made by Diocleciano Fernandes das Neves who traded and hunted in the interior during the 1850s and 60s. Das Neves' did not travel light. He was accompanied by over 200 porters and 20 heavily armed elephant hunters. The cross may also be associated with one of Joao Albasini's Portuguese mail runners. Located near Letaba.

De le Porte's Windmill: a typical windmill named after an early ranger. De la Porte was stationed at Skukuza during World War 1, while JSH was doing military service.

'Dipeni' Dipping Tank: a dip tank built during the Foot and Mouth disease outbreak in 1938. All foot traffic (human and animal) had to wade through the disinfectant dip before crossing the border with Mozambique. The name is a mixture of Afrikaans and XiTsonga, meaning 'at the diptank'. Located near Shingwedzi.

Doispane Outspan: a resting place on the wagon road between Doispane and Skukuza.

Duke's Windmill: an early wind pump named after an early ranger, Thomas Duke, of Lower Sabie.

Engelhard Plaque: commemorative plaque to American millionaire Charles Engelhard, who sponsored the construction of the eponymous dam.

Fever Tree Forest: a flat plain along the Shingwedzi River covered with hundreds of vivid yellow Fever Trees. Located in the Pafuri.

Filamanzi (Hidden water): a well-known outspan point on The Old Transport Road.

First Borehole: the first borehole in the park was dug at Sabi Bridge (now Skukuza rest camp)

Founders Memorial: a large frieze depicting the three men who are traditionally recognized as the founders of the KNP. The sculpture has pride of place outside the Skukuza reception building.

Frans de Kuiper's Attack Site: de Kuiper's expedition from Delagoa Bay to Ciremandelle (Phalaborwa) was rudely interrupted when Chief Dawano attacked the European party at Gomondwane. Heavy fighting ensued and De Kuiper had to retreat back over the Lubombo. He is also recorded as Francois de Cuiper or de Kuyper. Located near Crocodile Bridge.

Gaza Grey's Outpost: a member of Steinaecker's Horse, Gray was one of the first men that JSH visited, to better gauge conditions in the Lowveld. Located near Lower Sabie.

Glen Leary Site: in July 1926, Harold Trollope (a wealthy park benefactor) camped at Fihlamanzi outspan on the Old Transport Road, accompanied by his father-in-law, John Glen-Leary. A few days later, Glen-Leary was fatally injured by a leopard on a tributary of the Hlambanyathi spruit.

Grave Sites: hundreds of people, black and white, have met their maker in the unforgiving bush of the Kruger Park. In fact, the KNP is liberally sprinkled with the graves of men and women, both famous and unknown. Researchers have even found the grave of a person of either Indian or Arab ethnicity, buried at Pembe. This is unusual because the Asian seafarers did not generally venture inland. But, whatever the provenance, most of the old grave sites are long forgotten, lost in the wild.

Grobler Plaque: memorial plaque to Piet Grobler, a relative of Paul Kruger, who introduced the National Parks Act to parliament in 1926. Overlooking Piet Grobler Dam, located near Timbavati picnic site.

Harold Trollope Hut: tourist hut in Malelane rest camp, named in honour of Big Game hunter and landowner, Harold Trollope, who supported the establishment of the Kruger and Addo Elephant National Parks.

Hippo Pools and Rock Art: a spot on the banks of the Crocodile River, near the rest camp, where hippos are commonly seen lazing in the shallows. Bushman paintings can also be viewed, if a guide is present.

Isivivane: the Zulu name for a traveller's cairn. Custom states that you must place a rock on the pile each time you pass, as a sign of gratitude and good fortune. As they grow in size, these inviting stacks of stones act as waymarkers through the bush. They are commonly found throughout South Africa. In the KNP, there are old Isivivane marking the ancient foot paths to Matukwala as well as Sofala and Inhambane.

James Stevenson-Hamilton Memorial Library and Museum: extensive archive of books and papers relating to every aspect of the KNP, located at Skukuza. Also contains an interesting museum about the park, with memorabilia and exhibits.

Jock of the Bushveld Plaques: starting at Numbi Gate, a series of plaques, branded with an image of the famous dog, identify various locations along the Old Transport Road, immortalised by Percy Fitzpatrick's popular novel 'Jock of the Bushveld'. The waymarkers were erected at the suggestion of Cecily Niven, Fitzpatrick's daughter.

Joe Ludorf Plaque: memorial plaque to the first chairman of the National Parks Board, set into the distinctive Napi boulder. Located between Pretoriuskop and Skukuza.

John Fernandez Shop: small store run for the Makuleke community (1954-1969). Located in the Pafuri.

Josikhulu Drift: an overnight station for black porters, who carried trade goods through the KNP. As part of Joao Albasini's empire, the eponymous Josikhulu was installed as the resident tribal authority. Later, the station was run by Thomas Hart, who was killed by local tribesmen after an argument over a stolen rifle. He was 22 years old. Located near Pretoriuskop.

Klopperfontein Drift: a little oasis in the bush, used as a camp by hunters on the Ivory Trail, including Cecil 'Bvekenya' Barnard. Named after Hans Klopper, who often camped here. Located near Punda Maria.

Komapite Windmill: early windmill, built in 1933. In fact, as tourist attractions go, it's a bore hole. Located near Pretoriuskop.

Kruger Statue: controversial, glowering sandstone bust of President Paul Kruger, erected just outside Kruger Gate in 1972.

Kruger Tablets: a rather self-serving memorial plaque, erected by the National Parks Board in 1933 to "commemorate the institution of the national parks of the union. Sabi Game Reserve declared by President Paul Kruger in 1898. National Parks Act introduced by Mr. PGW Grobler, Minister of Lands, in 1926." Located between Skukuza and Tshokwane picnic site.

Lanner Gorge: a natural heritage site, one of the most dramatic view points in the KNP. It is only accessible as part of the overnight Nyalaland Hiking Trail, or through one of the concessionaires in the Makuleke Contract Park.

Letaba Elephant Hall: excellent museum dedicated to all things pachydermal. Contains the remains of the 'Magnificent Seven'. Located inside Letaba rest camp.

'Mafourteen' Footpath: leading from Letaba to the Mozambique border, this path was used by labour trains from the 1920s to the 1970s.

Makahane: ruins of an African iron-age settlement, ruled over by the cruel Makahane. Related to Thulamela, but more recent. Located near Punda Maria.

Makhadzi Picnic Site: new picnic spot built to serve traffic between Letaba to Giriyondo border post. Contains an interesting series of info boards on the cross-border region and Steinaecker's Horse (the irregular troop that patrolled the area during the Anglo-Boer War).

Mangalane Footpath: a migrant labour route in use between 1920 and 1960. Located near Lower Sabie.

Manungu's Kraal: a nominal chief, Manungu, was installed in the vicinity of Pretoriuskop by Joao Albasini to oversee his lucrative trade network.

Masorini Archaeological Museum: rewarding open-air museum that re-creates an African iron-age settlement, in the style of the BaPhalaborwa. Located close to Phalaborwa Gate.

Mining Sites: early iron-age African villagers were actively mining copper, gold, mica, ochre and other useful materials in the KNP for centuries. In more recent times, Europeans entered the region looking for diamonds, gold, copper and anything sparkly. There were certainly plenty of gold rushes nearby – Pilgrim's Rest, Barberton, Leydsdorp – but most KNP treasure seekers left with empty hands and broken hearts.

Mitomeni Dam: the first concrete dam in the KNP, built by M. Roland Jones, supervisor of Pretoriuskop, at Mtomani Spruit in 1931/32.

Nellmapius Ford: an old drift across the Crocodile River, used by wagons on the Transport Road to Delagoa Bay. Built by a contractor, Alois Nellmapius, the drift was in use from 1872-1892, until the opening of the Delagoa Bay railway line, when it fell in to disuse. Located between Malelane and Crocodile Bridge.

Old Gorge Rest Camp: decommissioned rest camp and drift over the Olifants River.

Old Pafuri Campsite: an old campsite in the far north (1939-1948).

Old Sabie River Pontoon: before a causeway was built, vehicles were ferried across the Sabie on a raft, based in Skukuza rest camp.

Old Saliji Ranger Post: located near Lower Sabie.

Old Shawu Picnic Site: disused picnic site and tea room, named after one of the area's famous 'Big Tuskers'. Located near Boulders.

Old Transport Road: route of the main wagon road from Lydenburg to Delagoa Bay. Several historical markers can be found along the route, most pertaining to the days of the transport riders. Starts near Pretoriuskop and ends around Crocodile Bridge.

Orpen Memorial: a rather measly commemorative bird bath erected within the small Orpen Gate rest camp, in honour of James and Eileen Orpen.

Orpen Rocks: a commemorative plaque set into boulders "to honour... and in gratitude to Mrs Eileen Orpen for her generous gift of seven farms for inclusion in the Kruger National Park, total area 28 633 morgen. This bears testament to her love of nature and the natural world. Erected 1944." Very nice of her. Located between Skukuza and Tshokwane picnic site.

Outspan Plaque: marks a popular outspan point on the Old Transport Road. A large leadwood tree on the edge of the camp was used for target practise around 1845.

Pet Cemetery: burial place for all the beloved pets of Kruger Park staff, not like the one in Stephen King's book. Located in Skukuza.

Phabeni Gate: entrance gate opened in 2002 to improve access for guests arriving from Gauteng. Named after a Swazi chief who gave his name to the adjacent stream.

Potgieter's Route: a commemorative marker, located within Punda Maria rest camp, celebrating the Bronkhorst-Potgieter Voortrekker journey - basically, a reconnaissance party passed this way in 1836, in search of the missing Van Rensburg party.

Pretorius' Grave: burial place of Willem Pretorius, a member of Carel Trichardt's 1848 expedition to Delagoa Bay. Pretoriuskop is named in his honour. He was interred here by Albasini. The grave is just visible in the long grass, a short distance from the road. However, this is lion country and it is not recommended that you get out of your car to view Pretorius' final resting place, or it might become yours too.

Prospectors Graves: a forlorn graveyard for prospectors who were active in the area during the 1870s. Located near Skukuza.

Rabelais Dam: a defunct reservoir, built before environmental assessments were common and located in a region with sensitive soils. After a destructive flood in 2000, it was decided to demolish the dam and allow a smaller pan to develop naturally. Located near Orpen Gate.

Rabelais Hut: an old entrance gate to the park, operational from in 1926 until 1954, when the KNP was expanded. The original 'reception' hut still stands, and contains a number of interesting info boards about the Orpens and the early days of Kruger. Check out the prices in 1932: 2/6 for the use of the rest camp hut, mattresses were a shilling and blankets cost sixpence. Located near Orpen Gate.

Red Rocks: 'Ribye ra gubyane' – potholes formed in soft Karoo sandstone. In the dry season, fish get trapped in the isolated pools. Located near Shingwedzi.

Reitz Pontoon: location of the old pontoon across the Olifants River. Located in Balule rest camp.

Sabie River Bridge: old railway bridge over the Sabie river, constructed as part of the Selati Railway. Best viewed from the Skukuza promenade.

Sardelli's store: Sardelli was a trader who ran a shack near the Zenga-Zenga Mountain in the Lubombo. His most popular product was a home-brewed liquor made from the fruit of the Marula tree. It is rumoured that he also operated a gang of bandits who ambushed Shangaan mineworkers and stole their wages. Located near Crocodile Bridge.

Sausage Trees: the Sausage Tree *(Kigelia africana)* gets its name from its heavy, frankfurter-like fruit, which is used by traditional healers as a purgative. A good example can be found in the Letaba parking lot, where motorists are advised to watch out for falling sausages.

Selati Steam Engine: a handsome looking steam engine, left over from the days of the Selati line. It used to house a restaurant but now stands empty in its lonely siding at Skukuza.

Shipikane Archaeological site: the KNP is dotted with the remains of old African settlements, which were gradually abandoned after the park was declared. The only ones which have been restored are Thulamela and Masorini. Perhaps other, more recent, remains will be resurrected in the future. Located near Letaba.

Skukuza Clock Tower: built in 1937, this clock tower made of sandstone blocks is in memory of Herbert Boshof Papenfus KC, 1865 – 1937. Member of parliament, friend to all animals and birds, and a founding member of the Parks Board. Located in Skukuza.

Soltke's Grave: a member of a Transport crew in the 1880s, Soltke accidentally shot himself in the leg and died of the wound, aged 23. Located near Pretoriuskop.

Steinaecker's Horse Camp: campsite used by the irregular force that patrolled the region during the 2nd AB War. Located near Pretoriuskop. Various other forts and campsites relating to Steinaecker's Horse have been identified in the region.

Stevenson-Hamilton Memorial: after his death, the ashes of renowned warden, James Stevenson-Hamilton, were scattered from atop Shirimantanga koppie. The views from the boulder are wonderful. Located near Skukuza.

Stolz' Grave: in 1886, Gert Frederik Coenraad Stolz went hunting near the Bukweneni River. He contracted malaria and died in the wilderness. The Stolz family were famous wagon makers from the White River area. Located between Pretoriuskop and Berg-en-Dal.

Struben Cottage: an old guest house in Skukuza rest camp, named after Fred and Harry Struben, two pioneers of the Witwatersrand gold fields. Built in 1937, it has now been restored and is available for hire.

Theba Recruitment Station: gathering point for Mozambican workers *en route* to the mines of the Witwatersrand, part of the WNLA labour route. Located at Pafuri border post.

Thompson's Shop: old store built by Alex Thompson and William Pye for the benefit of travellers in Crooks' Corner. Also known as Makuleke store. Operational from 1910-1954.

Thulamela: a stunning archaeological site, Thulamela is a stone-walled iron age settlement, located on top of a tall hill. It is only accessible as part of a guided tour from Punda Maria.

Trichardt's Memorial: route marker for the 'epic' trek of Louis Trichardt in March 1838. Located between Tshokwane picnic site and Satara.

Tshokwane Picnic Site: "In 1902 a large number of native kraals stood in the vicinity, but a series of drought years had gradually pushed them westwards to the better-watered country outside the reserve. By 1910 only old man Tshokwane himself, with his family, remained. He was a man of between 70 and 80 and a mine of local history. After Tshokwane's death, in about 1915, his family moved away, and the place was left entirely to the wild animals." JSH – South African Eden

Von Wielligh's Baobab: GR Von Wielligh surveyed the eastern boundary of the KNP, along the Mozambique border, and carved his initials into the bark of this baobab at 'Camp 19' in 1891. Located near Olifants.

WA Campbell Tourist Hut: one of the early huts for overnight visitors at Skukuza. It was built in 1929 at a cost of R300, and was sponsored by WA Campbell, one-time owner of MalaMala.

William Lloyd's Grave: grave of William Lloyd, one of Satara's early rangers.

William Pye's Grave: final resting place of a Crooks' Corner incorrigible.

WNLA posts at Letaba and Nwanetsi: holding camps and rest stops for migrant labour trains from Mozambique, organised by the Witwatersrand Native Labour Association (WNLA).

Wolhuter's Lion Attack: site of the famous struggle between Ranger Harry 'Lindandla' Wolhuter and two ferocious lions. Several plaques detail the life and death struggle. Located near Tshokwane picnic site.

Wolhuter Tourist Hut: one of the old rondawels that housed the early visitors at Pretoriuskop, named after the famous ranger. Built in 1930, the lop-sided little hut is preserved within the grounds of the modern rest camp.

Wolhuter's Windmill: Harry Wolhuter used this place at Doispane as an outpost from 1903–1940. Located near Pretoriuskop.

THE GREAT LIMPOPO TRANSFRONTIER CONSERVATION AREA (TFCA)

ZIMBABWE

GONAREZHOU
NATIONAL
PARK

ZINAVE
NATIONAL
PARK

PAFURI
BORDER

BANHINE
NATIONAL
PARK

LIMPOPO
NATIONAL
PARK /
PARQUE
NACIONAL
DO LIMPOPO

GIRIYONDO

KRUGER
NATIONAL
PARK

MASSINGIR

PHALABORWA

SOUTH
AFRICA

MOZAMBIQUE

EXISTING
CONSERVATION
AREAS

PROPOSED
TFCA
EXPANSION

NELSPRUIT

KOMATIPOORT

MAPUTO

INDIAN
OCEAN

SWAZILAND

MAP NOT TO SCALE

Part Two:

Exploring Kruger

The Circus, the Zoo and the Wilderness

There are many different Kruger National Parks; the bush speaks in a multitude of voices and therefore appeals to a diverse group of people. So, the vast KNP attracts birders, game spotters, nature lovers, hikers, campers, rich safari junkies and ordinary holiday makers in equal measure.

But, even within these interest groups, the bush experience is often a singular one, depending on the personal predilections of each visitor. That's why individuals are encouraged to discover their own game reserve and to form a unique personal bond with the wilderness.

With dozens of activities and attractions on offer, the tourism potential of the KNP is huge and some visitors may be overwhelmed by the scale of this enormous conservation area. So, the best advice for KNP newbies is to visit the park for yourself and seek out the things that interest you the most. And rest assured that whatever aspect of the park you choose to explore, it's all good. No-one can say that one kind of bush experience is more 'authentic' than another. They are all equally worthy and it's up to you to select a slice of Kruger that you will enjoy.

The information contained in this 'Exploring Kruger' section will hopefully help you discover the KNP that is right for you, so that you can optimise your time in the park. Things are changing all the time, however, so check online for the latest details. The KNP-related online forums and Facebook pages are very active too – just don't make them angry...

When you're in the park, for the latest game viewing news, chat to your fellow visitors and the knowledgeable KNP staff. Local conditions and game spotting recommendations change with the seasons and there are few hard and fast rules about where to see what – despite all the books claiming otherwise. So, ask around and be prepared to modify your plans to be in sync with the restless face of the KNP.

The first thing to consider when planning your trip to Kruger is the distance you can cover in a day. Once inside the park, you cannot drive very fast as the speed limits are low and, as a rule of thumb, you should plan on covering no more than 25km in an hour, and this doesn't include long stops to view game. In any case, it would be plain stupid to gallop through a game reserve. So, choose an area or rest camp and stick to it. Don't be too ambitious.

To help you make your decision about where to go, some Kruger-ites have divided the reserve into three sections: the circus, the zoo and the Wilderness.

The South, they say, is the Circus. It is the closest region to the Gauteng metropolis (between 4 and 5 hours away, depending on your entry gate) and is accordingly the busiest part of the KNP with highest density of cars and day trippers. However, the south also has a lot of game, especially the Big Five, and the spotting can be excellent. The landscape is varied, ranging from lush riverine environments to bushy mountains and open plains (the latter being ideal for game spotting). As is to be expected, the rest camps in the south are both large and well equipped. But, in the busy holiday seasons, prepare yourself for hectic crowds and traffic jams around every elephant.

The Central region is called the Zoo. The game spotting is good and the tourism infrastructure is well developed but not overwhelming. This part of the KNP is not as busy as the south, but can get crowded at peak times, especially over school holidays. The habitat is characterised by open, grassy plains, which are great for game spotting. Orpen and Phalaborwa gates are between 5 and 6 hours from Gauteng.

The north of the KNP can quite legitimately be called the Wilderness. It is far from any major cities and feels much more remote than the bustling southern regions. The landscape in the North is also more dramatic; boasting mountains, broad river valleys, thick forests and sandy flood plains. Yet there is good game here, including the regionally-specific nyala, eland and the ubiquitous elephant, and the human traffic is very light. There are only a couple of rest camps in the north but, if you've got a bit of extra time, it's well worth exploring this pristine part of the KNP. Punda Maria and Pafuri gates are between 6 and 7 hours from Gauteng.

What You Should Know

Climate

In spring/summer (October to March), the subtropical Lowveld is hot and humid with daytime highs often hovering around 30 and rising up to 40 degrees. This climatological dispensation reaches its height in January and February when the weather in the KNP can be downright beastly.

Summer is also the rainy season and there will be sporadic thunderstorms and downpours across the park during these wet months. However, the sun rises early and sets late, so the entrance gates are open for longer and you will have more time to drive around.

The Lowveld winters (April to October) are mild and pleasant during the day, with clear blue skies. Mornings and evenings can be cold, however, and you should bundle up if you're going out in an open game viewing vehicle because it can get pretty damn nippy after the sun sets. The chances of rain are slim during the dry season.

When to Visit

In terms of game spotting, the best time to visit the park is late winter and early spring (July to October). The days are pleasant and the grass is low, so you can see further into the bush. The park is also dry in the winter, so the animals tend to congregate around the available water holes, making the game easier to spot.

Of course, summer is nice too. This is when the grass is long and luxuriant and nature is in full flower. The park is therefore much more colourful during the wet season, especially when compared to the limited palette of browns and khaki that characterise the park in winter.

The breeding season begins in spring, offering lucky visitors the chance of witnessing a birth or spotting newly born babies. Autumn is the mating season and, if you're discreet, you may see some action in the bushes.

Birders will have a fine time throughout the year, although the summer months (specifically December and January) are considered optimal.

Do note, during the South African school holidays, the crowds are at their peak and the KNP can become quite unpleasant. The park usually operates at capacity throughout the vacation month of December, and this leads to overcrowded camps, congested traffic and outbursts of road rage that would normally only occur in the urban jungle. The number of day trippers allowed into the park may also be limited at peak times, so arrive early or risk getting turned back. The winter season is also very popular with dedicated game spotters and retirees, so it's always a good idea to book your accommodation well in advance.

Kruger Culture

No person is an island, and the KNP authorities want to encourage their guests to reach out to one another and share their experiences. So, do simple things such as waving to cars that you pass on the road; pass on information to fellow visitors about what you've spotted and where; participate in camp fire discussions; and share your knowledge and experiences with others. Collaborating with other tourists will definitely enhance your appreciation of the park.

Kruger Time

One KNP staffer told me that animals are just like us; they like to be comfortable and don't enjoy wandering around in the heat of the day. So, whether you are a birder, game spotter or just a rest camp layabout, the ideal daily routine goes something like this: wake up early (before sunrise) and take yourself on a game drive soon after the rest camp gate opens. The game is quite active in the cool mornings and this is when many of the best spots are made.

Temperatures begin to rise as the sun climbs higher, so return to camp around nine or ten and chill out in the shade of your veranda or around the pool. Enjoy a relaxed lunch or have a snooze in the early afternoon, then get back in the car a couple of hours before sunset (when the game is once again active) for another round of spotting.

Evenings can be spent around a braai, at the rest camp's restaurant or sitting on the stoep of your bungalow, drinking in the nocturnal symphony.

Driving in Kruger

The KNP has strict speed limits: 50kmph on tar roads and 40kmph on gravel roads. It would be foolish to exceed these limits for a number of reasons: you won't see any game if you travel at speed; you'll annoy your fellow game spotters; it's dangerous for the animals; it's disruptive; it's noisy; it's dusty, etc. You will also get a heavy fine if you exceed the specified speed limits and, yes, there are speed traps inside the KNP.

I know this for a fact because I was caught speeding by an old policeman with khaki shorts and knobbly knees, wrinkled to perfection by years of sitting in the hot sun. In my defence, I was running very low on petrol and was coasting downhill, hoping to reach the next rest camp before my car shuddered to a halt.

Then, just when I least expected it, I saw a glint in the bushes and the above-mentioned officer leapt out into the road. He listened to my story sympathetically, but was unmoved by my plight and issued me with a huge fine.

I eventually got the fine reduced by writing a heart-rending letter to the police department based at Skukuza, but this is not an experience that I recommend. As a general rule of thumb, plan on covering no more than 25km in an hour of driving, and this does not include any long stops. So, don't be too ambitious.

Game Spotting

Most rest camps have a spotting board, which pinpoints the locations where specific species have been spotted in the last day or two. Take a look at this board, usually in the reception area, to improve your game spotting strike rate.

You can also ask the rangers and other guests that you meet along the way for additional leads. And be patient. Sometimes waiting at a watering hole for a couple of hours is a better strategy than driving around like a lunatic, searching for a lion.

Of course, luck also plays a big role in the process as there are simply no guarantees when it comes to wild animals. You should also take along a couple of game spotting guides so that you can identify what you are looking at!

SANParks.org

Things change all the time, so consult the comprehensive SANParks website for all the latest KNP information. It contains a wealth of content, and the online reservation and payment system is comprehensive. There are plenty of other KNP-related websites out there, some good and some bad, but only sanparks.org is official.

Gate Times

Private vehicles are not allowed to drive through the park after sunset and before sunrise. To enforce this rule, entrance gates and rest camp gates both have fixed opening and closing times and these are not negotiable. Heavy fines will be imposed on those people who miss the gate closing times, so make sure you plan your day carefully and don't get caught too far away from your home gate when the sun starts to set. If you are late and have to drive fast to reach the gate in time, you will probably be fined for speeding.

Gate times correspond with sunrise and sunset and therefore shift with the seasons (between 04:30 and 06:00 in the morning, and between 17:30 and 18:30 in the evenings).

And, if you are late, don't think that you'll be able to talk your way out of it. The guards at the gates are not pushovers, and they have their orders. I once mistimed a drive and arrived back at camp about 15 minutes past curfew. The guard was apoplectic and was adamant that he was going to call the camp manager. I eventually won him over with my pleas of ignorance and a bag of naartjies.

Entrance Fees

Every person who enters the KNP must pay a daily conservation fee. This applies both to day visitors, overnight guests and people staying at one of the concession lodges. The cost of this conservation fee is generally not included in any quoted prices and must be calculated in addition to your other KNP expenses. The conservation fees are an important part of the park's revenue stream and help to maintain the reserve.

The current conservation fees (valid to 31 October 2017) are:

South African citizens and residents (with valid ID): R76 pppd / R38 per child under 12

Southern African Development Community (SADC) nationals (with valid passport): R152 pppd / R76 per child under 12

International visitors: R304 pppd / R152 per child under 12

Wild Card

If you are planning to spend a few days in the park, it may be worthwhile buying a SANParks WILD Card. This is a very effective loyalty programme whereby, in exchange for a single annual fee, Wild Card holders do not pay any daily conservation fees at selected SANParks, Ezemvelo KZN Wildlife, Msinsi, CapeNature and Swaziland's Big Game Parks' reserves – depending on which 'cluster' you buy. You can also get cards for individuals, couples, families or international guests.

Current rates range start at R515 for an individual Wild Card that includes access to over 80 parks around southern Africa. So, if you plan on spending more than six or seven days in any reserve over the course of a year, it's a no-brainer.

Day Visitors

Visitors with their own vehicles are welcome to enter the park and explore it for the day. This is a popular excursion for locals and people holidaying in the park's environs. Just make sure that you are out of the park before the specified gate closing time.

All the main rest camps have facilities for day visitors. These usually include a braai area and often a swimming pool. The rest camp restaurants, viewing decks and shops are also generally open to day visitors. Please note, however, that the accommodation areas of the camp are reserved for overnight guests only. Private bush camps and concession lodges are not open to day visitors.

There are also many picnic spots and other view sites throughout the park where day guests can get out of their cars and enjoy the bush. Various shops, restaurants, information boards and other activities are available at some of these picnic sites. Most rest camps also have a shop where day visitors can buy meat and picnic supplies.

Please note: to maintain the atmosphere of a tranquil nature reserve, there is a quota on the maximum number of vehicles that can enter the park each day. If this threshold is reached, only visitors with pre-booked permits or overnight accommodation will be permitted access. Such situations tend only to arise during peak periods, such as public holidays and during the holiday month of December. Arrive at the gate early during these times to ensure that you get in, or book an advance day visitor permit through central reservations or the SANParks website.

Picnic Sites

There are several picnic sites scattered throughout the KNP. These are excellent places to stop the car, stretch your legs and get a snack. Monkeys and birds are plentiful at the picnic spots, and several sites overlook riverine environments, offering visitors the promise of seeing bigger game. I also enjoy indulging in a bit of human spotting at the picnic sites and, if you keep your eyes peeled, you might see a lesser-spotted Crimplene Warbler, a common Khakipant or even the endangered Crested Mullet.

Gas skottels (mobile frying pans on stands) can be hired at most picnic sites for a nominal fee. The picnic site attendant will wash these on your departure, so you don't have to worry about scraping off the grease.

Airports

Flights to the KNP land at the Kruger-Mpumalanga international airport (KMIA). It's located between Nelspruit and White River, about 50km away from the southern KNP gates. The flight from Joburg takes about 50 mins (1 hour from Durban and 2.5 hours from Cape Town). Tickets from Joburg start around R2500 return.

There are also smaller airports in Hoedspruit and Phalaborwa, serviced by SA Airlink.

Banks and ATMs

There is a bank and ATM at Skukuza rest camp and an ATM at Letaba. No other cash withdrawal facilities are available. You can, however, use your credit card (preferably Visa / Mastercard) to pay for food, accommodation and activities throughout the KNP.

You can also pay for most accommodation and activities in advance, through the SANParks website.

Cellular and Wi-Fi

Thoroughly defying Maslow's traditional Hierarchy of Needs, our urgent desire to be connected at all times is now fundamental to life as we know it. Although the Kruger isn't really the place to stare at a smart phone, cellular reception is available in patches around the major rest camps (but don't count on high-speed data).

There are also internet cafés with wi-fi networks located at Berg-en-Dal and Skukuza.

Spiders, Snakes and Scorpions

A constant source of terror for many people, these poisonous beasties will probably not harm you as long as they don't feel threatened. To minimise the risk of stepping on one, always carry a torch when you walk around the rest camp at night.

If you do come across a snake, do not try to catch it! Rather back away very slowly and report it to the Manager on duty or to reception. The cautious among you may also want to check your shoes before putting them on in the morning...

Cheeky Monkeys

Monkeys and baboons are very cute and can be entertaining for young and old alike. My father (being both young and old) can sit and watch them for hours. But please do not feed the primates!

Remember that by feeding the monkeys, you are signing their death warrant as they tend to become aggressive and a nuisance once they start associating humans with food and, in many cases, this necessitates their elimination. They are also adept thieves, so don't leave food unattended and, before going out in the morning, make sure that you have locked your doors, closed the windows and securely packed away all your foodstuffs.

Seriously, you don't want a monkey inside your room – they'll trash everything and probably crap all over the place.

Bats and Insects

At night, light from the rest camps attracts many flying insects and, with these insects, come their predators, including bats and frogs. So, remember to keep the screen doors of your bungalow closed as this will prevent these unwanted creatures from entering your room.

Should a bat fly into your room by mistake, do not panic! The KNP website suggests that you calmly place a towel over the bat and release it outside. A more likely course of action would be to go to reception and ask for assistance.

Similarly, if you are standing outside, the night air is often teeming with flitting and flapping bats. If a bat touches you while standing around the braai, once again, don't panic! Bats are just like cute little mice with wings and will not bite unless they mistake you for a juicy bug. They are also adept flyers with a sophisticated radar system that helps them avoid collisions.

Malaria

The KNP is located in a malaria-endemic area. But what does this mean, and how seriously should you take the threat? Well, it's not something to be taken lightly, but some foreign folks get downright hysterical. So, let's get a couple of things straight about the spectre of malaria.

The disease is caused by a single-celled parasite called *Plasmodium.* It can live in the blood of birds, reptiles and mammals, and it is transmitted to humans by the female *Anopheles* mosquito (the genus name derives from a Greek word that translates as 'useless'). There are four strains of human malaria found around the world. They each vary in their severity. One of the most dangerous strains, *Plasmodium falciparum,* is found in the Lowveld.

The early symptoms of malaria are similar to those of the flu: feeling weak, dizzy, muscular pain, fever, vomiting, diarrhoea. These symptoms can be efficiently treated with medication and, provided the diagnosis is made quickly, there should be little lasting effect on the patient (although the disease can reoccur under certain circumstances). However, if neglected, the malaria can get 'complicated' and induce more severe symptoms. Ultimately, this could lead to cerebral malaria, respiratory problems, comas and even death.

If you have visited a malaria-endemic area, you should watch out for any flu-like symptoms for up to three weeks after you leave (or even longer). If any symptoms do occur, consult a doctor immediately and get tested for malaria. Always tell your doctor that you have been in a malaria area to avoid an incorrect diagnosis.

Now for the good news... Most of South Africa is free from malaria. Cape Town, Durban and Johannesburg are all well out of the danger zone, and you are only at risk once you descend the Eastern Drakensberg mountains into the Lowveld (the offending parasites cannot complete their life cycle in the cooler temperatures associated with higher altitudes).

Furthermore, not every mosquito in the KNP carries malaria. The *Plasmodium* parasite has to undergo a certain development process in the mosquito before it becomes infectious, and this only happens in certain *Anopheles* mosquitoes. So, getting a mosquito bite does not mean that you are definitely going to get malaria.

There's also been a substantial decrease in malaria transmission rates across Mpumalanga province over the years. In fact, historically, the incidence of malaria in the KNP is relatively low. Nevertheless, the risk is there. So, what should you do to protect yourself?

Here's some advice from the experts.

First, prevention is better than cure. Take precautions to avoid being bitten by mosquitoes. Malaria mosquitoes generally bite after dark, so wear long sleeves and trousers in the late afternoon and evening, and do not stand outside unnecessarily. Use insect repellent on exposed skin. Your ankles are particularly vulnerable.

When you turn in for the night, continue to be aware of precautionary measures. If you are camping, try to sleep under a bednet or in a netted tent. If you are staying in a rest camp hut or caravan, make sure that all the doors and windows are fitted with mosquito screens and check that all the screens are closed and intact. You can also spray insecticide aerosols and/or burn a mosquito coil at night.

In addition to these precautionary measures, it is highly recommended that you use a suitable medical prophylaxis in malaria-risk areas. This usually entails taking pills to protect your body from the parasite, should you get bitten (alternative therapies such as wristbands and the like haven't been proven to be particularly efficacious).

There are several treatments available, but malaria is becoming resistant to some of them, and you may experience side effects with others. Moreover, no one treatment is 100% effective (some can even mask the symptoms until the disease is far advanced). So, before you leave for the KNP, it is important that you consult your doctor, pharmacist or a reputable travel clinic to make sure you get the medication that is right for you and appropriate for the area you will be visiting.

In no particular order, here are the most commonly available treatments for areas with incidence of *P. falciparum,* such as the KNP:

Atovaquone/ Proguanil (sold under the brand names Malanil or Malarone). This is a modern, effective and relatively safe treatment with few documented side effects. The drawback is that it's also the most expensive (at least until a generic version is released). Paediatric tablets are available, but it's not suitable for pregnant or breast-feeding women, or people with severe renal (kidney) impairment. Dosage is one tablet a day, starting one day before you leave and continuing for seven days after you return. Always take the tablet after a meal to avoid nausea.

Mefloquine (sold under the brand names Lariam or Mefliam). This treatment is effective, although there are regions where the disease has built up resistance to mefloquine. There may also be strong side effects. It is not recommended for pilots, scuba divers or people with certain psychiatric conditions, cardiac abnormalities or seizure disorders, but it can be used during pregnancy. You are required to take one pill a week, starting two weeks before you leave and continuing four weeks after you return. Take the pills on a full stomach or you might spew!

Doxycycline is an antibiotic treatment that is effective and very inexpensive. However, Doxy can cause skin sensitivity to sunlight and other side effects, especially in pregnant women and children under 10. It has also been known to render birth control pills ineffective when the two are taken simultaneously, so additional prophylactics may be necessary! You take one pill every day, starting one day before you leave and continuing for a month after you return. Pills should be taken on a full stomach.

Remember those old-fashioned, hideously bitter **Chloroquine** pills that we used to take as kids? Well, they are no longer popular because they don't clear the parasite from your system and, moreover, the disease has developed wide-spread resistance to the treatment. I mention this to emphasise that pharmaceutical regimes change with time, so stay up to date and do some research before choosing a treatment.

In any case, the question remains: should you take a chemical prophylaxis or should you just slap on the bug spray and hope for the best? Well, that is up to you. Some long-term residents of the KNP don't take any medication at all, preferring to rely on simple preventive measures, as described above. You also get more resistant to the disease every time you get it, so if it doesn't kill you, it makes you stronger?

You should also consider the season during which you will be visiting the park. The mosquitoes are much more active in the hot, wet summer months (December to April) and visitors during this time should definitely take precautions. The low rainfall and cooler temperatures in the winter months reduces the number of mosquitoes, and therefore lowers the risk of infection, so many visitors do not take pills during this time. But don't be fooled, the mosquitoes do not just disappear during winter, their numbers just go down.

In any case, pregnant women and young children should be particularly cautious. They are particularly susceptible to the disease and may weaken rapidly. If you are pregnant or travelling with young kids, you may want to revise your travel plans until the kids are older.

Just remember, if you do choose to take prophylactic medication, make sure that you complete the course, as prescribed. If you miss pills or abandon the regime before it is finished, the disease may flare up. And don't think, "Well, I didn't get bitten, so I can stop taking the pills." They call the female *Anopheles* the 'silent killer' because she does not buzz in your ear and does not leave behind much of an itchy bite. So, you may not notice that you've been bitten until after the symptoms develop.

As diseases go, malaria is a big problem. The World Health Organisation estimates that half the world's population is at risk, with about 212 million malaria cases and 430 000 fatalities in 2015 alone. 90% of these cases were in sub-Saharan Africa. While the highest mortality rate is among children under 5, there has been a 29% overall reduction in malaria-related deaths since 2010 – thanks, in part, to large-scale public health programmes and private initiatives by organisations such the Bill and Melinda Gates Foundation.

Economic studies have also shown that malaria-related illness incurs a high social cost. Families affected by malaria harvest a fraction of their crops compared to healthy families and this is said to slow economic growth in Africa – suggesting a strong link between malaria and poverty. The direct and indirect costs of malaria in Africa are also huge, accounting for up to 40% of all public health spending in Africa.

Unfortunately, one of the most effective methods of fighting the parasite and its vector (mosquitoes) is chemical spraying with powerful poisons, such as DDT. Although once widespread through the western world, this practise is now considered environmentally unsound as the DDT toxin can seep into the ground and poison the water table. There is now a general moratorium on the use of

DDT around the world, and there is strong pressure to ban the pesticide altogether. In Africa, however, the situation is complicated by the fact that malaria kills hundreds of thousands of people each year and impacts heavily on the socio-economic health of the continent. There are therefore moves to begin a new campaign of DDT spraying, but this remains controversial.

Accommodation in Kruger

There is a wide variety of accommodation options available in the KNP, ranging from camping to bungalows to luxury lodges. Apart from the concession lodges, all overnight facilities are operated by SANParks. These rest camps are generally comfortable but basic, and have been developed to blend into the rustic, natural environment.

At the SAN Park rest camps:
- All bookings (except for the concession lodges) can be made through SANParks Central Reservations (012 428 9111 / 082 233 9111) or their website: www.sanparks.org
- All accommodation, ablution and kitchen facilities are serviced by cleaning staff on a daily basis.
- Vehicle fuel is available at all the main rest camps in Kruger (credit cards are now generally accepted for fuel purchases).
- Bedding is supplied in all overnight accommodation. Campers, however, need to be self-sufficient.
- Cooking utensils, stoves and refrigeration facilities are provided in most accommodation units. Exceptions will be indicated when booking.
- For the purposes of tariff information, 'Adult' is 12 years or above, 'Child' is 2-11 years, and kids under 2 years stay free.
- A charge of 1% will be added to all accommodation or activity costs for the Community Fund.

Main Rest Camps and Satellite Camps

The major rest camps are the cities of the KNP. Although specifics differ slightly, they all have a full range of tourist facilities and activities, a variety of accommodation options from camping to guest houses, and a central dining/viewing/retail area. Many also have information centres and holiday programmes for kids.

Satellite Camps have more limited facilities (no shop, no restaurant) but they do usually have a communal kitchen, ablutions and other basics for camping.

Balule (satellite)

Originally the only camp where 'non-white' people could stay, Balule is one of the most rustic camps in the park. There is no shop, no electricity and no restaurant, so guests have to be entirely self-sufficient (although lanterns are provided). This disconnection makes the camp peaceful and untouched, and it is now one of the most sought-after camps in the park. The camp is also very small and the surrounding bush is always visible through the thin game fence, so it really feels like you are part of the park. There are only a couple of basic rondawels in the camp, but it is very popular with caravaners and campers.

The name is an abbreviation of 'rimbalule', the original Tsonga name for the Olifants river, but the meaning of this name is now lost. To add to the confusion, the camp was originally known as Olifants, but that name was transferred to the new 'white' rest camp that was built on the other side of the river in 1961.

The camp is also the site of the old Balule pontoon that ferried vehicles and people across the river before the causeway was constructed. The location of the pont is marked by a memorial plaque that contains a good deal of illuminating historical background.

Berg-en-Dal

Berg-en-Dal is a relatively modern camp, established in the early 1980s. Instead of the traditional round rondawels, accommodation is in large, square, face-brick structures. These may lack the character of the older units, but they are certainly more spacious. They are also redolent with the utilitarian aesthetic of the old *vakansie oorde* (government-affiliated vacation resorts) that so characterised the Nationalist regime.

The camp is also unusual because has a mountainous setting. This makes for beautiful views and attractive drives, but it does impact on the density of game. Nevertheless, Berg-en-Dal (meaning 'Hill and Dale') is very attractive, with lush lawns and a profusion of plant life.

Another attraction is the Rhino Perimeter Trail – an interpretive walking trail that runs along the inside of the perimeter fence. The first section of the trail is wheelchair friendly and part of the trail caters for the visually impaired with Braille info boards.

Crocodile Bridge

Crocodile Bridge is a small rest camp located on the south-eastern border of the park. It is located close to the crumbling railway bridge that used to span the Crocodile River as part of the Selati railway line. The name of the river is a direct translation of the indigenous appellation (Mokwena to the Sotho and Ngwenya to the Swazi and Tsonga) which suggests that the water has always been teeming with crocs.

The camp is situated right next to the entrance gate, so it is a good place to stay if you are going to arrive late in the day. The gate is reached via a low-level causeway over the river, which offers attractive views across the wide watercourse. On one occasion, I had just crossed the river and was approaching the camp when a large elephant burst out of the bushes and nearly collided with my car. I'm not sure who was more surprised, but it was probably not the elephant.

You should also check out the Hippo Pool, located a short distance off the main road on the banks of the river. It offers visitors the opportunity to get a close-up look at hippos and other water life. A ranger might be in attendance to guide you to the river and to the nearby rock art site, but you may not leave your vehicle unless the ranger is present.

Letaba

Situated on a sweeping bend of the Letaba River (meaning 'river of sand'), this is a very worthwhile camp to visit. The famous Letaba lawns are green and inviting, and the vegetation is decidedly tropical. Although there are quite a few huts in Letaba, it doesn't feel cramped and the whole place has a laid-back atmosphere that really appeals. The central restaurant area overlooks the sandy riverbed and is an excellent location for game viewing. The short riverside interpretive trail is also very appealing.

Letaba is best known for its elephant population, which thrive in the surrounding mopane veld. The wonderful Elephant Hall museum, located in the camp, is the best place in the KNP to learn about these ponderous pachyderms, and you'll be amazed by the full-size elephant skeletons on display, including the remains of the 'Magnificent Seven'. And check out those weird bat-houses, built on top of tall poles to stop the little critters from nesting in the rondawels' roofs.

Lower Sabie

A very popular camp, Lower Sabie has a spectacular location on the banks of the Sabie River, about 43km downstream (east) from Skukuza. The central restaurant and viewing platform has a terrific view of the river and weir, and sunsets over the water are miraculous. The name of the river is derived from the Swazi word 'sabisa', which means 'to be careful'. The precise reason why people were told to be cautious when crossing the river remains unclear, but the sentiment was probably entirely justified.

Lower Sabie is a large camp with all the facilities you could need. Rondawels are well spread out and many face the perimeter fence for extended views into the bush. It is well regarded for the density of the game.

With a great location plus several large dams and view sites in the area, Lower Sabie is one of the most popular camps in the park.

Malelane (satellite)

A very small camp, located right on the southern border of the KNP, Malelane is more of a stop-over than a destination. If you are going to arrive late, this is a good place to book your first night as it is very close to the entrance gate. Unfortunately, it is built right on the Crocodile River and the unmistakable signs of civilisation on the far bank are clearly visible through the perimeter fence.

With only a couple of rondawels and a comfortable camping area, this is a low-key camp that offers a peaceful and intimate atmosphere. It is also one of the earliest tourist camps in the KNP and, although it has been greatly reduced in size, a restored tourist hut from the bygone days remains as a reminder of the site's illustrious past. The name is derived from a Swazi regiment of warriors (Malalane) who guarded the river on behalf of their king, Mswati II.

Mopani

Like Berg-en-Dal in the South, Mopani is a relatively recent camp (only completed in 1991) which eschews the old rondawel idiom in favour of square, face-brick constructions. This makes the accommodation spacious but somewhat bland. The lack of atmosphere is more than compensated by the excellent location on the banks of the Pioneer Dam, with lovely views out over the water. The camp is named after the Mopani tree *(Colophospermum mopane)*, which is very common in the area.

The Tropic of Capricorn is also a short drive away from the camp, on the parallel of latitude at 23° south of the equator. This is the southern boundary of the tropics and it marks the farthest point south at which the sun can be seen directly overhead at noon. It might not be the Greenwich Meridian, but it is a nice photo opportunity.

Olifants

Renowned for its wonderful view, Olifants is located high on the crest of ridge overlooking the Olifants River. The huts are arranged in terraces, centred around the central lookout deck and restaurant area. Although the accommodation is rather old-fashioned, the views more than make up for it. Olifants also offers several unusual activities, such as mountain bike trails and astronomy game drives. It's also famous for its aloes.

Sadly, Olifants has had a somewhat difficult past. The camp has been damaged by fire twice, in 1960 and in 1972, and has been rebuilt several times.

Orpen (with satellites Maroela and Tamboti)

Orpen is a small rest camp, located very close to the Orpen Gate. It is not a particularly inspiring setting, but it is convenient if you're going to arrive late. The camp is named after a generous couple, James and Eileen Orpen, who donated a total of eight farms to the KNP in order to expand the park's western border.

Characterised by scattered trees and wide-open plains, the Orpen area is covered by sweet grass which attracts many browsers, and their predators (including cheetah, lion and leopard). Elephant, rhino, buffalo, wild dog, zebra and giraffe are also common in this area.

And don't forget to pop into the Rabelais Hut – an old entrance gate that has been converted into a small museum documenting the park's early days.

Orpen rest camp is also the check-in point for two satellite camps: Maroela and Tamboti. There are no shops or restaurants at either of these tiny bush camps, so you need to be entirely self-sufficient, but they are deeply integrated into their surroundings for a truly immersive bush experience. And they both overlook the Timbavati River (derived from the Tsonga term 'ku bava', which translates as 'bitter or brackish water').

Maroela has no permanent accommodation structures and is only suitable for campers or caravanners. It's named after the Marula tree *(Sclerocarya birrea)*. Tamboti (named after the semi-poisonous Tamboti tree, *Spirostachys africana)* has permanent safari tents, a central boma and an in-camp bird hide. It is also very popular with Kruger cognoscenti, so book well ahead.

Pretoriuskop

The oldest tourist camp in the KNP (established in 1928), Pretoriuskop is set in a dramatic landscape, studded with enormous granite domes. It's an excellent 'beginners' camp for newbies to the park, as it is close to Joburg and offers lots of activities.

Although it contains a large number of huts, Pretoriuskop is nicely spread out across expansive lawns, with numerous tall trees and colourful bushes. Many of these plants are exotic, planted back in the days when the drive for indigenous vegetation was less fervent. Despite the current drive to remove all alien species from the KNP, the vegetation at Pretoriuskop was allowed to remain for nostalgic reasons and because it was deemed to be non-invasive.

The camp has all the usual facilities: restaurant, take-away, shop, open-air cinema, petrol, etc. When I was there, the shop had a particularly good selection of children's books and games, which indicates that it is popular with families. However, it is not situated close to water and there is no significant view site within the camp.

The mountainous scenery around the camp is distinctive and unusual, however. The granite outcrops form large bulbous hills and the roads around Pretoriuskop loop around these mammoth globs of stone, offering great views. Many of the roads, which were originally laid out by ranger Harry Wolhuter, are quite short and don't stray too far from the rest camp. This makes them ideal for quick game drives, which can be useful if you are travelling with young children or impatient adults.

The camp is situated at an altitude of 500m, which is quite high for the KNP. This means that the climate is milder in summer and the threat of malaria is somewhat reduced.

The camp is named after Pretoriuskop hill, located about 2.5km west of the rest camp. This 'peak' was named after a member of Carel Trichardt's Voortrekker expedition of 1848, who apparently died *en route* and was buried here by Joao Albasini. You'll find a small plaque alongside the Napi Road (H1-1), close to the Numbi gate, which identifies the grave of the unfortunate Pretorius. The grave itself is located a short distance off the road and, if you look carefully, you can just see the little gravestone, rather forlorn and lost, poking out of the long grass.

The camp also has the Sable Trail – an interpretive walk that leads around the inside perimeter of the rest camp – and a great swimming pool (built many years ago with corporate sponsorship from the Rembrandt Foundation). The pool incorporates a large granite boulder and kids will enjoy clambering over this natural water feature.

And don't forget to drive The Voortrekker Road – an old transport route from the days of the transport riders, which includes interesting historical sites including several 'Jock of the Bushveld' landmarks and Ship Mountain, a prominent geographical feature that is supposed to look like the upturned hull of a ship.

Punda Maria

One of the KNP's older rest camps, Punda Maria is a compact little site built on the slopes of a hill, offering nice views out over the undulating landscape. The camp was named by a former ranger, J.J. 'Ou Kat' Coetser, who corrupted the Swahili term 'punda milia' (Swahili for 'striped donkey' or zebra) into Punda Maria, in honour of his wife who had a striped dress. JSH, reportedly, wasn't a fan of the 'gasbag' Coetser, who was dismissed for shooting animals and eventually killed by an elephant.

Although the accommodation is somewhat basic and a little bit cramped, it does have a sparkling swimming pool and offers guests an opportunity to explore the wild and wonderful far-north of the KNP. The Sandveld eco-system around the camp is known as the 'botanical garden' of the KNP because of its remarkable bio-diversity. Fever trees, ilala palms and statuesque baobab trees are particularly abundant.

Guided tours to the fascinating Thulamela Archaeological Site, which has links to Mapungubwe and Great Zimbabwe, depart from Punda Maria. History buffs should also check out Crooks' Corner. Once the haunt of hunters, smugglers and other ne'er-do-wells, the remote site now offers visitors a terrific view over the wide, sandy flood-plain of the Limpopo River. And keep an eye out for Baobab Hill - a KNP heritage site, this distinctive hill was the first stop on the Wenela labour route through the KNP.

Satara

Satara is a busy camp, and not without reason. It is situated in an excellent game viewing area characterised by open, flat plains. The knobthorn veld around the camp is ideal for grazing and attracts large herds of herbivores, along with their predators.

The camp itself is large, but all the rondawels are set out in a series of circles, so it never becomes claustrophobic. The camp is not near water, but there are lots of trees and prolific bird-life. It has all the usual facilities, including a refreshing swimming pool.

It is a very old camp, originally built in 1928, and its name is derived from the Hindi term 'satrah' (meaning 'seventeen'). This rather obscure etymology is somewhat explained by the fact the original surveyor of the land, W.H. Gilfillan, had an Indian assistant. Lloyd's Grave, the final resting place of the first Satara ranger, is located inside the camp.

I should also mention the elephants who often frequent the area - especially the Nwanetsi water hole, situated adjacent to the H7 towards Orpen Gate. This medium-sized reservoir is close to the road and, if you're lucky, you'll see a herd or two cavorting in the cool, buoyant water. I spent more than an hour here, unable to take my eyes off the joyous sight of half a dozen elephants splashing about and wrestling with each other in a genuine expression of joy. A particularly big baobab is also located close-by, down a short gravel road.

Shingwedzi

Shingwedzi is a relatively large and dusty camp, built along the bank of the eponymous river. It is spacious and rustic, offering guests an unfussy and authentic KNP experience. It is one of the best places from which to explore the rugged and remote far-north of the KNP.

The camp was established in the mid-1930s and its name comes from the Tsonga term 'ngwetse', which inexplicably translates as 'the sound of metal objects rubbing against each other'.

Skukuza

Skukuza is the KNP's capital city. It is the largest rest camp and the park's administrative headquarters. Nicely situated on the southern banks of the Sabie

River, this is the same site where the long-serving warder of the park, James Stevenson-Hamilton, established his main base camp. Indeed, the name 'Skukuza' is a corruption of the Zulu 'sikhukhuza', meaning 'he who sweeps or scrapes clean', which was Stevenson-Hamilton's nickname among the local people.

In addition to the usual amenities, Skukuza also has a post office, a bank, an ATM, a landing strip, a golf course, an extensive research library, a museum, wildlife displays and a delightful indigenous nursery. Although many Kruger nuts eschew Skukuza as too big and too noisy, it is a practical and popular overnight destination with good game viewing opportunities.

The central restaurant and retail area is built along the river bank and wooden walkways give visitors the chance to promenade along the Sabie. The disused Selati railway bridge straddles the river and enhances the scene. All in all, Skukuza is a (comparatively) bustling and attractive rest camp that should satisfy all members of the family.

A large and well-equipped day visitor centre and swimming pool has been built a short distance downstream from the rest camp.

Other attractions include the Stevenson Hamilton Memorial Library, which contains a large collection of literature on the KNP, as well as some interesting display cases detailing the park's early history. There's also the somewhat melancholy animal graveyard – the final resting place for many of the dogs, horses and other animals who served with distinction in the KNP. Sadly, the Selati Restaurant, housed in a restored steam engine with carriages, is currently defunct.

The area around Skukuza has several memorial plaques and tablets embedded in the distinctive boulders dotted around the place. These honour the founding of the park, as well as several founding members of the Parks Board. Joe Ludorf's plaque can be found on the H1-1, between Pretoriuskop and Skukuza, the Orpen plaque and the Kruger Tablets are located on the H1-2, between Skukuza and Tshokwane picnic site. And the Stevenson Hamilton Memorial on Shirimantanga boulder marks the place where the ashes of James Stevenson-Hamilton were scattered after his death in 1957. When I was there, the memorial plaque affixed to the bottom of the boulder was missing. The view from the top of the boulder, however, is marvellous. Another great viewpoint is Grano Hill, located on the H1-1, which overlooks the rolling bushveld plains.

Tzendze Camp Site
Tsendze Rustic Camping site is situated close to Mopani Rest Camp. Its development was based on a philosophy that one should 'touch the earth lightly', and the campsites are carefully laid out between the ancient trees. The name

comes from the Tsonga term 'tsendzeleka' which, rather charmingly, translates as 'to ramble around like someone lost in the bush'.

Bush Camps

Bush camps are smaller, more remote rest camps with accommodation in simple, rustic structures that blend in with the environment. They don't have shops or restaurants, and electricity may be limited. But the units do have an equipped kitchen, private toilets, an open veranda and game drives can be arranged. Access to all bushveld camps is restricted to overnight visitors, so it's very private.

- Bateleur
- Biyamiti
- Shimuwini
- Sirheni
- Talamati

Bush Lodges

A bush lodge is a private lodge that can only be booked out as a single unit. Designed for families or larger groups, the lodge has an equipped kitchen, several bedrooms, bathrooms and braai facilities. There are no shops or restaurant facilities – check in is at the nearest main camp reception.

- Boulders (nearest camp is Mopani)
- Roodewal (nearest camp is Satara)
- Pafuri Border Camp (nearest camp is Punda Maria)

Concession Lodges

An important part of the KNP's revenue stream is the income generated from private concession areas. These are large pieces of land within the KNP that are contracted out to private companies for a predetermined number of years. The concession holders then have the right to build a lodge, which tend to be of the expensive and luxurious kind. Concessionaires also have exclusive use of the game-viewing roads in the concession area, as these are closed off to the general public.

Within these exclusive enclaves, five-star lodges flourish and those lucky few who are able to pay the hefty tariffs will be able to enjoy the finest in food, wildlife and service in comfortable seclusion. All concession lodges offer game drives, walks and other activities, as guided by expert rangers.

- Imbali Safari Lodges
- Jock Safari Lodge
- Lukimbi Safari Lodge
- Rhino Walking Safaris
- Shishangeni Private Lodge
- Singita Lubombo Private Game Lodge
- Lion Sands Kruger (including Tinga and Narina lodges)
- The Outpost (Makuleke Concession Park)
- Pafuri Camp (Makuleke Concession Park)

Overnight Hides

If you want to try something different, why not spend a night or two at a waterside bird hide? During the day, these facilities are open to the public, but book it for the evening and you'll have the run of the place; basking in the moonlit spectacle of the Kruger at night.

Facilities are pretty basic – a fold-down bed base and mattress are supplied, along with an 'environmental toilet'. Bedding kits are available at the reception, or bring your own. You also need to bring all your own food, wood, water, cooking utensils and equipment. A boma with braai facilities is available for overnighters (gas braais are not permitted), but there is no electricity so bring your own lights. And don't leave the enclosure at night. It's wild out there!

The hides must be reserved in their entirety and accommodate a minimum of 2 people, up to a maximum of 9.

- Sable (reception at Phalaborwa Gate)
- Shipandani (reception at Mopani)

Sable is particularly enticing, located on one of the largest public dams in the central region of the park, with a capacity of 221 mega litres and a catchment area of 1900 ha. It was built as part of the Kruger National Park Tar Road project during the 1970s. The Dam supplied water to the construction teams who were working on the tar road between Phalaborwa Gate and Letaba rest camp. Construction of the dam began on the 5 September 1972 and was finished in the same month.

Camping and Caravans

Most rest camps have a number of sites suitable for tents, caravans or motorhomes. Campsites usually have power points available for those who want to plug in. Communal ablution blocks and cooking facilities are also provided. Campers will need to bring along all their own cooking utensils, cutlery, sleeping equipment etc.

Eating in Kruger

In the past, the quality of the catering inside the park varied greatly. Then they tried the concession approach, where one company had the contract to run just about every restaurant, café and picnic spot in Kruger. The result was standardisation, but often at the expense of culinary excitement.

Now, as part of their Commercialisation as Conservation strategy, a variety of vendors have been given licenses to operate the various restaurants and take-away joints, located in rest camps through the park. Current operators include South African stalwarts such as Mugg and Bean, Wimpy and Cattle Baron, as well as several independents.

Depending on the size of the rest camp, catering options range from budget delis and take-aways to upmarket restaurants – often featuring an evening buffet. Eating out is not your only choice, however. If you are staying in the park for any length of time, it's a good idea to bring along your own supplies so that you can prepare a few home-cooked meals for yourself. All accommodation is self-catering, with suitable kitchen facilities and cooking utensils supplied, and all the rest camps have well-stocked shops where you can buy any additional supplies that you might need.

In fact, everyone who visits the KNP should indulge in that quintessentially South African pastime – the braai. So, stock up on some boerewors, grab your tongs and enjoy your very own barbeque under the stars. You'll find yourself in good company. Every night, like clockwork, dozens of fires ignite across the rest camp lawns, as beers are pulled from the fridge and the smell of smoke and braaivleis (grilled meat) fill the air. It's an integral part of Kruger Culture, so get involved.

As a side note: vegetarians might struggle a bit in the park because, for some reason, restaurants in conservation areas feel compelled to serve huge hunks of animal flesh to their voracious patrons. Diners, for their part, usually respond in kind by demonstrating an insatiable desire for meat after a busy day of game spotting. The irony of the game reserve buffet, where visitors gleefully devour the same game species they spent the day admiring, seems to escape everyone. Perhaps it's a matter of becoming a predator by proxy.

Activities in Kruger

Drive Yourself Wild

Be warned, the KNP can make people go crazy. I mean it. The game reserve has a strange power which transforms normally mild-mannered accountants into binocular-bearing, bird bothering boffins! Nice, respectable German tourists just have to enter the Lowveld and they become blood-ravening beasts, baying for a lion kill. While formerly considerate husbands and mothers often force the entire family to sit in a hot car for hours, waiting for a wild dog at a water hole.

Yes, game spotting can become an obsession. If you don't believe me, just witness the queue of cars that line up inside the camp gates every morning, waiting for opening time. I know of several people who wake up hours before the sun rises so that they can be the very first in line, as if they are trying to buy tickets for a big rock concert. Then, as soon as the gates are flung open, they race out into the murky dawn with their guide books at the ready, hoping to be the first to spot that elusive cheetah.

Now, before we go any further, I have a confession to make. I was not always a huge fan of the Kruger Park. I mean, I like animals and I support just about every conservation initiative. But, for me, the Kruger was kinda like a 24-hour convenience store: I don't really need milk at three in the morning, but I'm glad to know that the facility is there, just in case.

In the course of researching the book, however, I have changed my mind somewhat. Like so many others before me, I have now been bewitched by the solitude, silence and complexity of this natural wonderland. The susurrations of wind through the acacia leaves have become music to my hurried, harried urban ears. The hot, still, timeless afternoons are a balm to my frazzled city nerves. I've even come to enjoy the hours of driving around, looking for game (which, by the way, hate me and hide away whenever I approach).

So, I'm a Kruger convert (relatively speaking). I now find game drives to be therapeutic and enchanting, as I relax, breathe deeply, and try to appreciate everything from trees, to birds, to scenery, to grass, to insects.

As I've briefly mentioned, I am not a very lucky game spotter. Perhaps it's my innate impatience, or the fact that I simply cannot wake up early enough to catch the dawn procession. But, whatever the reason, the only things I tend to see are ABI (Another Bloody Impala), giraffe, waterbuck, zebra, the ubiquitous elephant, grumpy buffalo and the odd rhino. Nevertheless, the promise of spotting a rare wild dog, lazy lion, reclusive leopard or shadowy cheetah is tantalising enough to keep me motivated – after all, who knows what lies in wait around the bend...

To give you an idea of just how unpredictable game spotting can be, allow me to recount one remarkable spot. It occurred after a 5-day research trip to the park, during which I had seen nothing but the usual suspects. I was, in fact, thoroughly fed up and quite ready to head home. With this in mind, I gratefully left Skukuza rest camp and headed out on the busy main road towards Kruger gate.

It was a beautiful late afternoon. The sun was setting directly in front of me, hanging low and red in the sky. I hunkered down and prepared myself for the long drive home. Then, just a few hundred metres outside Skukuza gate, I saw a strange shape walking across the road. It was strongly silhouetted against the flaming sky and it took me a couple of moments to realise that it was a leopard.

In the time it took me to pick my jaw off the floor and reach for my camera, the stealthy predator had loped across the roadway and crept into the grassy verge. I slowly pulled up alongside the big cat and watched as it crouched in the long grass. The leopard paid me no mind as it was intently monitoring two unsuspecting Red hartebeest who were happily grazing close to the Skukuza fence.

For the next 15 minutes, nothing happened. The leopard lay in wait, poised but patient, while dozens of cars sped past on the road above. Both my fellow motorists and the hartebeest were totally unaware of the drama that was playing out just inches from the thoroughfare. Then, in a flash, the leopard bolted from its hiding place and charged the hapless antelope. In a flurry of fur and fangs, the leopard and its prey dashed off into the trees. I couldn't see the kill, but I could hear an ominous series of crashes and cracks as the animals smashed their way through the bush.

After that little performance, I felt totally energised. Despite my previous avowal that I had had more than enough of the KNP, I was now ready to turn around and spend another week in the reserve, hoping to repeat the experience. All in all, it was a most gratifying end to my trip and a tacit lesson that, no matter how carefully you plan your visit, sometimes you just have to be in the right place at the right time.

Some common hand-signals used in the KNP (that I just made up):
- *Palms up:* 'Seen any lion?'
- *Shrugging of shoulders:* 'I haven't seen any lion'
- *Pointing:* 'Shut up and look there!'
- *Shaking of fist:* 'Slow down, this isn't Joburg'
- *Hand outstretched on the forehead:* 'I've left my sunglasses at home'
- *Lazy wave:* 'Lekker, hey?'
- *Slap on forehead:* 'Why have they stopped? There's nothing there! Must be Birders.'

Birding

If the fanatical game spotters are a bunch of loonies, then the bird watchers are even worse. They can spend an entire day driving ever-so-slowly through the reserve with their binoculars pointed to the sky, trying to catch sight of the lesser-spotted twitterfinch, or something like that.

Over-eager birders, also known as 'twitchers', will have a field day in the KNP, with over 500 local and migrant species having been recorded in the reserve. So, if you are looking to get some 'mega-ticks' or some 'lifers', bring along the bird book and hit the road. I have been assured by several avi-tourism experts that you will not be disappointed.

Speaking for myself, however, I don't get it. The only birds I can identify are the ostrich, the pigeon and the African hornbill; all the others are just a mystifying collection of feathers, wings and chirpy noises. Nevertheless, if you are interested in learning more about birding, there are several excellent books on the subject and well-informed guides can be hired to escort you through the reserve.

Bird and Game Hides in Kruger

There are about a dozen bird/game-viewing hides in Kruger National Park and several more are earmarked for construction if sufficient funds become available. There are also in-camp hides at Bateleur, Punda Maria, Sirheni, Talamati and Tamboti. Private hides have been built at Letaba for the exclusive use of guests at the Fish Eagle Guest House, and at Shingwedzi for visitors staying at Rentmeester Guest House.

The hides are usually situated on a river bank or alongside a waterhole, and this means that almost anything can turn up during the course of the day. Hippo and crocodile are resident at most hides, as are large selection of water birds such as herons, fish eagles, storks, kingfishers and crakes. Leopard sightings are also quite common, so pack a lunch and spend some time secreted away in one of the hides. You'll be amazed at how much you can see if you stand still for a while.

There are no toilets at most of the hides, so do the necessary evacuations before you leave the camp. If you find yourself in a spot of bother, don't panic because most of the hides are located close to rest camps or picnic sites, where you'll find the necessary ablution facilities.

Most of the hides are designed to be accessible to people in wheelchairs, but some of the older hides were built before this became a consideration. In particular, Kanniedood is situated up a ladder, while people with mobility difficulties may require assistance at Lake Panic and Matambeni.

If you are going to enter a hide, please be aware of proper hide etiquette. Remain as quiet as possible when exiting your vehicle and walking towards the hide. Do not walk outside the enclosed area and do not approach the waters' edge. Remember that this is a Big Five Reserve and there is always the danger of predators in the area. Game rangers also do regular patrols of the Bird Hides to ensure that these rules are enforced.

Once inside the hide, keep your voice as low as possible as any kind of commotion could scatter the birds and game, much to the consternation of your fellow hidees. Conversation should be kept to a minimum and don't drop things on the wooden floors or else you might get aggressively shushed!

Photography is a popular activity at the hides, so bring along your camera and zoom lens and get in on the action. However, you might want to prepare yourself for a bit of lens-envy, as some of the pros have enormous equipment.

Game Drives

Looking for game by yourself is all well and good, but the expert eye of a trained ranger will definitely enhance your chances of spotting something. All the KNP camps offer morning and evening game drives, and these are highly recommended. The evening game drives are particularly memorable because they are the only way to witness the nocturnal life of the park. Private cars are not allowed outside the rest camps after sunset.

Game drives are conducted on board 10-seater or 22-seater game drive vehicles in the company of an experienced and armed guide. Morning drives leave at around 04:30 in summer and 05:30 in winter. Night drives leave from reception between 17:00 and 19:00. Drives usually lasts between 3-4 hours. All-day drives are available on request, where guests can hire a vehicle and driver for the entire day.

Guests should wear comfortable clothing on the game drives, and it is recommended that you dress in layers. Things can get pretty cold in the back of the open vehicle, especially in the early morning and at night. Blankets are usually provided, but bring along a warm jacket or jersey – and maybe something fortifying in a thermos. You'll also want to bring along your camera and binoculars. The viewing vehicles are usually equipped with several hand-held spot lights, so guests can contribute to the night drive experience by shining lights into animals' eyes as they pass.

Drives can be booked through central reservations or at the rest camp's reception office. Costs are between R300 to R400 per adult and half-off for kids.

Bush Braais

A nice twist to the standard game drive, Bush Braais take guests to 'an open area filled with burning lanterns where, whilst listening to the sounds of the bushveld and the distant animals calling, the food is grilled on open fires'. After your meal (with a cash bar) there's another short game drive back to the rest camp. Enquire at the rest camp reception if this activity is on offer.

Astronomy Game Drives

For a night drive with a difference, try out this exciting new activity available at Olifants Camp. The experience starts with a late afternoon guided game drive in an open safari vehicle to Nwamanzi Lookout Point on the banks of the Olifants River, where you'll be treated to drinks and snacks. This is followed by a talk on stars, planets and African folklore, while the guide points out celestial objects which are visible that evening. Guests then have the opportunity to view the night sky through a telescope. The total duration of the experience is 3 hours and guests should confirm departure times and availability at Olifants Camp Reception.

Tree Spotting

Yes, tree spotting is definitely a thing and there are several guide books to prove it. And, unlike birds or animals, trees stay put so you'll always know where to find them. While the KNP is awash with many different tree species, here is a quick intro to two of the park's most iconic specimens.

Baobabs

The iconic baobab tree *(Adansonia digitata)* is found throughout the Lowveld, starting around the Tropic of Capricorn and moving northwards. It is an amazing and unmistakable botanical life form, growing up to 30 metres tall with an expansive circumference of 10 metres or more.

The species was first described by Adanson, a French botanist, who studied them on the Cape Verde islands. While we only have one species of baobab in Africa *(digitata)*, there are actually eight species of *Adansonia* – six of which are found in Madagascar and one in Australia.

Baobabs begin life as a curious, smooth-barked sprout with a bulbous bottom and narrow neck. As they grow, they store considerable amounts of water in their trunks, which causes the trees to swell and buckle as they mature. The bark also develops many knots and ripples, and reminds me of an elephant's rough hide. Many of the older baobabs eventually develop a hollow centre, which are often large enough to offer animals and even humans a shady refuge on a hot day. There's even one tree in Limpopo Province that functioned as a novelty saloon in the gold mining days.

Their great size suggests great age, but there is some disagreement about how slow a baobab grows. Most people assert that they grow slowly and can reach an age of several thousand years. Others dispute this and claim that they are much younger than they look. However, unlike most trees, baobabs do not form annual growth rings, so botanists will just have to keep a close watch.

Baobabs are deciduous trees, which lose all their leaves in winter. This reveals a mass of angular branches that reach out to the sky in an arthritic embrace. The distinctive shape of these denuded branches has given the baobab one of its nicknames: the upside-down tree, so called because it looks like the tree has been flipped on its head, with the roots sticking up into the sky.

Just about every part of the baobab can be utilised by humans. The leaves can be boiled and eaten. The pollen of the flowers can be made into a kind of glue. The wood can be used to make rope or paper. Medical unguents and remedies can be concocted. Even the seeds can be sucked for flavour or ground into a palatable coffee (apparently).

The fruit pod also contains tartaric acid, which can be collected and made into a yoghurty, sherbet-like dessert. This is the source of the Afrikaans name for the tree: *kremetert,* which I foolishly thought meant 'Cream tart' but actually translates as 'cream of tartar'. In other parts of the world, the baobab is also known as the Monkey-bread tree and the Sour-gourd tree.

The Shepherd's Tree

The Shepherd's Tree *(Boscia albitrunca)* is a relatively common evergreen species that is found throughout the KNP region. It gets its name because it is a favourite resting place for local folk who are tending their herds. Their choice is a good one as the tree has thin leaves, which offer shade while still letting the breeze blow through. The components of the Shepherd's tree also have several medicinal properties.

Apart from its practical uses, the tree has considerable social significance. It is renowned as a tree of reconciliation. So, when there's a problem in the village, people take a branch from the Shepherd's Tree and place it in the middle of the meeting to help them find a resolution to the conflict. Perhaps we should plant a Shepherd's Tree in the middle of parliament!

Guided Walks

There's no better way to experience the bush than to walk through it. The crisp bite of a morning breeze, the subtle smell of the grass, the delicious threat of lions lurking in the underbrush; it's an invigorating and enlightening experience. All walks are guided by two armed rangers, who will both protect you and interpret the bush as you walk.

With untamed nature in such close proximity, these little strolls can become quite thrilling. One time, when I was on an early morning walk, we heard lions roaring close by. Our ranger got us all to settle down and we carefully went off in search of the beast. With hearts beating fast, we stalked our prey, hoping that the tables wouldn't be turned on us. We continued creeping through the bush for some time, but we didn't find anything. I'm sure that any lion worth its salt would have heard us stomping through the veld from a mile away. But it was terribly exciting.

Daily early morning and afternoon guided walks are available from most camps and depart from reception. A maximum of 8 people can be accommodated on each trail. The walk itself is relaxed and is suitable for anyone with a moderate degree of fitness. Guests should wear comfortable walking shoes or boots, and clothing applicable to the prevailing weather conditions. You should also bring your own cameras and/or binoculars. No children under 13 are allowed. Appropriate accommodation must be booked for the previous/upcoming night at the camp from where you'll be departing.

Typically, trails last between 3 and 4 hours. The cost is currently between R400 and R500 per person.

Wilderness and Backpack Trails

There's nothing quite like hiking through the untamed bushveld. In addition to the short day-walks mentioned above, the KNP offers a variety of guided multi-day walking trails. Wilderness trails are three-night excursions that include wholesome meals, bedding and accommodation in basic hiking cabins or tents. Backpack trails are more rustic affairs where walkers have to bring all their own food and equipment.

Wilderness trails currently cost between R4150 and R4500 per person, while backpack trails cost between R2450 and R2700 per person.

4x4 Eco Trails

There are several tempting 4x4 self-drive trails in the KNP. These give you the opportunity to explore areas that are generally inaccessible to the public. The trails are designed primarily as nature experiences and not as extreme off-road adventures. In fact, a 4x4 is required mainly to reduce environmental impact, and not because the roads are bad. Some riverbeds and dongas will have to be negotiated, however. The trails are weather sensitive and may not be operational during the wet season.

All the trails are led by an experienced guide, and each vehicle must be fully equipped with tent, water, food, cooking equipment, etc. The eco-trails range from a short overnight excursion to a 5 night, 500km expedition along the Lubombo

Mountains. The cost ranges from R1250 and R9000 per vehicle (max. 4 occupants).

Mountain Bike Trails

One of the latest adventure activities on offer in the KNP is mountain biking. Now, I can't stand any form of bicycle – they make my bum sore, and one of them tried to kill me once. But if that's your thing, Olifants has guided trails available and they include backpacks, water bottles, helmets (compulsory), snacks and juice. The cost is around R715 if you bring your own bike, and R965 if you want them to supply a bike.

Golf

It's not the first thing you think of doing when you visit the game reserve, but you can indeed play golf in the KNP. And a very pretty course it is too. Set amid lush indigenous trees, this nine hole/18-tee golf course gives golfers the unique opportunity to play a round in the middle of Big Five country. It's a 'close-to-nature golf experience', complete with a family of warthogs who totter around the greens. The course is a Par 72, and is 5950m (6450 yards) for men and 5059m (5480 yards) for women.

Built in 1972, the golf course was originally intended as a recreational facility for Skukuza personnel who lived at the nearby staff village (a pleasant settlement with neat homes set in lush gardens). Since the course is not fenced-in, hippo, impala and baboons often invade the links, but this only adds to the excitement. Various natural water hazards have been incorporated into the course and, although it has no bunkers, the proliferation of trees around the course form formidable 'aerial bunkers'.

Tee-off times are available for visitors in the mornings between 07:00 and 11:00 from Sunday to Friday, and standard golf dress code applies. The golf course naturally has a club house and bar, which serves drinks and snacks on a pleasant veranda throughout the day. For bookings, contact the club directly.

Skukuza Indigenous Nursery and Boardwalk

In August 1975, Harry Matthysen established the Skukuza Nursery. All he had was a piece of ground 100m x 45m, 3100 plants and a single garden hose with 28 leaks. Nevertheless, his mandate was to cultivate grass and other indigenous plants, which would be used to beautify the various rest camps. He also offered advice to the resident park staff who wanted to plant indigenous plants in their own gardens.

Within a couple of years, the demand for plants was such that the nursery was opened to the public. At that time, impala lilies cost R2.00 and cycads were a princely R10.00. As the facility expanded, it became one of the largest indigenous nurseries in South Africa and it played an important role in educating the public about the benefits of indigenous plants.

In 1983, a new nursery was built next to the Skukuza staff village. The area was so dense with vegetation that Matthysen and his team were chased by three lions when they went to inspect it.

Today, the nursery is flourishing. It contains thousands of indigenous and endemic plants, and a broad selection of Lowveld species can be purchased. With the exception of cycads, all seed is collected in the Park and sent to the nursery for drying and cultivation. There are also satellite nurseries in Pretoriuskop, Malelane Gate and Letaba.

The nursery is still actively involved in a number of educational activities, and children from the surrounding areas are often taken here for environmental awareness programmes.

Furthermore, the nursery is currently concentrating on the collection and cultivation of indigenous plants with medicinal value. In collaboration with local communities and traditional healers, the nursery is working to supply samples of important plants, which can then be cultivated in their home villages. This eliminates the need for herbalists to 'poach' plants from within the reserve. The initiative is in line with the concept of sustainable utilization of natural resources as put forward by organizations like the IUCN (World Conservation Union) and the Department of Environmental Affairs and Tourism (DEAT), and was officially launched on 10 September 2004.

The latest addition to the Skukuza nursery is an elevated wooden boardwalk that was opened in September 2006. Sponsored by Working for Wetlands, the walkway has several interpretive boards which will educate visitors about the surrounding plants and vegetation.

The Skukuza nursery is located 4 km from Skukuza camp on the main Kruger Gate road, close to the Golf Club. Entrance is free and it is a delightfully shady place in which to stroll around.

Weddings and Conferences

Although beyond the scope of this book, various conference facilities are available at Skukuza, Berg-en-Dal and Shingwedzi. Smaller group-meeting rooms are available at Letaba and Bateleur.

SANParks is also open to hosting 'weddings or special family events, with unique surroundings, tranquil settings, superb facilities and enthusiastically helpful staff'. Sounds like a plan to me!

Getting There

The South / Marula Region

	Distance from Joburg	Rest Camps
Crocodile Bridge Gate	452km (via Nelspruit)	Crocodile Bridge Lower Sabie Biyamiti
Malelane Gate	406km (via Nelspruit)	Berg-en-Dal Malelane
Numbi Gate	- 391km (via Nelspruit and White River) - 432 (via Dullstroom and Hazyview)	Pretoriuskop
Phabeni Gate	- 415km (via Nelspruit and White River) - 428km (via Dullstroom and Hazyview)	Pretoriuskop Skukuza
Paul Kruger Gate	- 444km (via Nelspruit and White River) - 457km (via Dullstroom and Hazyview)	Skukuza

Places of Interest

Dullstroom

One of SA's premier trout fishing districts, the Dullstroom area has dozens of lodges and cosy cottages set amid the trout dams. If you're just passing through, the main street has a good selection of restaurants, clothes and curio shops, and quaint farm stalls that sell home-made produce.

Hazyview

A veritable boom town, Hazyview is a busy commercial centre that serves the densely populated Acornhoek / Bushbuckridge area. Recently, several strip malls have been erected to cater for visitors to the KNP and here you will find every conceivable amenity. A good place to stock up on supplies.

Kaapsehoop (Kaapschehoop)

If you want to take a detour off the beaten track, leave the N4 at the stinky paper plant called Ngodwana and drive for 13km up the mountainside to the idiosyncratic village of Kaapsehoop. Located high in the mountains, amid jagged spikes of weathered sandstone, this tiny village has only a few quirky shops and a couple of restaurants. But it is beautiful here, and you'll fall in love with the famous herd of wild horses who wander blissfully through the town.

There's also a fantastic walk through the rocks to the edge of escarpment, offering unforgettable views. From Kaapsehoop, you can return to the N4 or you can continue on the back roads to Nelspruit (about 30km).

Nelspruit

The major town in the Lowveld and provincial capital of Mpumalanga, Nelspruit is a good place to stock up on provisions. There are several new malls, supermarkets, car dealerships and even a casino on the outskirts of town, with all the trimmings.

If you have time, stroll through the tranquil National Lowveld Botanical Gardens, located close to the casino. Wooden boardwalks wind through the lush surroundings and info boards will help you identify the beautiful plants of the region. The suspension bridge over the waterfall and rapids is a particular highlight of the gardens.

Panorama Route / R532 (Graskop / God's Window / Blyde River Canyon)

If you have time, you simply must explore the Panorama Route, one of the most dramatic drives in South Africa (and one of my favourite parts of the country). Starting at the lovely town of Graskop (famous for its pancakes and African art), the Panorama runs along the edge of the eastern Drakensberg escarpment.

Stop off at the viewing points known as God's Window and Wonder View for a breathtaking lookout over the Lowveld (if the weather is clear). Next up is the spectacular Bourke's Luck Potholes, with a paved walking path and graceful bridges spanning the deep, smooth 'potholes' that were formed by the erosive rolling of rocks in the river bed.

Further along, the gaping Blyde Rivier Canyon (3rd largest in the world) demands a stop – there are several outstanding viewpoints but don't miss Three Rondawels for the most iconic vista. Additional stops can be made at the dramatic Lisbon and Berlin waterfalls, the riverside tea garden, and other historical markers (mainly dedicated the doughty Voortrekkers).

From the Blyde River Canyon, you can access Hoedspruit and the central gates, via the beautiful pass through the Abel Erasmus tunnel. Or you can re-trace your steps to Graskop and follow Kowyn's Pass down to Hazyview and the Kruger or Phabeni Gates.

Pilgrim's Rest

Another place to visit if you have the time, 'Pilgrim's' is a turn-of-the-century gold mining town that has been maintained in its original condition. All the houses date back to the gold rush period, and all the shops and restaurants have been restored to maintain the gold rush theme.

Set deep in the rugged mountains, accessed down a wonderfully twisty road, this village is a priceless place – although it's had some ups and downs of late. Don't miss the evocative Royal Hotel, the gold panning demonstrations and the eerie graveyard set high on the slopes above the town.

Sabie

Once the centre of the region's timber trade, Sabie is a pretty town set amid grand scenery. There are dozens of waterfalls in the area, which can be visited as part of a day drive. Check out the eclectic shops and restaurants on the main street. The Sabie Museum has an exhibition on the town's timber roots.

Sudwala Caves

A spectacular series of grottos, dripping with limestone formations. Located a short distance off the N4. A little over-developed, unfortunately, but great for the kids. And the adjacent dinosaur park (which I remember from my distant childhood) is still awesome.

White River

A charming little town, White River has grown from a sleepy little dorp into a booming tourist centre with dozens of tourist attractions. Don't miss the outstanding Casterbridge Centre, with dozens of interesting shops, a large activity area for kids, vintage car museum, boutique hotel, homemade chocolate shop, deli, restaurants, theatre, internet café and an art-house cinema! A number of fine-dining establishments and up-market accommodation options are also available for people who want to break their trip to the KNP with a stopover.

The Centre / Nkayeni Region

	Distance from Joburg	*Rest Camps*
Orpen Gate	- 466km (via Dullstroom and Hoedspruit) - 559km (via Polokwane and Tzaneen)	Satara Orpen Maroela Tamboti Talamati Roodewal
Phalaborwa Gate	- 497km (via Dullstroom and Hoedspruit) - 525km (via Polokwane and Tzaneen)	Olifants Balule Letaba Roodewal Shimuwini Boulders Tsendze Mopani Bateleur Shingwedzi

Places of Interest

Abel Erasmus Tunnel

A truly beautiful road that runs along a steep ravine, taking you down from the escarpment to the Lowveld plains. Stop at the large curio stall by the entrance to the short tunnel and marvel at the orange and yellow-flocked cliffs that surround you. The views up the massif from the bottom of the pass are equally staggering.

Echo Caves

Guided tours through 2km of subterranean tunnels.

Hoedspruit

This is a popular stepping off point for Kruger, with a wide selection of restaurants, curio shops, supply stores, lodges and banking facilities. It is surrounded by dozens of private game reserves and wildlife sanctuaries, including the Hoedspruit cheetah project and the Swadini reptile park.

Lydenburg (Mashishing)

A functional transit town, with all the necessary facilities. Check out the Lydenburg museum for their fascinating exhibit of the mysterious Lydenburg heads - strange terracotta masks that were created over 1000 years ago by a little-known African iron-age culture (although the original heads are at the South African Museum in Cape Town). The town's name translates as 'place of suffering' as it was established after a malaria epidemic in Andries-Ohrigstad forced the inhabitants to move here, away from the mosquitos. The town's new (friendlier) official name is Mashishing, meaning 'place of long, green grass'.

Phalaborwa

A prominent if somewhat homely mining town, known mainly for its copper, Phalaborwa has all the facilities that a tourist could wish for. A good place to stock up before plunging into the bush. The town also has lots of accommodation options for those in transit to or from the park.

The North / Nxanatseni Region

	Distance from Joburg	*Rest Camps*
Punda Maria Gate	- 553km (via Polokwane and Giyani) - 564km (via Polokwane and Louis Trichardt) - 591km (via Polokwane, Magoebaskloof and Tzaneen)	Punda Maria Shingwedzi Sirheni Bateleur
Pafuri Gate	614km (via Polokwane and Louis Trichardt)	Makuleke Concession Lodges (The Outpost and Pafuri Lodge)

Places of Interest

Leydsdorp
A once-flourishing gold mining town, Leydsdorp went bust after the Witwatersrand gold fields were discovered. It is now a ghost town and the remaining buildings were converted into an idiosyncratic lodge offering a (very) quiet and remote vacation experience. The fate of the lodge is now unclear, but you can check out the nearby hollow Baobab tree, which was used as a bar back in the gold mining days.

Louis Trichardt (Makhado)
An up-and-coming market town, Louis Trichardt is a good place to get lunch or supplies. Main access point to explore the Soutpansberg.

Magoebaskloof / Haenertsburg
A beautiful mountain pass through lush indigenous forests, Magoebaskloof is a delightful drive. Start by exploring the adorable town of Haenertsburg, located at the top of the pass, and take time to stop at all the farm stalls and restaurants on the way down. You can also explore George's Valley, a parallel road down to Tzaneen. The Zion Christian Church's mammoth headquarters at Moria is close by and the road can be VERY busy over the Easter weekend. If you have the time, take the detour to Duiwelskloof and wander through the legendary Queen Modjadji's cycad reserve.

Musina (Messina)
The most northerly town in South Africa, Musina is located just a few kilometres south of the Beit Bridge border post with Zimbabwe. As such, the town is a major

transit stop for cross-border traffic and offers all the necessary facilities to tourists and truckers alike.

Polokwane (Pietersburg)

The provincial capital of Limpopo province, Polokwane is a large, bustling business centre with plenty of shops and accommodation. The town has a casino, for those who feel like a flutter before entering the wilderness.

The Soutpansberg

An enigmatic and beautiful mountain range that extends from east to west across the otherwise flat plains. The N1 highway traverses the mountains via the Verwoerd tunnel. Much of the area is maintained as a conservation area.

Tshipise

A good, old-fashioned holiday resort, Tshipise is built around a fiendishly hot mineral spring that bubbles out of the ground halfway between Musina and Pafuri Gate. Terrifically popular with the old folk, who flock here in the winter months, Tshipise is a good place to soak away the dust after a long jaunt through the KNP.

Tzaneen

Situated at the bottom of Magoebaskloof pass, Tzaneen is an attractive but practical town, renowned for its fruits and nuts. If you have the time, visit the stunning Debengeni Falls for a picnic.

Venda (Giyani and Thohoyandou)

Although the former homeland known as Venda does not have a well-developed tourism infrastructure, this is a fascinating part of the country. With a rich cultural history, the region is just waiting to be explored. Check out the sacred Lake Fundudzi, visit the Dzata Ruins and museum, take a dip in the hot mineral springs, or just wander through the crazy urban sprawl of Thohoyandou.

Quick Contacts

SANParks Central Reservations: 012 428 9111 / 082 233 9111
Website: www.sanparks.org

KNP Camp Contact Numbers:
- Bateleur: 013 735 6843
- Berg-en-dal: 013 735 6145/06
- Biyamiti: 013 735 6171
- Crocodile Bridge: 013 735 6012
- Letaba: 013 735 6636/7
- Lower Sabie: 013 735 6056/7
- Malelane: 013 735 6152
- Mopani: 013 735 6535/6
- Olifants: 013 735 6606/7
- Orpen: 013 735 6355/5127
- Pretoriuskop: 013 735 5128/5132
- Punda Maria: 013 735 6873
- Satara: 013 735 6306/7
- Shimuwini: 013 735 6683
- Shingwedzi: 013 735 6806/7
- Sirheni: 013 735 6860
- Skukuza: 013 735 4196
- Talamati: 013 735 6343

Entrance Gate Contact Numbers:
- Crocodile Bridge Gate: 013 735 6012
- Kruger Gate: 013 735 6012
- Malelane Gate: 013 735 6152
- Numbi Gate: 013 735 5133
- Orpen Gate: 013 735 0237
- Pafuri Gate: 013 735 5574
- Phabeni Gate: 013 735 5890
- Phalaborwa Gate: 013 735 3547
- Punda Maria Gate: 013 735 6870

Kruger Park Data File

General

- Size: 19,633 km² / 1 962 362 hectares
- Dimensions: North to South: 345km, east to west: average 54km
- Annual visitor numbers: 1.7 million approx.
- Sections: Nxanatseni (northern region), Nkayeni (central region), Marula (southern region)
- Total number of beds: 4200
- Total number of camping sites: 3000
- Road network: 882km (tarred), 1703km (gravel)

Number of species (2005 census)

- 505 birds
- 336 trees
- 118 reptiles
- 53 fish (including 3 exotic species)
- 35 amphibians
- 148 mammals

Mammal Genera

- Insectivora (shrews etc.): 9
- Chiroptera (bats): 42
- Primates: 5
- Carnivora: 27
- Perissodactyla: 3 (2 rhinos, 1 zebra)
- Hyracoidea (dassies): 2
- Tubulidentata (aardvark): 1
- Proboscidae (elephant): 1
- Artiodactyla: 26 (2 pigs, 1 Giraffe, 1 Hippo, 22 antelopes)
- Pholidota (pangolin): 1
- Rodentia (rodents): 25
- Lagomorpha (hares): 3
- Macroscelidae (elephant shrews): 3

Insects

A complete list of insect species has not been completed, but it is estimated the total biomass of insects is greater than the combined biomass of all the other animals in the park.

Total plant taxa: 1990

- Mosses: ±3
- Ferns: ±32
- Sedges: ±74
- Aloes: ±18
- Grasses: ±224
- Trees and Shrubs: ±404
- Others (herbs, lianes, succulents etc.): 1234

Game estimates (2010-2011)

- Lion: 1 620 – 1750
- Leopard: 1000
- Cheetah: 120
- Wild dog: 120
- Spotted hyena: 5340
- Elephant: 13 750
- Burchell's zebra: 23 700 – 35 300
- Hippopotamus: 3100
- Warthog: 3100 - 5700
- Giraffe: 6800 – 10 300
- Buffalo: 37 130
- Eland: 460
- Roan antelope: 90
- Sable antelope: 290
- Greater kudu: 11 200 – 17 300
- Nyala: >300
- Waterbuck: 3100-7800
- Reedbuck: 300
- Mountain reedbuck: 150
- Blue wildebeest: 6400 – 13 100
- Tsessebe 220
- Impala: 132 300 – 176 400
- Crocodile: 4420

Big Lists

- The Big Five: Buffalo, Elephant, Leopard, Lion and Rhino
- The Little Five: Buffalo Weaver, Elephant Shrew, Leopard Tortoise, Ant Lion and Rhino Beetle

- Birding Big 6: Ground Hornbill, Kori Bustard, Lappet-faced Vulture, Martial Eagle, Pel's Fishing Owl and Saddle-bill Stork
- Big Five Trees: Baobab, Fever Tree, Knob Thorn, Marula, Mopane

Selected Bibliography

Braak, LEO. 2003. *Globetrotter Kruger National Park.* New Holland Publishing

Bryden, Bruce. *A Game Ranger Remembers – 30 years in the Kruger National Park.* Jonathan Ball Publishers.

Bulpin, TV. 1965. *Lost Trails of the Transvaal.* Thomas Nelson and Sons.

Bulpin, TV. 1967. *The Ivory Trail.* Books of Africa.

Carnaby, Trevor. 2005. *Beat About the Bush – mammals and birds.* Jacana Maps

Carruthers, Jane. 1995. *The Kruger National Park – a social and political history.* University of Natal Press

Carruthers, Jane. 2001. *Wildlife and Warfare – the life of James Stevenson-Hamilton.* University of Natal Press

Dennis, Nigel. 2000. *Getaway guide to where to watch game in the Kruger National Park*

Fitzpatrick, Percy. 1907. *Jock of the Bushveld.* Longman

Fleminger, David. 2005. *Back Roads of the Cape.* Jacana Media.

Fleminger, David. 2006. *Mapungubwe Cultural Landscape – Southbound pocket guide to the world heritage sites of South Africa.* 30 Degrees South Publishing.

Hall-Martin, Anthony and Carruthers, Jane. 2003. *South African National Parks – A Celebration.* Horst Klemm Publications.

Hilton-Barber, Brett and Berger, Lee R. *The Prime Origins Guide to Exploring Kruger.* Prime Origins

Hopkins, Ron. 2013. *Field Guide to the Historical Sites of Kruger National Park.* Ron Hopkins Publishing.

Jacana Media. 2004. *Lowveld and Kruger Guide.* Jacana Maps

Joubert, Salomon. 2007. *The Kruger National Park – a history* (3 volumes). High Branching.

Kloppers, JJ and Bornman, Hans. 2005. *A Dictionary of Kruger National Park Place Names.*

Kruger, Kobie. 1994. *Mahlangeni – stories of a game ranger's family.* Penguin Books.

Kruger, Kobie. 2002. *All Things Wild and Wonderful.* Penguin Books.

Magubane, Peter. 1998. *Vanishing Cultures of South Africa.* Struik

McCracken, Donal P. 2008. *Saving the Zululand Wilderness – an early struggle for nature conservation.* Jacana Media.

Meiring, Piet. 1976. *Kruger Park Saga.* Piet Meiring Publishers.

Oakes, Dougie (ed). 1988. *Illustrated History of South Africa – the real story.* Readers Digest.

Paton, Anthony. 2006. *Transformation of the myth and the myth of transformation: Over 100 years of guiding in South African   game reserves.* MA Thesis, unpublished.

Paynter, David. 1987. *Kruger - portrait of a national park.* Southern Book Publishers

Pringle, John A. 1982. *The Conservationists and its killers - the story of game protection and the Wildlife Society of Southern Africa.* Books of Africa

Roderigues, Jan. 2005. *The Game Rangers* (3rd edition). JA Roderigues Publishers.

Stevenson-Hamilton, James. 1929. *The Lowveld: its wildlife and its people.* Cassel and Company (1934 edition, with an introduction by Jan Smuts).

Stevenson-Hamilton, James. 1937. *South African Eden - from Sabi Game Reserve to Kruger National Park.* William Collins and Sons (1974 edition).

Stokes, C. S. 1944. *Sanctuary.* The 'Sanctuary' Production Committee

Wolhuter, Harry. 1948. *Memories of a Game Ranger.* Wildlife Society of South Africa.

Acknowledgements

This book was a long time in the writing, or not writing as was more often the case. When I did finally submit my first manuscript, many months late, the original publisher abandoned the project as they didn't think a popular history about the Kruger would be commercial (to be fair, they were expecting a travel guide).

A similar aversion was expressed by several other local publishers I subsequently approached. So, I decided to go it alone. And this (finally) is the result.

Over the course of the nearly ten years of Life that intervened between starting and publishing this work, many things have changed and I have tried to update the text accordingly. However, while every effort was made to ensure a high degree of accuracy throughout, I'm sure some errors have crept in. I rely on sharp-eyed readers to point out any mistakes or omissions I may have made.

In terms of thanks, there are many, but I'll be brief. To my long-suffering family and friends – your support and love is always appreciated, but I'd never say that to your faces. Edgar Neluvhalani and Kevin Moore at SANParks helped me out during my original research phase, as did Raymond and Rene Travers at the KNP (although that was so long ago, I doubt they remember me). Anthony Paton generously let me read his PhD thesis on Game Guiding in South Africa. Wilderness Safaris kindly offered me a complimentary stay at Pafuri Lodge (which they ran back then), and Lambson Makuleke gave of his time for an illuminating interview about the region.

Thanks also go to Norman Fleminger, Flora Fleminger and Hilary Fine who gave the manuscript a quick once over, and Ilan Mizrachi, who created the maps and designed the cover.

Finally, I'd like to thank all the KNP staff and random people who swapped stories, shared a meal or helped me make the most of Kruger. While I still remain more of a mountain person, to be honest, writing this book has given me a deep appreciation of the Wild and the tremendous effort required to keep it safe.

About the Author

David is a writer and director, working in the media industry for the last 20 years. His passion for travel began as a child, when his family would pile into a motorhome and drive around South Africa for their holidays.

His interest in travel writing grew out of an open curiosity about people, a love of history in all its gory, and an insatiable desire for the open road.

A long-standing film buff, David is currently developing screenplays and sitcoms. And he's going to start working on his novel, tomorrow. David is a lifelong Joburger and walks his dogs in the park every day.

25439936R00123

Printed in Great Britain
by Amazon